An Introduction to English Fiction, Poetry and Drama

小说、诗歌
与戏剧探寻之旅

——英语文学导读

高奋 编著

ZHEJIANG UNIVERSITY PRESS
浙江大学出版社

图书在版编目（CIP）数据

小说、诗歌与戏剧探寻之旅——英语文学导读/高奋
编著. —杭州：浙江大学出版社，2013.3（2023.7 重印）
ISBN 978-7-308-11212-3

Ⅰ. ①小… Ⅱ. ①高… Ⅲ. ①英语－阅读教学－高等
学校－教材②英语文学－高等学校－教材　Ⅳ. H319.4：I

中国版本图书馆 CIP 数据核字（2013）第 033750 号

小说、诗歌与戏剧探寻之旅——英语文学导读
An Introduction to English Fiction, Poetry and Drama
高　奋　编著

责任编辑	诸葛勤
封面设计	周　灵
出版发行	浙江大学出版社
	（杭州市天目山路 148 号　邮政编码 310007）
	（网址：http://www.zjupress.com）
排　　版	浙江时代出版服务有限公司
印　　刷	广东虎彩云印刷有限公司绍兴分公司
开　　本	710mm×1000mm　1/16
印　　张	14.5
字　　数	351 千
版 印 次	2013 年 3 月第 1 版　2023 年 7 月第 3 次印刷
书　　号	ISBN 978-7-308-11212-3
定　　价	30.00 元

前　言

"生命是一束纯净的火焰，我们依靠自己内
心看不见的太阳而生存。"

托马斯·布朗

　　当我们静下心来，回想我们走过的生命历程时，我们会发现文学阅读在我们生活
的时空中占据着很重要的位置。幼年的时候，我们陶醉在祖父母、父母讲述的故事里，
兴致勃勃地在他们动听的讲述中捕捉着由语言编织的美丽想象；童年和青年的时候，
我们在阅读和欣赏各类课文、读物、作品中学会了表达、书写和思考，逐渐形成对社
会和自我的理解和认识。可以说，我们心灵的成长在很大程度上是体验和感悟的过程，
而在这一过程中文学作品以其灵动的想象、真挚的情感、深刻的人文关怀深深地渗透
到我们的思想和灵魂之中，成为我们感知世界、自我和历史的最重要的途径。

　　我们应该已经阅读了不少中国文学名著，比如《红楼梦》《西游记》《三国演义》
等等，但是一提起英语文学作品，许多读者可能依然一脸无奈和困惑。这种无奈和困
惑是由多种原因造成的，比如文化的差异、语言的隔阂等等，其中英语文学导读类书
籍的缺乏也是导致读者无法进入英语文学天地的重要原因之一。

　　**本教材是为学习者轻松地跨入英语文学的殿堂而编写的。它的目的不仅在于拓展
学习者的通识范畴，加深理解力和提高品位，而且在于为学习者提供英语小说、诗歌
和戏剧的基础知识、分析技能、赏析范例，为英语文学学习提供良好的基础能力训练，
有效提升学习者的实力。**

　　作为导读类教材，本书拟解决的核心问题是：如何阅读英语文学作品？围绕这个
问题，本教材系统地介绍和展示了阅读和批评英语文学作品的基础知识、解读过程和
分析方法。全书根据作品体裁的不同分为三个部分，即：阅读小说、阅读诗歌和阅读
戏剧。每一章节都在简要介绍和简要分析某个特定的基本要素的基础上，精选优秀的

英语文学作品,并对其进行详尽的分析或赏析。编著者希望通过分层次提供基础知识、分析技能、赏析范例,为学习者提供阅读、欣赏、感悟和研究文学作品的平台。

依据小说、诗歌和戏剧的不同特性,本教材的三个部分各有侧重:"阅读小说"部分主要围绕小说的人物、主题、情节、背景、叙述视角、反讽等小说的基本要素展开;为了更贴近生活,对小说的选择基本限定在现代文学;为了更好地了解分析过程和方法,对小说的赏析大都包含三种不同的批评方法。"阅读诗歌"部分主要围绕诗歌的措辞、句法、基调、修辞方法、节奏、音韵等基本要素展开;为了凸现英语诗歌悠久的历史,对诗歌的选择范围没有特定的限制,并且提供了诗歌类型的介绍;为了更好把握诗歌阅读的精妙,部分分析是用母语进行的,重在唤醒我们对语词的感觉。"阅读戏剧"部分主要围绕戏剧的主要种类喜剧、悲剧展开;为了真正了解英语戏剧的底蕴,选择了莎士比亚的著名悲剧作为阅读对象;由于篇幅的限制,只能选择莎剧的一部分,因此无法对莎剧作细致的赏析;不过,这样可能更切合实际,我们可以将学习重点放在阅读和表演上,以便更好地体验戏剧。

本教材的主要特点是:

(一)从读者阅读的立场出发,用形象的方式,将学习、思考和研究放置在同一个平台上,使学生轻松入门。在综合英美文学界对基本文学术语所作的研究的基础上,对这些基本术语作出精练而明确的界定,并对它们作了简明扼要的述评,便于学习者理解和把握。同时,用多角度的批评范文揭示英语文学中的小说、诗歌、戏剧文本的分析过程,让读者轻松地理解和掌握阅读文学作品的基本技能和方法。

(二)从文学欣赏的立场出发,以体验的方式,使学生在细读多篇原汁原味的英语诗歌、小说和戏剧作品的过程中,真正了解文学作品的精妙。每一个章节都围绕一个问题展开,力求以生动、形象的方式就文学阅读和批评中的主要问题进行讨论和引导,旨在引发读者的兴趣和更多的问题,为他们进一步的研究打开窗户。

(三)从批评解惑的立场出发,在解读诗歌、小说的阅读过程和阅读技巧的基础上,为文学文本提供西方批评界普遍采用的多种批评方法和视角,为学习者提高自己的鉴赏和思考能力,增强的文本研究能力提供参考模板。

本教材中所采用的部分赏析文章由王霞、王金、刘鎏、姚依东、余华、孙艳艳等撰写,特此表示感谢。本教材是《英语文学阅读导论》的修订版,特别感谢浙江大学出版社诸葛勤先生的绝妙建议和细致编辑,特别感谢我历届学生们在本课程学习中的积极参与和热烈讨论。没有你们,本教材的出版将变得不可能。

高 奋

2013 年春

Contents

Section 1 Reading Fiction
第一部分 阅读小说

> No man is an island, entire of itself; every man is a piece of the continent, a part of the main… Any man's death diminishes me, because I am involved in mankind, and therefore never send to know for whom the bell tolls; it tolls for thee.
>
> John Donne

  在快节奏的现代生活中，我们是否有必要阅读小说？为什么要阅读小说？我们的回答是：小说能够给人带来愉悦和感悟。小说丰富的想象力和曲折的情节，可以给平淡的生活注入生机和活力，这是毫无疑问的。不过，小说更重要的作用在于：它可以加深我们对生活的感知，并且帮助我们深入了解我们的"自我"。借助于想象的翅膀，小说能够使我们透过现实生活表面的物象世界，潜入到"真实"的世界之中，了解生活中"基本的、持久的、本质的东西"（约瑟夫·康拉德语）；凭借感悟的触角，小说能够使我们突破"自我"的堡垒，感知人类共同的"集体无意识"，真正把握"自我"与"世界"的关系。小说是一种探索，它用文字照亮我们的生活和行为；小说是一种洞见，它用意识提炼我们对生存本质的瞬间理解；小说是一位朋友，它通过"人物"向我们展示了"他者"的世界和"他者"的价值体系，使我们在体验中建构"自我"的世界。

  什么是小说？英语的"小说"有两种称谓，即"fiction"和"novel"。"fiction"是对虚构作品的总称，通常包括小说、故事、寓言等叙事作品，它大都以散文体的形式出现，但是"fiction"同时又是"novel"的同义词。"novel"是指一种特定的叙事体裁。

简要介绍：

Novel, nearly always an extended fictional prose narrative, although some novels are very short, some are non-fictional, some have been written in verse, and some do not even tell a story. Such exceptions help to indicate that the novel as a literary genre is itself exceptional: it disregards the constraints that govern other literary forms, and acknowledges no obligatory structure, style, or subject-matter. Thriving on this openness and flexibility, the novel has become the most important literary genre of the modern age, superseding the epic, the romance, and other narrative forms. Novels can be distinguished from short stories and novellas by their greater length, which permits fuller, subtler development of characters and themes. There is no established minimum length for a novel, but it is normally at least long enough to justify its publication in an independent volume, unlike the short story. The novel differs from the prose romance in that a greater degree of realism is expected of it, and that it tends to describe a recognizable secular social world, often in a skeptical and prosaic manner inappropriate to the marvels of romance. The novel has frequently incorporated the structures and languages of non-fictional prose forms (history, autobiography, journalism, travel writing), even to the point where the non-fictional element outweighs the fictional. It is normally expected of a novel that it should have at least one character, and preferably several characters shown in processes of change and social relationship; a plot, or some arrangement of narrated events, is another normal requirement. Special subgenres of the novel have grown up around particular kinds of character (the spy novel), setting (the historical novel, the campus novel), and plot (the detective novel); while other kinds of novel are distinguished either by their structure (the epistolary novel, the picaresque novel) or by special emphases on character (the Bildungsroman) or ideas. —It is the publication in Spain of the first part of Miguel de Cervantes's *Don Quixote de la Mancha* in 1605 that is most widely accepted as announcing the arrival of the true novel. —In England Daniel Defoe is regarded as the founder of the English novel with his *Robinson Crusoe* (1719) and *Moll Flanders* (1722). The novel achieved its predominance in the 19th century, when Charles Dickens and other writers found a huge audience through serial publication, and when the conventions of realism were consolidated. In the 20th century a division became more pronounced between the popular forms of novel and the various experiments of modernism and postmodernism—from the stream of consciousness to the anti-novel.[1]

简　析：

上面的界定用简洁的语言对小说作了全面的勾勒：

1）从形式上看，小说是开放而灵动的，它在语言、篇幅、结构、风格、题材等方面都没有特别的规定和限制。

2）从内容上看，小说以主题和人物为核心向外拓展，具有一种独立的整体性。

3）从构成上看，小说基本的要素包括人物、主题、情节、背景、叙述视角、反讽等。

4）从类型上看，小说由于突出某个要素而构成一种特别的类型。比如，突出人物的小说有：流浪汉小说、成长小说等；突出情节的小说有：侦探小说、言情小说、科幻小说等；突出背景的小说有：历史小说、校园小说、社会小说、宗教小说等。当然，这种分类是主观的，其中有重叠的成分。

5）从历史发展角度看，英语小说从 18 世纪小说家笛福的伪自传体小说《鲁滨孙漂流记》开始，经历了 19 世纪的现实主义小说和 20 世纪的现代主义小说，到 20 和 21 世纪的后现代主义小说，已经走过了 3 个世纪的历程。

经历了 3 个世纪的发展，小说的形式、内容、类型都经历了很多的变化，唯独它的基本要素依然保留。本部分将在简要介绍小说的基本要素的基础上，对部分短篇小说进行赏析，帮助读者形成自己的阅读和批评方式。

Elements of Fiction (小说的要素):

- ◆ Plot: author's deliberate arrangement of events and actions
- ◆ Character: the persons created in the literary work
- ◆ Setting: time and place and social context
- ◆ Point of view: the way a story is told
- ◆ Irony: basic tone of the story
- ◆ Theme: the central idea of a story

Questions:

1. What do you think of the definition offered?

2. Please tell your understanding of the novel based on your reading of novels.

3. What is the relationship between the novel and our life?

---

1 Baldick, Chris. *Oxford Concise Dictionary of Literary Terms*. 上海：上海外语教育出版社，2000: 151-152.

Chapter 1　Plot

第一章　情节

> I have always felt that the first duty of a writer was to ascend—to make flights, carrying others along if he could manage it.
>
> E. B. White

简要介绍：

The **Plot** refers to the author's deliberate arrangement of events and actions in a dramatic or narrative work, which are manipulated as a coherent and unified whole to achieve particular artistic and emotional effects.

The plot is different from the story. The plot is the selected and manipulated version of events and actions as presented to the reader or audience in a certain order and duration, whereas the story is the chronological sequence of events in their "natural" order and duration. Therefore, the story is the "raw material" of events, which is used by the author to reconstruct the plot.

The events and actions of the plot are performed by particular characters in a work, for instance, protagonist (the chief character in a plot), antagonist (the character against protagonist), villain (evil antagonist), and are the means to reveal moral and values of the characters through their relationship.

The plot mostly develops with conflicts, with suspense and surprise used to elicit the interest of reader and audience. The conflict may be that of person against person, or of person against environment, or of person against himself/herself, which may be physical, mental, emotional or moral.

The order of a plot is a continuously sequence of beginning, middle and end, as Aristotle pointed out in his *Poetics*, and all the parts are closely connected into a unified whole. The basic elements of the traditional plot generally include the following four parts:

　　1. Exposition: which depicts the initial setting, who are the characters, where does the story take place, when does the story happens, what is the social background;

　　2. Elaboration: the actions develops into conflict;

　　3. Climax: the conflicts develop into a crisis;

　　4. Denouement (resolution, ending): the crisis is resolved with either a happy ending or an unhappy ending or an indeterminate ending.

　　Although there are four parts in the plot, yet it does not mean that all novels must have all of them. Generally speaking, there are three kinds of plot patterns:

　　1. Common type: the story is narrated with four basic parts;

　　2. In *medies res*: the story is narrated without an exposition;

　　3. Opening ending: the story is narrated without an ending.

简　析：

　　关于"情节"，我们需要注意的是：

　　1）情节不同于故事，不像故事一样按照事件自然发生的顺序发展，而是作家根据自己的意图和构思对事件的取舍和安排。因此，情节安排本身已经隐藏了对生活的理解和感悟。

　　2）自亚里士多德以来，情节通常被分为三个部分：开端、发展和结尾。为了分析的方便，也有批评家将情节分为四个部分：开端、发展、高潮、结尾。所有这些部分共同组成一个有机整体，用于有效表达作品的主题。

　　3）传统小说情节的发展是围绕冲突进行的，这些冲突可能是关于人与人之间的、人与环境之间的或人与自我之间的。现代小说和后现代小说是反情节的，因此冲突不再显现，许多时候以顿悟（epiphany）的方式取而代之。

　　4）情节的发展是由人物推动和完成的，因此情节的发展是与人物个性的全方位展开和小说主题思想的发展同步进行的。

作　品：

KATHERINE MANSFIELD
[1888—1923]

The Fly

　　"Y'are very snug in here," piped old Mr. Woodifield, and he peered out of the great, green leather arm-chair by his friend, the boss's desk, as a baby peers out of its pram. His talk was over; it was time for him to be off. But he did not want to go. Since he had retired, since his... stroke, the wife and the girls kept him boxed up in the house every day of the week except Tuesday. On Tuesday he was dressed up and brushed and allowed to cut back to the City for the day. Though what he did there the wife and girls couldn't imagine. Made a nuisance of himself to his friends, they supposed... Well, perhaps so. All the same, we cling to our last pleasures as the tree clings to its last leaves. So there sat old Woodifield, smoking a cigar and staring almost greedily at the boss, who rolled in his office chair, stout, rosy, five years older than he, and still going strong, still at the helm. It did one good to see him.

Wistfully, admiringly, the old voice added, "It's snug in here, upon my word!"

"Yes, it's comfortable enough," agreed the boss, and he flipped the *Financial Times* with a paper-knife. As a matter of fact he was proud of his room; he liked to have it admired, especially by old Woodifield. It gave him a feeling of deep, solid satisfaction to be planted there in the midst of it in full view of that frail old figure in the muffler.

"I've had it done up lately," he explained, as he had explained for the past—how many?—weeks. "New carpet," and he pointed to the bright red carpet with a pattern of large white rings. "New furniture," and he nodded towards the massive bookcase and the table with legs like twisted treacle. "Electric heating!" He waved almost exultantly towards the five transparent, pearly sausages glowing so softly in the tilted copper pan.

But he did not draw old Woodifield's attention to the photograph over the table of a grave-looking boy in uniform standing in one of those spectral photographers' parks with photographers' storm-clouds behind him. It was not new. It had been there for over six years.

"There was something I wanted to tell you," said old Woodifield, and his eyes grew dim remembering. "Now what was it? I had it in my mind when I started out this morning." His hands began to tremble, and patches of red showed above his beard.

Poor old chap, he's on his last pins, thought the boss. And, feeling kindly, he winked at the old man, and said jokingly, "I tell you what. I've got a little drop of something here that'll do you good before you go out into the cold again. It's beautiful stuff. It wouldn't hurt a child." He took a key off his watch-chain, unlocked a cupboard below his desk, and drew forth a dark, squat bottle. "That's the medicine," said he. "And the man from whom I got it told me on the strict Q.T. it came from the cellars at Windsor Castle."

Old Woodifield's mouth fell open at the sight. He couldn't have looked more surprised if the boss had produced a rabbit.

"It's whisky, ain't it?" he piped feebly.

The boss turned the bottle and lovingly showed him the label. Whisky it was.

"D'you know," said he, peering up at the boss wonderingly, "they won't let me touch it at home." And he looked as though he was going to cry.

"Ah, that's where we know a bit more than the ladies," cried the boss, swooping across for two tumblers that stood on the table with the water-bottle, and pouring a generous finger into each. "Drink it down. It'll do you good. And don't put any water with it. It's sacrilege to tamper with stuff like this. Ah!" He tossed off his, pulled out his handkerchief, hastily wiped his moustaches, and cocked an eye at old Woodifield, who was rolling his in his chaps.

The old man swallowed, was silent a moment, and then said faintly, "It's nutty!"

But it warmed him; it crept into his chill old brain—he remembered.

"That was it," he said, heaving himself out of his chair. "I thought you'd like to know. The girls were in Belgium last week having a look at poor Reggie's grave, and they happened to come across your boy's. They're quite near each other, it seems."

Old Woodifield paused, but the boss made no reply. Only a quiver of his eyelids showed that he heard.

"The girls were delighted with the way the place is kept," piped the old voice. "Beautifully looked after. Couldn't be better if they were at home. You've not been across, have ye?"

"No, no!" For various reasons the boss had not been across.

"There's miles of it," quavered old Woodifield, "and it's all as neat as a garden. Flowers growing on all the graves. Nice broad paths." It was plain from his voice how much he liked a nice broad path.

The pause came again. Then the old man brightened wonderfully.

"D'you know what the hotel made the girls pay for a pot of jam?" he piped. "Ten francs! Robbery, I call it. It was a little pot, so Gertrude says, no bigger than a half-crown. And she hadn't taken more than a spoonful when they charged her ten francs. Gertrude brought the pot away with her to teach 'em a lesson. Quite right, too; it's trading on our feelings. They think because we're over there having a look around we're ready to pay anything. That's what it is." And he turned towards the door.

"Quite right, quite right!" cried the boss, though what was quite right he hadn't the least idea. He came round by his desk, followed the shuffling footsteps to the door, and saw the old fellow out. Woodifield was gone.

For a long moment the boss stayed, staring at nothing, while the grey-haired office messenger, watching him, dodged in and out of his cubbyhole like a dog that expects to be taken for a run. Then: "I'll see nobody for half an hour, Macey," said the boss. "Understand? Nobody at all."

"Very good, sir."

The door shut, the firm heavy steps recrossed the bright carpet, the fat body plumped down in the spring chair, and leaning forward, the boss covered his face with his hands. He wanted, he intended, he had arranged to weep...

It had been a terrible shock to him when old Woodifield sprang that remark upon him about the boy's grave. It was exactly as though the earth had opened and he had seen the boy lying there with Woodifield's girls staring down at him. For it was strange. Although over six years had passed away, the boss never thought of the boy except as lying unchanged, unblemished in his uniform, asleep for ever. "My son!" groaned the boss. But no tears came yet. In the past, in the first months and even years after the boy's death, he had only to say those words to be overcome by such grief that nothing short of a violent fit of weeping could relieve him. Time, he had declared then, he had told everybody, could make no difference. Other men perhaps might recover, might live their loss down, but not he. How was it possible! His boy was an only son. Ever since his birth the boss had worked at building up this business for him; it had no other meaning if it was not for the boy. Life itself had come to have no other meaning. How on earth could he have slaved, denied himself, kept going all those years without the promise for ever before him of the boy's stepping into his shoes and carrying on where he left off?

And that promise had been so near being fulfilled. The boy had been in the office learning the ropes for a year before the war. Every morning they had started off together; they had come back by the same train. And what congratulations he had received as the boy's father! No wonder; he had taken to it marvellously. As to his popularity with the staff, every man jack of them down to old Macey couldn't make enough of the boy. And he wasn't in the least spoilt. No, he was just his bright natural self, with the right word for everybody, with that boyish look and his habit of saying, "Simply splendid!"

But all that was over and done with as though it never had been. The day had come when Macey had handed him the telegram that brought the whole place crashing about his head. "Deeply regret to inform you..." And he had left the office a broken man, with his life in ruins.

Six years ago, six years... How quickly time passed! It might have happened yesterday. The boss took his hands from his face; he was puzzled. Something seemed to be wrong with him. He wasn't feeling as he wanted to feel. He decided to get up and have a look at the boy's photograph. But it wasn't a favorite photograph of his; the expression was unnatural. It was cold, even stern-looking. The boy had never looked like that.

At that moment the boss noticed that a fly had fallen into his broad inkpot, and was trying feebly but desperately to clamber out again. Help! help! said those struggling legs. But the sides of the inkpot were wet and slippery; it fell back again and began to swim. The boss took up a pen, picked the fly out of the ink, and shook it on to a piece of blotting-paper. For a fraction of a second it lay still on the dark patch that oozed round it. Then the front legs waved, took hold, and, pulling its small sodden body up, it began the immense task of cleaning the ink from its wings. Over and under, over and under, went a leg along a wing, as the stone goes over and under the scythe. Then there was a pause, while the fly, seeming to stand on the tips of its toes, tried to expand first one wing and then the other. It succeeded at last, and, sitting down, it began, like a minute cat, to clean its face. Now one could imagine that the little front legs rubbed against each other lightly, joyfully. The horrible danger was over; it had escaped; it was ready for life again.

But just then the boss had an idea. He plunged his pen back into the ink, leaned his thick wrist on the blotting-paper, and as the fly tried its wings, down came a great, heavy blot. What would it make of that? What indeed! The little beggar seemed absolutely cowed, stunned, and afraid to move because of what would happen next. But then, as if painfully, it dragged itself forward. The front legs waved, caught hold, and, more slowly this time, the task began again.

He's a plucky little devil, thought the boss, and he felt a real admiration for the fly's courage. That was the way to tackle things; that was the right spirit. Never say die; it was only a question of... But the fly had again finished its laborious task, and the boss had just time to refill his pen, to shake fair and square on the new-cleaned body yet another dark drop. What about it this time? A painful moment of suspense followed. But behold, the front legs were again waving; the boss felt a rush of relief. He leaned over the fly and said to it tenderly, "You artful little b..." And he actually had the brilliant notion of breathing on it to help the drying process. All the same, there was something timid and weak about its efforts now, and the boss decided that this time should be the last, as he dipped the pen deep into the inkpot.

It was. The last blot fell on the soaked blotting-paper, and the draggled fly lay in it and did not stir. The back legs were stuck to the body; the front legs were not to be seen.

"Come on," said the boss. "Look sharp!" And he stirred it with his pen—in vain. Nothing happened or was likely to happen. The fly was dead.

The boss lifted the corpse on the end of the paper-knife and flung it into the waste-paper basket, but such a grinding feeling of wretchedness seized him that he felt positively frightened. He started forward and pressed the bell for Macey.

"Bring me some fresh blotting-paper," he said sternly, "and look sharp about it." And while the old dog padded away he fell to wondering what it was he had been thinking about before. What was it? It was... He took out his handkerchief and passed it inside his collar. For the life of him he could not remember.

Questions:

1. In terms of the plot, "The Fly" is constructed in three parts: the boss with old Woodifield, the boss's memory of his dead son, and the boss and the fly. What is the connection between these parts?
2. The story is entitled "Thy Fly", is it appropriate? Is it of symbolic meaning?
3. Is there any conflict in the story?
4. What helps form the unity of the story?
5. What does the ending indicate?
6. Does the plot help the expression of the theme successfully?

赏　析：

Three Critical Approaches to Mansfield's "The Fly"

1. Traditional Approach to "The Fly": *Biographical Indications in "The Fly"*

Complying with the tradition of English novel, Katherine Mansfield always bases her works on her own experiences and daily affairs "heightened by sensitivity and good writing". She writes of nothing that doesn't directly happen to her, even when appearing to "be at her most imaginative and fanciful"[1]. This constitutes one of the main characteristics in her literary creation. Thus, in many of her works, there always contains some biographical elements. For example, "A Birthday" (1911), one of her early works, is an epitome of her own birth, with the setting bearing much resemblance to Wellington where she was born; "Something Childish but Very Natural" (1914) is "evidently her and Murry's love-in-a-cottage situation projected back to a couple of youngsters"[2]; "The Canary" (1921) is her self-portrait at a time when she was greatly threatened by the approaching death. And "The Fly" is of no exception to such a feature.

The story begins with old Mr. Woodifield's visit to the boss in his cozy and warm office. The two old men were chattering desultorily in a mood of leisure and slight sentiment. However, as soon as the boss's dead son was mentioned, the ambience turned to be tense. And the boss began to be immersed in the memory of his beloved young son who died in the war. When he came back to reality, he helped a fly from the inkpot, but finally drowned it with several ink blots.

Like many of her other short stories, "The Fly" is featured with simple plot and little direct introduction to those characters. But with a deeper insight into the story and some knowledge of Mansfield's life, we'll find that the story greatly draws on her complex family background. Primarily named as Kathleen Beauchamp, Katherine Mansfield was born in 1888 in Wellington, New Zealand. Her father, Harold Beauchamp was a merchant who later became very successful and was even appointed as the director of the Bank of New Zealand. Her mother was a "gentle" and feeble lady whose ambition was to be engaged in various social activities. As the third child of the family, Mansfield had three sisters and a younger brother. Quite clever as she was, she didn't gain much popularity among most family members, due to her rebellious behaviors. But she had established a rather close relationship with her brother, Leslie Beauchamp, who always helped her. Such a large family together with the complicated relationship within has a great impact on Mansfield's writing. And as far as "The Fly" is concerned, the backdrop of the Beauchamp family mainly functions in two

---

1 Gordon, Ian A. Katherine Mansfield. In: Scott, Ian and Kilvert, ed. *British Writers* (Volume VII). New York: Charles Seribner's Sons, 1984: 177.
2 Ibid, 173.

aspects.

Firstly, most of Mansfield's families, to a great extent, are archetypes of many characters in the story. The boss is a reflection of her father, Harold Beauchamp, who also had already achieved great success in his business life. And since Mr. Beauchamp lost his beloved young son in late 1915, which is "six years" before the early 1922 when the story was written, the main happenings to the boss exactly coincides with those to him in reality. Correspondingly, the image of the boss's son is drawn from Mansfield's younger brother. As the only son of the family, Leslie Beauchamp was highly expected to take over his father's business and was bound to have a bright future. Obeying the father's decision, he went to work as an apprentice in the company. But then when serving in the army during the First World War, he died of accident in a drill. All these tally perfectly with the picture of the boss's son as is drawn by the old man's memory. Besides, old Woodifield's wife is an echo of Mansfield's mother. Though absent in the story, Mrs. Woodifield is indirectly depicted as no more than a caring wife who took good care of her palsied husband. She didn't allow him to drink whisky which might be harmful to his health, and dressed and brushed him for his visit to old friends. These descriptions correspond to the very image of Mrs. Beauchamp whose whole attention was paid to Mr. Beauchamp. As an "ideal" wife, she devoted all her time to helping, understanding and looking after him, though being reluctant to take up those daily house-hold chores. In all, in terms of the characters, the story has an inerasable relation to the author's family.

In addition, the short story is also strongly indicative of Mansfield's different relationships with her kin. In the story, the author writes about two family circles: the boss's family with the boss and his son, and the Woodifields with Mr. Woodifield, his wife, the girls and Reggie. These two families even develop kind of contrast in accordance with the two fathers' diverse reactions to their sons' death. Since such characters as Mrs. Woodifield, the boss and his son respectively originate from Mansfield's mother, father and brother, such a fictional arrangement actually excludes the mother from the circle constituted by the other two, and thus implies that the author may have disparate attitudes toward her mother on one side and the father with brother on the other.

The implication is soundly supported by the real situation of her family life. Generally speaking, Mansfield was not thought well of by most of her families. Always defying her parents' decisions, she was never considered to be a good and obedient daughter. However, she was always bearing genuine and enthusiastic love for her father, which can be seen from her frequent letters to him. And she constantly adored her younger brother whose death had profound influence on her view of life as well as writing interest. On the contrary, she didn't develop a good rapport with her mother. Though probably being a good wife, Mrs. Beauchamp was never a competent mother. She didn't know how to take care of her children. Nor did she even know how to love them. Thus, brought up by the grandma, young Mansfield was always distanced from her mother. For most of the time, she felt lonely and gradually formed the idea that no one but grandma loved her, which made her sometimes quite annoying and not so pleasant. What's more, her premature genius of keen observation and scathing critiques led to the further loss of her mother's favor for her. From then on, the mother-daughter relationship had been in a state of tension, subtlety and unnaturalness. Even when hearing the daughter was heavily ill, Mrs. Beauchamp showed more sympathy then motherly love for her, which can be learned from her letter in 1918. Meanwhile, we may also have a glimpse of Mansfield's not so favorite attitude towards the mother in her lifeless and love-disabled characterization of mother figures in her stories on childhood.

As a whole, "The Fly" characterizes wide reference to Mansfield's main family members as well as delicate implication of the complex interpersonal relationship thereof. And such great emphasis on the biographical background is closely connected with author's personal conditions during the writing period. As being assured of her contracting tuberculosis in 1918, Mansfield had always been enduring the fear of death and the torture of loneliness. The mental pains together with physical agony impelled her to re-consider the meaning of life and look back upon her bygone days, which had her realize the importance of families more deeply than ever. And during that time, she even wrote quite some sentimental letters to her father, in hope of being forgiven and getting a little fatherly love from him before her death. Thus, with those autobiographical grains, "The Fly" constitutes part of Mansfield's review over her whole life. Furthermore, by explicitly employing the image of her father and brother, the story signals her eagerness for family love, especially the fatherly love—the only possible one that can be obtained from the loose, broken family.

To sum up, from the historical-biographical point of view, "The Fly" is saturated with elements of the author's family background. It takes in those images of her father, mother and brother, and discloses her different relationships with the three family members. Thus, the story presents a general and somewhat complete picture of the Beauchamp family in Mansfield's eyes. And it also partially reflects her final meditation on the meaning of life—the return to family love.

2. Formalistic Approach: *Life-death Metaphors in "The Fly"*

Praised by Ian Gordon as James Joyce in short story writing[3], Katherine Mansfield is renowned for her innovative development of writing techniques like fragmentation of time line, symbols and images, constant shifts of point of view and so on. And in the case of "The Fly", the main formal device lies in symbols and images, through which the eternal theme of life and death is explored.

As one of the representative works of symbolism, the story is characterized by ingenious use of metaphors, which leads to various interpretations of it. And generally, a major part of critics agree that

---

3 "凯瑟琳·曼斯菲尔德之于短篇小说艺术，犹如乔伊斯之于长篇小说艺术。"见：赵敏霞. 论曼斯菲尔德短篇小说的主题特征. 学术交流，1999，4: 132.

"The Fly" aims to reveal the futility of life and the harm war has done to human beings. However, when looking into the story, we may find that it not only expresses the idea of death's inevitability but also proposes a way out for the foreordination. Thus, in this analysis, we'll probe into those life-death metaphors in the story, in order to have a more complete view of Mansfield's meditation on life and death. These metaphors will be mainly approached from two aspects: respective metaphors of life and death, and those of the life-death unity.

1) Respective Metaphors of Life and Death

Throughout the story, there are abundant images of life as well as death. For example, images of green armchair, new carpet and new furniture all symbolize the vitality of life. For, green is the color of life, the armchair is compared to a pram which is the embodiment of birth and new life, and new things are always endowed with the hint of being vigorous. While the first half of the story is comparatively full of life metaphors, the second half is saturated with death images, such as the photo of the boss's son. Since the son is revealed dead, his photograph, besides being used for commemoration, also becomes the sign of the doom to death that confronts everybody. And such an implication is further strengthened by the employment of these words like "grave" and "spectral" in describing the photo. Apart from the photo image, the story constantly refers to images of grave and dark inkpot which also symbolize the unfathomable abyss of death.

As a whole, the metaphors of life and death spread around the whole story, which evinces the main theme of the story—life and death.

2) Metaphors of the Life-death Unity

In addition to those respective metaphors of the dichotomy, the story boasts images which embody life and death at the same time. Mainly there are two such images: Mr. Woodifield and the fly. And they constitute the major tension in the story, for while the image of old Woodifield indicates the doom of human beings, the fly image advocates a proper living attitude to face up to it.

☐ Old Woodifield: the doom

Appearing in the first part of the story, old Mr. Woodifield embodies the paradoxical unity of life and death. Firstly, in terms of his addressing form, the name "Woodifield" primarily implies energy and vitality, for "woodifield" literally means a field full of woods and trees which are acknowledged symbols of life. However, the author constantly refers to him as "*old* Woodifield" or "*old* Mr. Woodifield". The addition of the adjective "old" to the name not only hints at the coming end of his life but also always reminds us of such a fact. Besides, in terms of the characterization, Mr. Woodifield is for one thing described as a baby, the symbol of new life. He is compared to a baby in the pram when sitting in the green armchair, and his daily life is allusively depicted as an infant one which is under the constant supervision and care from "the wife and girls", or the mother and sisters. Meanwhile, he is also presented as an average sick old man, which is generally achieved by the employment of such adverbs and adjectives as "feebly", "faintly", "dim" and "frail", as well as the repetitive reference to "old", like "old brain", "old voice", "old figure", etc. Trivial as they are, these words vividly create a feeble old figure who had been in his last days.

With these two treatments, the image of Mr. Woodifield symbolizes co-existence of life and death in human beings. Everyone lives along with the likelihood of death. Furthermore, as is indicated by comparing the old man in armchair to baby in pram, the place for the new life and that for the dying become one. And so do the beginning of life and the end of it. Thus, life is destined for death.

In all, the image of Mr. Woodifield embodies the unity of life and death, and is further employed to imply that life results in death, or to the extreme, that we live to die.

☐   The Fly: a positive living attitude

With the information conveyed by the image of Mr. Woodifield, one question may naturally emerge: since we are doomed to death, how shall we live our life and what kind of living attitude shall we adopt? And the answer may be found in the other image of the unity of life and death—the fly.

Depicted vividly in the story, the fly is presented as a brave life fighter. When firstly falling into the ink pot which is the physical threat to life, it "tried feebly but desperately to clamber out again". As being rescued, it plucked itself up to be ready for life. But soon another danger came over. An ink blot fell on its body! Immersed in the blot, it would naturally think that it was once again trapped in the pot and placed on the verge of the abyss of death. And it was "absolutely cowed, stunned and afraid to move". Thus, for this time what the blot really brought to the fly is not the physical threat but the mental one which is in fact more destructive and disastrous. Because while the former may only lead to pains for a short time, the latter has one tortured by the ubiquitous shadow of death and will ruin one's whole life. But our hero wasn't beaten. After a short time of being frightened, it came to life again. And it even got through a second blot. However, everyone has his limits. Confronted with the successive fatal blows, the fly finally wore itself out to death.

Throughout the struggling process, the fly manifests tremendous perseverance, fortitude and the strong will for life. It never submits to the fear of death but is strong-minded enough to go on with its life; and it never gives itself up till the last drop of its strength. All these suffice for its being the symbol of life. However, being a fly itself, its life is trivial and weak. It is easily trapped in danger and can be killed by several blots of ink. In its life, death always haunts. And in the story, the fly finally died due to its deficient life force. Thus, from another point of view, the fly also incarnates death and the fragility of life.

Embodying the unity of life and death, the image of fly, nevertheless, doesn't simply refer to the unavoidability of death. Instead, due to the story's greater emphasis on the fly's struggling process, it proposes a positive way of leading a life, facing dangers and confronting death. That is, "never say die". No matter how mighty difficulties are, how unpredictable the life is and how near the death is drawing, we should not give up our life, or rather the hope of life, but keep fighting till the last minute just as the fly did. And that's "the right spirit" and "the way to tackle things" including death.

The story was written in the early 1922. It was a time when Mansfield, suffering from tuberculosis, was disillusioned with traditional medical practice and had already realized that she was bound to die soon. But like the fly she didn't give up and stubbornly engaged herself in an expensive though almost useless X-ray treatment. For, shadowed with death, she was earnest for living. With such a writing background, the story with abundant life-death metaphors actually reflects the author's thinking on life and death. She holds that although death is doomed, it shall not be feared but confronted with immense struggling spirit. This is not only a life manifesto for the dying like Mansfield, but also an allegory for all the modern people who are continuously disillusioned, trapped and threatened by various ordeals in reality. Or in the boss's words, "never say die". And that's the exact truth of life.

3. Psychological Approach: *The Freed Instinct to Destroy*

Almost every reader of "The Fly" will encounter a puzzling question after finishing the story. That is, why would the boss torture the fly again and again till its death, while sympathizing and admiring it at the same time? Is it because he wanted to learn the truth of life from the fly's struggle in ink? If so, how could we explain his last two ink blots, for after the first blot he had already acquired the epiphany of life? Or, is it simply due to his curiosity of the limits of life? In our opinion, a more acceptable explanation may be that the boss's repeated afflicting the fly is the projection of his imbalanced psyche—the activation of the instinct of destruction and overt aggression that is part of the repressed id. And the character himself, in accordance with Freudian theory, is a destructive and sadist-inclined neurotic, which can be justified by two symptoms.

One lies in the boss's aggressive attitude toward old Woodifield. Though being an old friend, the boss bore more hostility than sympathy against the sick pal. As he had said to himself, Mr. Woodifield's collapse of health "gave him a feeling of deep, solid satisfaction". Such a surprising statement somewhat implies that in his inner mind, he was gratified with the friend's something being destroyed or was longing to destroy, and that the innate aggressive desire of the id had been revived. What's more, his inducing old Woodifield to have some whisky is a very realization of the natural drive. Since whisky is harmful to a paralytic, providing the wine equals wrecking the life of the old friend. And the author's use of such words as "swoop", "cry", "hastily" and "toss off" in describing the boss's serving and drinking the wine is further indicative of the uncontrolled devastating impulse in his psyche, for all these words have the common grain of violence and power. So, with a look into his unnatural thoughts and actions, we may apprehend that faced with the frail friend, the boss had left aside the natural human love and sympathy, but bore him "unprovoked" aggression which was virtually provoked by the inborn desire to destroy and damage.

Unlike the cryptic expression of the boss's aggressive drive in his attitude toward Mr. Woodifield, a more apparent symptom rests in his abnormal or morbid treatment of the fly. After he had rescued the fly from the inkpot, it is still him that threw it back in danger time and time again. By dripping the ink bots on the fly, he was cornering it in the abyss of death symbolized by the dark ink, which thus constitutes the exact process of life-destroying. Besides, it is also driven by the freed instinct to destroy the fly despite his conscious respect and admiration for it. Though holding such excuses as "what would it make of it" and "what about it this time", he was in fact deep trapped in the instinctual gratification achieved by afflicting it and seeing it suffer, struggle. And whenever the fly cleaned itself and got rid of the danger of death, the boss dripped the blot. Such timing is exactly the manifestation of his unconscious desire to ruin others' life and happiness. As is agreed by many critics, the fly represents the whole mankind. Thus, the boss's maltreatment of it is never an accidental case of killing a small animal, but evinces the terrible human instinctual passion to destroy everything and everyone.

In all, according to these two symptoms, the boss can be diagnosed as a neurotic suffering from the over-activity of the aggressive instinct in the id. Then how comes the neurosis? We hold that it indirectly results from his tremendous grief of losing the beloved son. As can be seen in the middle part of the story, the boss felt unparalleled affection for his only son who was his sole promise of life. Thus, it's easy to imagine what a heavy blow the son's death would bring to him. Ever since the day when hearing the sad news that the son was dead, he had become "a broken man", and his life "had come to have no other meaning". Such great sorrow together with the loss of hope for life becomes the very inducement of the potential psychic imbalance, as is the circumstance with many neurotic cases. And since those strong emotions could not be let out timely, psychological problems emerge. In the case of the boss, six years after the son's death, he had already been incapable of having "a violent fit of weeping" which was the only way for him to relieve. Consequently the sorrow was internalized and there came up the psychic disturbance. As healthy psyche always consists in the balance of id and superego, psychic disturbance characterizes either the over-activity or deficiency of certain part in the psychic zones. And as for the boss, the imbalance leads to the activation of the instinct to destroy, which is manifested through his violent action, aggressive attitude and unconscious inclination for sadism.

However, we shall not confine the interpretation of Mansfield's characterization of the boss to a description of a sadist-inclined neurotic. As a writer who is concerned with human life, she goes beyond it. Saralyn Daly once said that Mansfield was always paying attention to the latent human violence[4]. Thus in "The Fly", by writing of such a figure as the boss, she discloses the destructive instinct that is ingrained with every human being, and hints at its possible consequence—the extermination of the mankind, as is exemplified by the death of the fly. For, whenever the instinct is in

---

4　"萨拉琳·戴利指出'曼斯菲尔德一直关注人类的潜在暴力'……"见：徐凯. 巧妙的象征·深刻的内涵. 名作欣赏，2000，5: 58.

control, those sincere human relations like love and sympathy give way and everyone becomes the destructor. A most representative example is the war in which the aggressive instinct is amplified and human life is freely trampled. So in this sense, the story can also be regarded as an indictment of the ruthless war, the degeneration of the civilized society.

References:

[1] Guerin, Wilfred L. et al. *A Handbook of Critical Approaches to Literature.* Beijing: Foreign Language Teaching and Research Press, 2004.

[2] Scott, Ian and Kilvert, ed. *British Writers (*Volume VII). New York: Charles Seribner's Sons, 1984.

[3] Ward, A. C. *Longman Companion to Twentieth Century Literature*. Essex: Longman House, 1981.

[4] 阿尔伯斯 A. 一次轻率的旅行：凯瑟琳·曼斯菲尔德的一生. 冯洁音译. 上海：知识出版社，1993.

[5] 付灿邦. 论曼斯菲尔德的《苍蝇》. 四川师范学院学报（哲社版），1994，4: 112.

[6] 傅子柏. 论曼斯菲尔德的《苍蝇》. 重庆师范学院学报（哲社版），1995，3: 73.

[7] 徐凯. 巧妙的象征·深刻的内涵. 名作欣赏，2000，5: 58.

[8] 张首映. 西方二十世纪文论史. 北京：北京大学出版社，1999.

[9] 赵敏霞. 论曼斯菲尔德短篇小说的主题特征. 学术交流，1999，4: 132.

(王霞)

Chapter 2　Character

第二章　人物

> Good fiction is made of that which is real, and reality is difficult to come by. So much of it depends upon the individual's willingness to discover his true self, upon his defining himself—for the time being at least—against his background.
>
> Ralph Waldo Ellison

简要介绍：

Characters are the persons created in a dramatic or narrative work, who are sketched by the writer as recognizable persons with particular moral, intellectual, and emotional qualities through their distinctive ways of saying—the dialogue—and their ways of doing—the actions.

Characters mostly share three principles. Firstly, characters are consistent in their speech and actions, and do not behave one way on one occasion and a different way on another unless there is a clear description for the inconsistency. Secondly, characters are motivated in their speech and actions grounded in their dispositions, desires, moral nature and values. Thirdly, characters are lifelike, with convincing human qualities. A character is usually a person, but it may not be a necessity. In Herman Melville's *Moby Dick*, the antagonist is a whale; while in Virginia Woolf's *Flush*, the protagonist is a dog. No matter a character is a person or an animal, one thing is in common, that is, he/it must have some recognizable human qualities.

Two types of characters are named after the publication of E. M. Forster's *Aspects of the Novel* (1927), that is, "flat" character and "round" character. A "flat" character refers to the one who remains essentially stable or unchanged in disposition, from beginning to end of a work, without much individuality (for instance, Woodifield in "The Fly"); while a "round" character is complex and less predictable in disposition, and may undergo a radical change, either through a gradual process of development or as the result of a crisis (for example, the boss in "The Fly").

The methods by which the writer creates distinctive characters in a dramatic or narrative work are called characterization. There are two ways of characterization, they are, showing and telling. In showing, the author simply presents characters' speech, actions, inner thoughts, and emotions directly, but with no authorial description and comment, and lets the reader infer by himself the characters' temperament. In telling, the author describes and analyzes directly characters' disposition and motives. The method of telling has the advantage of being clear and economical, but it has been considered a violation of artistry by modern writers and critics after Flaubert and Henry James, who advocated showing only, which seems more dramatic and lifelike.

简　析：

关于"人物"，我们需要注意的是：

1）人物是在情节的发展中完成塑造的，因此，除了作者直接的描写和评论外，人物自身的言行举止及其变化发展是理解和把握人物的关键。

2）与现实中的个体一样，小说中人物的个性具有同一性的特点——人物的言语和行动不会毫无理由地产生突变，人物的言行只是其内在性情、品质、价值观的冰山一角。因此，透过表层，感悟言行背后的深层动机是理解人物的重要途径。

3）人物根据其塑造是否全方位和全过程的而被分为"扁平人物"和"圆形人物"两种。"扁平人物"由于被局限在某种单一的观念之内而显得单薄、缺乏变化；"圆形人物"是一种立体塑造，不仅展现人物个性上的多面性，而且展现个性发展中的复杂性。一部作品中的主要人物通常都是"圆形"的，但是这并不是说"扁平人物"不重要。作品中的人物应该是一种组合，其取舍取决于创作的需求。

4）人物塑造有"讲述"和"展现"两种方法。"讲述"是指作者对对象的描述、评价，有较强的主观性；"展现"是指只记录人物的对话、行动、思想而让作者从作品中退出的写作模式，其主要特征是客观、真实，给读者较大的想象和参与空间，阅读的难度也增强。现实主义作品主要采用"讲述"模式，而现代主义作品主要采用"展现"模式。

作 品：

JAMES JOYCE
[1882—1941]

Araby

North Richmond Street, being blind, was a quiet street except at the hour when the Christian Brothers' School set the boys free. An uninhabited house of two storeys stood at the blind end, detached from its neighbours in a square ground. The other houses of the street, conscious of decent lives within them, gazed at one another with brown imperturbable faces.

The former tenant of our house, a priest, had died in the back drawing-room. Air, musty from having been long enclosed, hung in all the rooms, and the waste room behind the kitchen was littered with old useless papers. Among these I found a few paper-covered books, the pages of which were curled and damp: *The Abbot*[1], by Walter Scott, *The Devout Communicant*[2] and *The Memoirs of Vidocq*[3]. I liked the last best because its leaves were yellow. The wild garden behind the house contained a central apple tree and a few straggling bushes, under one of which I found the late tenant's rusty bicycle-pump. He had been a very charitable priest; in his will he had left all his money to institutions and the furniture of his house to his sister.

When the short days of winter came, dusk fell before we had well eaten our dinners. When we met in the street the houses had grown sombre. The space of sky above us was the color of ever-changing violet and towards it the lamps of the street lifted their feeble lanterns. The cold air stung us and we played till our bodies glowed. Our shouts echoed in the silent street. The career of our play brought us through the dark muddy lanes behind the houses, where we ran the gauntlet of the rough tribes from the cottages, to the back doors of the dark dripping gardens where odours arose from the ashpits, to the dark odorous stables where a coachman smoothed and combed the horse or shook music from the buckled harness. When we returned to the street, light from the kitchen windows had filled the areas. If my

---

1 英国小说家 Walter Scott (1771—1832) 的传奇小说。
2 英国方济各会（Franciscan）修道士 Pacificus Baker (1695—1774) 的宗教作品。
3 法国特工人员兼作家 Francois Jules Vidocq (1775—1857) 的回忆录。

uncle was seen turning the corner, we hid in the shadow until we had seen him safely housed. Or if Mangan's sister came out on the doorstep to call her brother in to his tea, we watched her from our shadow peer up and down the street. We waited to see whether she would remain or go in and, if she remained, we left our shadow and walked up to Mangan's steps resignedly. She was waiting for us, her figure defined by the light from the half-opened door. Her brother always teased her before he obeyed, and I stood by the railings looking at her. Her dress swung as she moved her body, and the soft rope of her hair tossed from side to side.

Every morning I lay on the floor in the front parlour watching her door. The blind was pulled down to within an inch of the sash so that I could not be seen. When she came out on the doorstep my heart leaped. I ran to the hall, seized my books and followed her. I kept her brown figure always in my eye and, when we came near the point at which our ways diverged, I quickened my pace and passed her. This happened morning after morning. I had never spoken to her, except for a few casual words, and yet her name was like a summons to all my foolish blood.

Her image accompanied me even in places the most hostile to romance. On Saturday evenings when my aunt went marketing I had to go to carry some of the parcels. We walked through the flaring streets, jostled by drunken men and bargaining women, amid the curses of labourers, the shrill litanies of shop-boys who stood on guard by the barrels of pigs' cheeks, the nasal chanting of street-singers, who sang a *come-all-you*[4] about O'Donovan Rossa[5], or a ballad about the troubles in our native land. These noises converged in a single sensation of life for me: I imagined that I bore my chalice safely through a throng of foes. Her name sprang to my lips at moments in strange prayers and praises which I myself did not understand. My eyes were often full of tears (I could not tell why) and at times a flood from my heart seemed to pour itself out into my bosom. I thought little of the future. I did not know whether I would ever speak to her or not or, if I spoke to her, how I would tell her of my confused adoration. But my body was like a harp and her words and gestures were like fingers running upon the wires.

One evening I went into the back drawing-room in which the priest had died. It was dark rainy evening and there was no sound in the house. Through one of the broken panes I heard the rain impinge upon the earth, the fine incessant needles of water playing in the sodden beds. Some distant lamp or lighted window gleamed

---

4 特指所有以 "Come all you Irishmen" 为开端的流行歌曲。
5 指爱尔兰独立运动领导人 Jeremiah O'Donovan (1831—1915)。

below me. I was thankful that I could see so little. All my senses seemed to desire to veil themselves and, feeling that I was about to slip from them, I pressed the palms of my hands together until they trembled, murmuring: *"O love! O love!"* many times.

At last she spoke to me. When she addressed the first words to me I was so confused that I did not know what to answer. She asked me was I going to *Araby*. I forget whether I answered yes or no. It would be a splendid bazaar, she said she would love to go.

"And why can't you?" I asked.

While she spoke she turned a silver bracelet round and round her wrist. She could not go, she said, because there would be a retreat that week in her convent[6]. Her brother and two other boys were fighting for their caps and I was alone at the railings. She held one of the spikes, bowing her head towards me. The light from the lamp opposite our door caught the white curve of her neck, lit up her hair that rested there and, falling, lit up the hand upon the railing. It fell over one side of her dress and caught the white border of a petticoat, just visible as she stood at ease.

"It's well for you," she said.

"If I go," I said. "I will bring you something."

What innumerable follies laid waste my waking and sleeping thoughts after that evening! I wished to annihilate the tedious intervening days. I chafed against the work of school. At night in my bedroom and by day in the classroom her image came between me and the page I strove to read. The syllables of the word *Araby* were called to me through the silence in which my soul luxuriated and cast an Eastern enchantment over me. I asked for leave to go to the bazaar on Saturday night. My aunt was surprised and hoped it was not some Freemason[7] affair. I answered few questions in class. I watched my master's face pass from amiability to sternness; he hoped I was not beginning to idle. I could not call my wandering thoughts together. I had hardly and patience with the serious work of life which, now that it stood between me and my desire, seemed to me child's play, ugly monotonous child's play.

On Saturday morning I remained my uncle that I wished to go to the bazaar in the evening. He was fussing at the hallstand, looking for the hat-brush, and answered me curtly:

"Yes, boy, I know."

---

6 她上学的那所女隐修会学校有一次静修（集体祷告和静思）。
7 共济会，国际上最大的秘密团体，旨在传授并执行秘密互助纲领。天主教会认为共济会是反天主教的团体。

As he was in the hall I could not go into the front parlour and lie at the window. I left the house in bad humour and walked slowly towards the school. The air was pitilessly raw and already my heart misgave me.

When I came home to dinner my uncle had not yet been home. Still it was early. I sat staring at the clock for some time and, when its ticking began to irritate me, I left the room. I mounted the staircase and gained the upper part of the house. The high, cold, empty, gloomy rooms liberated me and I went from room to room singing. From the front window I saw my companions playing below in the street. Their cries reached me weakened and indistinct and, leaning my forehead against the cool glass, I looked over at the dark house where she lived. I may have stood there for an hour, seeing nothing but a brown-clad figure cast by my imagination, touched discreetly by the lamplight at the curved neck, at the hand upon the railings and at the border below the dress.

When I came downstairs again I found Mrs. Mercer sitting at the fire. She was an old, garrulous woman, a pawnbroker's widow, who collected used stamps for some pious purpose. I had to endure the gossip of the tea-table. The meal was prolonged beyond an hour and still my uncle did not come. Mrs. Mercer stood up to go: she was sorry she couldn't wait any longer, but it was after eight o'clock and she did not like to be out late, as the night air was bad for her. When she had gone I began to walk up and down the room, clenching my fists. My aunt said:

"I'm afraid you may put off your bazaar for this night of our Lord."

At nine o'clock I heard my uncle latchkey in the hall door. I heard him talking to himself and heard the hallstand rocking when it had received the weight of his overcoat. I could interpret these signs. When he was midway through his dinner I asked him to give me the money to go to the bazaar. He had forgotten.

"The people are in bed and after their first sleep now," he said.

I did not smile. My aunt said to him energetically:

"Can't you give him the money and let him go? You've kept him late enough as it is."

My uncle said he was very sorry he had forgotten. He said he believed in the old saying: "All work and no play makes Jack a dull boy." He asked me where I was going and, when I had told him a second time, he asked me did I know *The Arab's Farewell to his Steed*[8]. When I left the kitchen he was about to recite the opening

---

8 英国诗人 Caroline Norton 的一首伤感的诗歌，大意是：一个阿拉伯人卖掉心爱的马匹后极为伤心。

lines of the piece to my aunt.

I held a florin tightly in my hand as I strode down Buckingham Street towards the station. The sight of the streets thronged with buyers and glaring with gas recalled to me the purpose of my journey. I took my seat in a third-class carriage of a deserted train. After an intolerable delay the train moved out of the station slowly. It crept onward among ruinous houses and over the twinkling river. At Westland Row Station a crowd of people pressed to the carriage doors; but the porters moved them back, saying that it was a special train for the bazaar. I remained alone in the bare carriage. In a few minutes the train drew up beside an improvised wooden platform. I passed out on to the road and saw by the lighted dial of a clock that it was ten minutes to ten. In front of me was a large building which displayed the magical name.

I could not find any sixpenny entrance and, fearing that the bazaar would be closed, I passed in quickly through a turnstile, handing a shilling to a weary-looking man. I found myself in a big hall girdled at half its height by a gallery. Nearly all the stalls were closed and the greater part of the hall was in darkness. I recognized a silence like that which pervades a church after a service. I walked into the center of the bazaar timidly. A few people were gathered about the stalls which were still open. Before a curtain, over which the word *Café Chantant*[9] were written in coloured lamps, two men were counting money on a salver. I listened to the fall of the coins.

Remembering with difficulty why I had come I went over to one of the stalls and examined porcelain vases and flowered tea-sets. At the door of the stall a young lady was talking and laughing with two young gentlemen. I remarked their English accents and listened vaguely to their conversion.

"O, I never said such a thing?"

"O, but you did!"

"O, but I didn't!"

"Didn't she say that?"

"Yes, I heard her."

"O, there's a …fib!"

Observing me, the young lady came over and asked me did I wish to buy anything. The tone of her voice was not encouraging; she seemed to have spoken to me out of a sense of duty. I looked humbly at the great jars that stood like eastern

---

9 （法语）音乐咖啡厅。

guards at either side of the dark entrance to the stall and murmured:

"No, thank you."

The young lady changed the position of one of the vases and went back to the two young men. They began to talk of the same subject. Once or twice the young lady glanced at me over her shoulder.

I lingered before her stall, though I knew my stay was useless, to make my interest in her wares seem the more real. Then I turned away slowly and walked down the middle of the bazaar. I allowed two pennies to fall against the sixpence in my pocket. I heard a voice call from one end of the gallery that the light was out. The upper part of the hall was now completely dark.

Gazing up into the darkness I saw myself as a creature driven and derided by vanity; and my eyes burned with anguish and anger.

Questions:

1. How much do you know about the protagonist? What are his chief qualities?
2. What is the character of the uncle? How does he influence the boy's disposition?
3. How important is setting in the story?
4. How do you understand the ending? Is there anything gained by the protagonist or the narrator through his frustration?

赏　析：

Three Critical Approaches to "Araby"

1. Traditional Approach to "Araby"

"Araby" is one of the fifteen short stories in James Joyce's collection, *Dubliners*. Although Joyce wrote the stories between 1904 and 1906, they were not published until 1914. The book *Dubliners* paints a portrait of life in Dublin, Ireland, at the turn of the twentieth century. Its stories are arranged in an order reflecting the growing process of a naïve child into a mature man. The first three stories are told from the point of view of a young boy, the next three from the point of view of an adolescent, and so on. "Araby" is the last story of the first set, and is told from the perspective of a boy just on the verge of adolescence.

1) The Genre and the Plot of the Short Story

"Araby" is a short story—that is, a relatively brief narrative of prose fiction (ranging in length from five hundred to twenty thousand words) characterized by considerably more unity and compression in all its parts than the novel—in theme, plot, structure, character, setting, and mood.[1] In the short story "Araby", several different microcosms are evident. The story demonstrates adolescence, maturity, and public life in Dublin at that time. As the story progresses, we learn gradually how this city has grown to destroy the young boy's holy hopes of life, and leave the boy with "anguish and anger". Breaking away from the traditional plot of "conflict—climax—dénouement", Joyce employs "epiphany" to culminate the climax as well as the déouement of the story, that is, in "Araby", the climax collapses with the dénouement. In Joyce's terms, an epiphany is a moment when the essence of a character is revealed, when all the forces that bear on his life converge, and we can, in that instant, understand him.[2] In "Araby", the meaning is revealed on a young boy's psychic journey from first love to disappointment and despair, and the theme is found in the boy's discovery of the discrepancy between the real and the ideal in life.

The story opens with a description of North Richmond Street, a "blind" "silent" street where the houses "gazed at one another with brown imperturbable faces". It is a street of decaying conformity, false piety and lethargy. The boy's house contains the same sense of an unanimated present and a lost past. The former tenant of their house, a priest, died in the back room, and his legacy—several old curled books, which the boy enjoys leafing through because the leaves are yellow, and a bicycle pump rusting in the backyard—symbolize the intellectual and religious vitality of the past. The boy, in the midst of such decay and spiritual paralysis, experiences his fantasy of first love and his awakening from his thorough romantic imagination.

Every morning before school the boy lies on the floor in the front parlor peeking out through a crack in the blind of the door, watching and waiting for the girl next door to emerge from her house and walk to school. He is shy and still boyish. He follows her, walks silently past, not daring to speak, overwhelmed with a confused sense of sensual desire and religious adoration. In his mind she is both a saint to be worshipped and a woman to be desired. He observes her so carefully that he appreciates the "white curve of her neck" and feels the light catch the white border of a petticoat... His eyes are "often full of tears", and one evening he goes to the back room where the priest had died. Clasping the palms of his hands together, he murmurs, "O love! O love!" in a prayer not to God, but to the concept of love and perhaps even to the girl, his lover. Walking with his aunt to shop on Saturday evenings he imagines that the girl's image accompanies him, and that he protects her in "places the most hostile to

1 Guerin, Wilfred L. et al. *A Handbook of Critical Approaches to Literature* 文学批评方法手册. 第4版. Beijing & Oxford: Foreign Language Teaching and Research Press & Oxford University Press, 1999: 52
2 Scholes, R. & A.W. Litz, ed. *Dubliners: Text, Criticism, and Notes*. New York: The Viking Press, 1969: 132.

romance". In the mixed symbolism of the Christian and the Oriental myths Joyce reveals the blindness of the boy in the story: "These noises converged in a single sensation of life for me: I imagined that I bore my chalice safely through a throng of foes." Drifting away from his schoolmates' boyish games, the boy has fantasies in his isolation, in the ecstasy and pain of first love.

Finally the girl speaks to the boy. She asks him if he is going to *Araby*. He replies that if he does he will bring her a gift. Exactly like any young boy or girl who indulged in the fantasy of their first love, the boy lives in his own imagination and cannot sleep or study well at all from that moment. The word *Araby* "cast an Eastern enchantment" over him, but on the night he is to go to the bazaar his uncle forgets to give him some money. Neither the aunt nor the uncle understands the boy's mood and anguish, thus his isolation and blindness are deepened. At last, when he gets the money and hurries to the dreamland—bazaar, he recognizes "a silence like that which pervades a church after a service" and finds the bazaar a mundane and dirty place where two men are "counting money on a salver" and he listens to "the fall of the coins". A young lady, bored with him and interested in flirting with two men, smites the boy's feeling of "Eastern enchantment". Suddenly from the trivialities here the boy experiences epiphany, a "sudden showing forth" in which his mind is flooded with light, with truth. He can see the parallel that exists between the girl here and "his" holy girl; he can see the cause of his feeling for her—physical attraction. Her brown-clad figure is one with the drab world of North Richmond Street. His love, like his quest for a gift to draw the girl to him in an unfriendly and cold world, ends with the epiphany that his pure and holy love exists only in his mind. Thus the theme of the story—the discrepancy between the real and the ideal reveals itself in the bazaar, a place of tawdry trade. The epiphany in which the boy finds his dream a falsity and himself driven and derided by vanity caused his "anguish and anger" to himself. The story ends with the boy's painful epiphany which may be experienced by every growing juvenile.

2) Historical-Biographical Considerations

Born in Dublin in 1882, James Augustine Aloysius was the eldest of the ten surviving children of John and Mary Jane Joyce. Well-known as a modernist novelist and noted for his experimental use of language, James Joyce published *Dubliners* in 1914, *A Portrait of the Artist as a Young Man* in 1916, a play *Exiles* in 1918 and *Ulysses* in 1922. In 1907 Joyce had published a collection of poems, *Chamber Music*. Joyce once told a friend, "One of the things I could never get accustomed to in my youth was the difference I found between life and literature."[3] Joyce dedicated his career to erasing it and in the process he has successfully revolutionized 20th century fiction. The life we read in his literature was chiefly his own. "Araby" is a short story that reflects Joyce's own life as a boy growing up in Dublin. Joyce uses the voice of a young boy as a narrator; however the narrator seems much more

---

3 Coulthard, A. R. *World Literature in Review*. (Internet) http://www.elibrary.com/id/2525/getdoc.cg...2D000&form= RL&pubname=explicator&puburl=0

mature than the boy in the story. And the mature narrator is the grown up Joyce. Joyce may portray the uncle according to his own father. Joyce's father was bad-tempered, witty, hard drinking and ruinously improvident. In the story, the boy's uncle doesn't come back home until 9 o'clock at the night when the boy was waiting for the uncle to give him the money to go to the bazaar. He has forgotten his promise to the little boy. And we can perceive that he goes to the pub after his work and get drunk. The aunt in the story resembles his mother, a devout Roman Catholic, helplessly watched her husband and family slide into near poverty and hoped for a happier life in the hereafter.

James' entire education came at the hands of the Jesuits. By the time the young Joyce graduated from University College, Dublin, in 1902, he decided he had learned enough to reject his religion and all his obligations to family, homeland and the British who ruled there.

He frequently employs the church related image in "Araby". For example, "the North Richmond Street was a quiet street except at the hour when the Christian Brothers' School set the boys free." When he arrived at the bazaar timidly, he recognized "a silence like that which pervades a church after a service". The church gradually lost its function and power in their mind despite that its rituals still tightly restricted the Irish. In "Araby", the former tenant, a deceased priest, who symbolizes the influence of the church, is shown to have been insensitive to the spiritual needs of his people. His legacy was a collection of books that showed his confusion of the sacred with the secular. And there is evidence that he devoted his life to gathering money and furniture. He left behind no evidence of a life of spiritual influence. In this sense, the Irish's religion and faith were paralyzed. Joyce uses a medical term—"paralysis"—to sum up the material and spiritual effects of the colonial dominance, he clearly believed that Ireland's colonial exploitation by England played a primary and determining role in engendering the disease.

> The economic and intellectual conditions that prevail in [Ireland] do not permit the development of individuality. The soul of the country is weakened by centuries of useless struggle and broken treaties, and individual initiative is paralyzed by the influence and admonitions of the church, while its body is manacled by the police, the tax office, and the garrison. No one who has any self-respect stays in Ireland...[4]

"Araby" seems to be a reflection of Joyce's own life in a repressive Dublin culture. Joyce described North Richmond Street as blind, cold and quiet, and the uninhabited house detached from its neighbors in a ground, indicating the decaying and deserted surroundings in Dublin. The boy and his companions go play behind their houses, along the "dark muddy lanes", to where the "rough tribes" dwell. The rough tribes indicate those who are uneducated, poverty-stricken and lacking in faith, not to

---

4 Mason, Ellsworth & Richard Ellmann, ed. *The Critical Writings of James Joyce*. New York: The Viking Press, 1964: 171.

say a holy religious belief. In the gardens odors arise from "the ash pits"—the dark dripping gardens and the ash pits are Joyce's symbols of the decay of religious faith of Irish people.

At that time, under the heavy pressure of the British colony, more than half of the Irish fled to foreign countries, leaving a deserted and paralyzed Ireland behind. The title "Araby" itself suggests escape. To the nineteenth-century European mind, the Islamic lands of North Africa, the Near East, and the Middle East symbolized decadence, exotic delights, escapism, and a luxurious sensuality. The story focuses on the boy's escape from the drab reality and his fantasy about the holy love in the "paralyzed" Dublin. And it may be a retrospective of Joyce's look back at his youthful life and the constant struggle between ideals and reality. Araby is an attempt by the boy to escape the bleak darkness of North Richmond Street. Joyce arranges an attempt to escape the "short days of winter", "where night falls early" and streetlights are but "feeble lanterns" failing to light the somberness of the "dark muddy lanes". Metaphorically, Joyce calls the street blind, a dead end, much like Dublin itself in the mid 1890s when Joyce lived on North Richmond Street as a young boy.

At the bazaar, the girl attending the stall, like Mangan's sister, becomes an object of faith. But when she speaks—like Mangan's sister whose words are trivial and worldly, in a sudden flash of insight the boy sees that his faith and his passion have been blind. His fantasy and dream are smitten by the girl who is speaking with English accent. This may imply that it is the English colonists who smite the life of the Dubliners. The boy also sees in the "two men counting money on a salver" a symbol of the moneylenders in the temple. He allows the pennies to fall in his pocket, indicating his dreams also fall. We can sense the Joyce's indictment to the English colony in it.

2. Irony in "Araby": A Formalistic Approach

According to *A Handbook of Critical Approaches to Literature*, the formalistic critic deals with organic unity and dominant image, irony and paradox, with ambiguity, with the tensions that result from multiple interactions within the organic form of the literary piece.[5] It's not difficult to find irony in James Joyce's story "Araby".

Despite the perfect conformation of external form with general content, there is an interesting discontinuity of sorts—a paradox—that might catch our attention. Although "Araby" is told from the first person viewpoint of its young protagonist, we do not receive the impression that a boy tells the story. Instead, the narrator seems to be a man whose mind is more mature than the boy. If a boy's mind had reconstructed the events of the story, he won't have called his then sacred thought and action stupid. It is a mature man's particular way of telling the story that enables us to perceive clearly the torment the boy experiences when ideals, concerning both sacred and earthly love, are destroyed by a sudden

---

5 Guerin, Wilfred L. et al. *A Handbook of Critical Approaches to Literature* 文学批评方法手册. 第4版. Beijing & Oxford: Foreign Language Teaching and Research Press & Oxford University Press, 1999:118.

epiphany of the actual world. The contrast between a man's mature thought and a boy's immature mind presents us with a remarkable "tension". The tension, which resolves itself into the organic form of the story, achieves a psychic distance between the hero and the narrator despite its first-person narrative style.

In this way, the reader won't be misled by the naïve boy. Instead, we can get an ironic view of the institutions and persons surrounding the boy from the mature man narrator. For example, the boy's view "Her image accompanied me (the boy) forms a paradox with the man's view even in places the most hostile to romance." The paradox here presents an irony for us. The ironic view would be impossible for the immature, emotionally involved mind of the boy himself. Only an adult looking back at the high hopes of "foolish blood" and its resultant destruction could account for the ironic viewpoint. Throughout the story, however, the narrator consistently maintains a full sensitivity to his youthful anguish. Throughout the story we can sense the two narrators rolling into one.

The opening paragraph, which sets the scene, prepares us for the view of the conflict between the loveliness of the ideal and the drabness of the actual. Descriptive words show the narrator's consciousness of the boy's response to beauty and the response of the neighborhood people, who are blind to beauty: North Richmond Street is "blind"; its houses, inhabited by "decent" people, stare indifferently at one another, and all this is under a sky of "ever-changing violet", in a setting of gardens marred by the "odors of ash-pits" and "dark odorous stables". The boy's own house, which had formerly been inhabited by a priest, is placed in a garden like that of Eden. It is a place of potential holiness, shown to us in the irony of the garden's barrenness and the priest's worldliness: the garden has now only a "central apple tree" and "a few straggling bushes"; the priest had died and left behind him evidence of his preoccupation with secular literature and with money and furniture.

Then appears a figure representative of the ideal into this setting, the girl. The immature boy narrator shows us in a subtly ironic manner that in his youthful adoration of Mangan's sister, she is the embodiment of all his boyish dreams of the beauty and of physical desire and, at the same time, the embodiment of his adoration of all that is holy. In his dark environment Mangan's sister stands out, a figure always shown outlined by light, with the power to set in him zeal to conquer the bleak and the unholy. Her image constantly makes him feel as though he bears a holy "chalice" through a "throng of foes"—the Saturday evening throng of drunken men, bargaining women, cursing laborers, and all the others who have no conception of the mystical beauty his young mind has created in this world of material ugliness.

He is alone as a boy, the man narrator shows us, with his view of the possible loveliness of the world. Even the aunt and uncle with whom he lives are insensitive to his burning need to go to the bazaar, which looms in his imagination as a place of mystical Eastern enchantment, to purchase a gift presenting to his beloved one. Looking back, the narrator can see that his uncle had been concerned with his daily, worldly tasks, his aunt with maintaining blindly the Christian rituals. From the vantage point of maturity the narrator can realize that the aunt and the uncle perhaps once possessed an awareness of the romantic, an awareness that has since been clouded by the drabness of North Richmond Street.

He has come alone on a deserted train; the bazaar, full of spurious wares, is tended by secular people who leave him even more solitude than he had been before; the young lady who should have waited on him ignores him to joke with two young men. The young lady's inane remarks to the young men reminded the boy of his adored one's remarks. Both are concerned with the material, the rude.

With his backward look, the narrator has supplied us with two apprehensions: the first is the boy's fully remembered and fully felt anguish of an epiphany when the disparity between a youthful dream of the mystic beauty of the world and his actual world revealed to him. The second is the irony implied in the man's view that can see the dream itself as a "vanity". Thus the ironies in "Araby" are achieved by the two narrative voices rolling into one.

3. Departure from Eden: A Mythological and Archetypal Approach to "Araby"

The universality of experience makes the story resorting to many people's interest, for they respond instinctively to an experience that could have been their own. It is a part of the instinctual nature of man to long for the happiness of Eden, which is the paradise for man and woman leading a carefree life harmoniously. For every man falling in love for the first time accidentally, to search for and find the "paradise" is believed to be possible. The development of theme in "Araby" resembles the archetypal myth of banishment from paradise.

In "Araby" Joyce works from a "visionary mode of artistic creation"—a phrase used by psychiatrist Carl Jung to describe the "visionary" kind of literary creation that derives its material from "the hinterland of man's mind—that suggests the abyss of time separating us from pre-human ages, or evokes a superhuman world of contrasting light and darkness. It is a primordial experience, which surpasses man's understanding and to which he is therefore in danger of succumbing."[6] Assuredly this describes Joyce's handling of the material of "Araby". The quest itself and its consequences surpass the understanding of the young protagonist of the story. He can only "feel" that he undergoes the experience of the quest and naturally is confused, and at the story's conclusion, when he fails, he is anguished and angered, somewhat resembles the anguish experienced by Adam and Eve when they were banished from Eden. The nameless boy was banished from his first imagined pure and noble love for the girl. Before their banishment, Adam and Eve were intellectually blind, just like the blindness of the nameless boy when he fell in love with Mangan's sister—an imagined image, to say it exactly.

---

6 Jung, Carl G. *Modern Man in Search of a Soul*. Trans. W. S. Dell and Cary F. Baynes. New York: [s.n.], 1933: 156-157.

Before Adam and Eve stealthily ate the fruit from the intelligence tree, they were intellectually blind and lived a happy life blindly. The repeated word "blind" in "Araby" imply the boy's blind first love. When he was blind in love, he was happy and a surge of hope filled him. However, he searched for light everywhere and regarded the girl as the light shining into his dull and dark life despite his dark circumstances. He even felt the girl's image in places the most hostile to romance: the market and the streets, among the "drunken men and bargaining women", amid "the curses of laborers, the shrill litanies of shop-boys". Everywhere in his dark surroundings the boy seeks the "light". He looks for it in the "central apple tree" which is the symbol of religious enlightenment, in the dark garden behind his home. The garden should be like Eden, but the tree in "Araby" is overshadowed by the desolation of the garden, and thus become the tree of the spiritual agony. The tree in "Araby" has become Joyce's individual archetype. However, the tree in Eden symbolizes the tree of intelligence which enlightened Adam and Eve from their blindness. In "Araby", the market Araby, where the boy disillusioned and found himself "a creature driven and derided by vanity", shares some similarity in function with the tree in Eden. Though the boy felt agonized and angry he got the insight, grew up and became mature spiritually. Though Adam and Eve ate the fruit from the tree and dispelled by God from Eden the paradise, they harvest intelligence and rich experience living as human being.

Just like Willa Cather once wrote in *O Pioneers!* "there are only two or three human stories, and they go on repeating themselves as fiercely as if they had never happened before."[7] The myth of Eden repeats itself day after day, year after year. So does the story "Araby" in which the boy can't help falling in love (cf: stealthily eat the fruit on the intelligence tree), then dispels from his dreamland (cf: dispelled from Eden) and gets mature and grows up (cf: capable of thinking and leading normal human life). Sharing the same collective unconsciousness, most boys have the same psychological and emotional experience on their process to growing mature. And one of the commonest repeating stories derived from the myth of Eden may be that human beings have to pay some price to acquire insight and intelligence.

References:

[1] Cather, Willa. *O Pioneers!*. 北京：人民文学出版社，2002.

[2] Coulthard, A. R. *World Literature in Review*. (Internet) http://www.elibrary.com/id/2525/getdoc. cg...2D000&form.

[3] Guerin, Wilfred L. et al. *A Handbook of Critical Approaches to Literature* 文学批评方法手册. 第 4 版. Beijing & Oxford: Foreign Language Teaching and Research Press & Oxford University Press, 1999.

---

7 Cather, Willa. *O Pioneers!*. 北京：人民文学出版社，2002: 130.

[4] Mason, E. & Ellmann R, ed. *The Critical Writings of James Joyce.* New York: The Viking Press, 1964.

[5] Scholes, R. & A. W. Litz, ed. *Dubliners: Text, Criticism, and Notes*. New York: The Viking Press, 1969.

(余华)

Chapter 3   Setting

第三章   背景

When romance do really teach anything, or produce any effective operation, it is usually through a far more suitable process than the ostensible one.

Nathaniel Hawthorne

简要介绍：

Setting is the context in which speech and actions of a narrative or dramatic work occur. The major elements of setting are place, historical time, and social environment that frame the plot and characters. The setting of Katherine Mansfield's "The Fly", for example, is in the City (London), on a certain Tuesday a few years after the First World War.

Setting displays reality in detail in which the characters act, persuade the reader of the validity of the work. These concrete representations of actual life illustrate universal truths about human experience, applicable not just in a certain place in that novel, but anywhere human beings live.

Setting generates the atmosphere of the work and sometimes symbolizes the emotional state of the characters. We are better able to understand the actions of the characters and their significance if we are sensitive to the description of setting.

Setting is relevant to the overall purpose of the literary work, and may be essential to meaning in works by writers such as William Faulkner, James Joyce, Virginia Woolf, for the physical details of setting are associated with the values, ideals, and attitudes of that place at that times. Just as one of the novelists said, setting is the "conductor of all the currents of emotion and belief and moral conviction that charge out from the story".

简 析：

关于"背景"，我们需要注意的是：

1）背景是情节发展和人物塑造的场所，主要由时间、地点和社会环境构成。背景的主要构成因素决定了它在作品中的重要作用：提供现实的场景，营造与人物情感相符的氛围和揭示特定时代的价值观、生活态度、生活方式。

2）背景为作品所提供的现实感为作品与读者的沟通提供基础。不论是写实作品还是虚构作品，作品大都会给出具体的时间、地点和社会背景，让读者根据自己的经历和知识来体验和理解作品中描写的生活和思想。相同的故事，变换了背景后很可能导致不同的理解，这说明了背景的重要性。

3）背景所描写的氛围与人物的情绪大致相符。背景常常预设了必要的氛围，使读者自然而然地调节情绪，很快进入情节和人物所需要的情绪，这显然有助于读者更好地理解作品。

4）背景以独特的方式暗示着作品的主要思想。背景描写隐含着特定时代的人们所持的价值观、理想、生活态度、生活方式，以及人物的情绪等，它们常常通过意象、隐喻、典故、神话、象征等创作技巧间接地传达着作者的思想，因此，准确领悟背景描写中细节的含义往往可以使读者比较快地读懂一部作品。

作 品：

VIRGINIA WOOLF
[1882—1941]

Kew Gardens[1]

From the oval-shaped flower-bed there rose perhaps a hundred stalks spreading into heart-shaped or tongue-shaped leaves half-way up and unfurling at the tip red or blue or yellow petals marked with spots of colour raised upon the surface; and from the red, blue or yellow gloom of the throat emerged a straight bar, rough with gold dust and slightly clubbed at the end. The petals were voluminous enough to be stirred by the summer breeze, and when they moved, the red, blue and yellow lights passed one over the other, staining an inch of the brown earth beneath with a spot of the most intricate colour. The light fell either upon the smooth, grey back of a pebble, or the shell of a snail with its brown, circular veins, or falling

---

1 Kew Gardens 位于伦敦市郊 Kew, Surrey，是英国皇家植物园。

into a raindrop, it expanded with such intensity of red, blue and yellow the thin walls of water that one expected them to burst and disappear. Instead, the drop was left in a second silver grey once more, and the light now settled upon the flesh of a leaf, revealing the branching thread of fibre beneath the surface, and again it moved on and spread its illumination in the vast green spaces beneath the dome of the heart-shaped and tongue-shaped leaves. Then the breeze stirred rather more briskly overhead and the colour was flashed into the air above, into the eyes of the men and women who walk in Kew Gardens in July.

The figures of these men and women straggled past the flower-bed with a curiously irregular movement not unlike that of the white and blue butterflies who crossed the turf in zig-zag flights from bed to bed. The man was about six inches in front of the woman, strolling carelessly, while she bore on with greater purpose, only turning her head now and then to see that the children were not too far behind. The man kept this distance in front of the woman purposely, though perhaps unconsciously, for he wished to go on with his thoughts.

"Fifteen years ago I came here with Lily," he thought. "We sat somewhere over there by a lake and I begged her to marry me all through the hot afternoon. How the dragonfly kept circling round us: how clearly I see the dragonfly and her shoe with the square silver buckle at the toe. All the time I spoke I saw her shoe and when it moved impatiently I know without looking up what she was going to say: the whole of her seemed to be in her shoe. And my love, my desire, were in the dragonfly; for some reason I thought that if it settled there, on that leaf, the broad one with the red flower in the middle of it, if the dragonfly settled on the leaf she would say 'Yes' at once. But the dragonfly went round and round: it never settled anywhere—of course not, happily not, or I shouldn't be walking here with Eleanor and the children. Tell me, Eleanor. D'you ever think of the past?"

"Why do you ask, Simon?"

"Because I've been thinking of the past. I've been thinking of Lily, the woman I might have married... Well, why are you silent? Do you mind my thinking of the past?"

"Why should I mind, Simon? Doesn't one always think of the past, in a garden with men and women lying under the trees. Aren't they one's past, all that remains of it, those men and women, those ghosts lying under the trees... one's happiness, one's reality?"

"For me, a square silver shoe buckle and a dragonfly—"

"For me, a kiss. Imagine six little girls sitting before their easels twenty years ago, down by the side of a lake, painting the water-lilies, the first red water-lilies I'd ever seen. And suddenly a kiss, there on the back of my neck. And my hand shook all the afternoon so that I couldn't paint. I took out my watch and marked the hour when I would allow myself to think of the kiss for five minutes only—it was so precious—the kiss of an old grey-haired woman with a wart on her nose, the mother of all my kisses all my life. Come, Caroline, come Hubert."

They walked on past the flower-bed, now walking four abreast, and soon diminished in size among the trees and looked half transparent as the sunlight and shade swam over their backs in large trembling irregular patches.

In the oval flower-bed the snail, whose shell had been stained red, blue and yellow for the space of two minutes or so, now appeared to be moving very slightly in its shell, and next began to labour over the crumbs of loose earth which broke away and rolled down as it passed over them. It appeared to have a definite goal in front of it, differing in this respect from the singular high stepping angular green insect who attempted to cross in front of it, and waited for a second with its antennae trembling as if in deliberation, and then stepped off as rapidly and strangely in the opposite direction. Brown cliffs with deep green lakes in the hollows, flat, blade-like trees that waved from root to tip, round boulders of grey stone, vast crumpled surfaces of a thin crackling texture—all these objects lay across the snail's progress between one stalk and another to his goal. Before he had decided whether to circumvent the arched tent of a dead leaf or to breast it there came past the bed the feet of other human beings.

This time they were both men. The younger of the two wore an expression of perhaps unnatural calm; he raised his eyes and fixed them very steadily in front of him while his companion spoke, and directly his companion had done speaking he looked on the ground again and sometimes opened his lips only after a long pause and sometimes did not open them at all. The elder man had a curiously uneven and shaky method of walking, jerking his hand forward and throwing up his head abruptly, rather in the manner of an impatient carriage horse tired of waiting outside a house; but in the man these gestures were irresolute and pointless. He talked almost incessantly; he smiled to himself and again began to talk, as if the smile had been an answer. He was talking about spirits—the spirits of the dead, who, according to him, were even now telling him all sorts of odd things about their experiences in Heaven.

"Heaven was known to the ancients as Thessaly[2], William, and now, with this war[3], the spirit matter is rolling between the hills like thunder." He paused, seemed to listen, smiled, jerked his head and continued:

"You have a small electric battery and a piece of rubber to insulate the wire—isolate?—insulate?—well, we'll skip the details, no good going into details that wouldn't be understood—and in short the little machine stands in any convenient position by the head of the bed, we will say, on a neat mahogany stand. All arrangements being properly fixed by workmen under my direction, the widow applies her ear and summons the spirit by sign as agreed. Women! Widows! Women in black—"

Here he seemed to have caught sight of a woman's dress in the distance, which in the shade looked a purple black. He took off his hat, placed his hand upon his heart, and hurried towards her muttering and gesticulating feverishly. But William caught him by the sleeve and touched a flower with the tip of his walking-stick in order to divert the old man's attention. After looking at it for a moment in some confusion the old man bent his ear to it and seemed to answer a voice speaking from it, for he began talking about the forests of Uruguay which he had visited hundreds of years ago in company with the most beautiful young woman in Europe. He could be heard murmuring about forests of Uruguay blanketed with the wax petals of tropical roses, nightingales, sea beaches, mermaids, and women drowned at sea, as he suffered himself to be moved on by William, upon whose face the look of stoical patience grew slowly deeper and deeper.

Following his steps so closely as to be slightly puzzled by his gestures came two elderly women of the lover middle class, one stout and ponderous, the other rosy cheeked and nimble. Like most people of their station they were frankly fascinated by other signs of eccentricity betokening a disordered brain, especially in the well-to-do; but they were too far off to be certain whether the gestures were merely eccentric or genuinely mad. After they had scrutinized the old man's back in silence for a moment and given each other a queer, sly look, they went on energetically piecing together their very complicated dialogue:

"Nell, Bert, Lot, Cess, Phil, Pa, he says, I says, she says, I says, I says—"

"My Bert, Sis, Bill, Grandad, the old man, sugar,

---

2 Thessaly:为希腊一地域名。
3 指第一次世界大战。

Sugar, flour, kippers, greens,
Sugar, sugar, sugar."

The ponderous woman looked through the pattern of falling words at the flowers standing cool, firm, and upright in the earth, with a curios expression. She saw them as a sleeper waking from a heavy sleep sees a brass candlestick reflecting the light in an unfamiliar way, and closes his eyes and opens them, and seeing the brass candlestick again, finally starts broad awake and stares at the candlestick with all his powers. So the heavy woman came to a standstill opposite the oval-shaped flower-bed, and ceased even to pretend to listen to what the other woman was saying. She stood there letting the words fall over her, swaying the top part of her body slowly backwards and forwards, looking at the flower. Then she suggested that they should find a seat and have their tea.

The snail had now considered every possible method of reaching his goal without going round the dead leaf or climbing over it. Let alone the effort needed for climbing a leaf, he was doubtful whether the thin texture which vibrated with such an alarming crackle when touched even by the tips of his horns would bear his weight; and this determined him finally to creep beneath it, for there was a point where the leaf curved high enough from the ground to admit him. He had just inserted his head in the opening and was taking stock of the high brown roof and was getting used to the cool brown light when two other people came past outside on the turf. This time they were both young, a young man and a young woman. They were both in the prime of youth, the season before the smooth pink folds of the flower have burst their gummy case, when the wings of the butterfly, though fully grown, are motionless in the sun.

"Lucky it isn't Friday," he observed.

"Why? D'you believe in luck?"

"They make you pay sixpence on Friday."

"What's a sixpence anyway? Isn't it worth sixpence?"

"What's 'it'—what do you mean by 'it'?"

"O, anything—I mean—you know what I mean."

Long pauses came between each of these remarks; they were uttered in toneless and monotonous voices. The couple stood still on the edge of the flower-bed, and together pressed the end of her parasol deep down into the soft earth. The action and the fact that his hand rested on the top of hers expressed their feelings in a strange way, as these short insignificant words also expressed something, words with short wings for their heavy body of meaning, inadequate to carry them far and thus alighting awkwardly upon the very common objects that surrounded them, and were to their inexperienced touch so massive; but who knows (so they thought as they pressed the parasol into the earth) what precipices aren't concealed in them, or what slopes of ice don't shine in the sun on the other side? Who knows? Who has ever seen this before? Even when she wondered what sort of tea they gave you at Kew, he felt that something loomed up behind her words, and stood vast and solid behind them; and the mist very slowly rose and uncovered—O, Heavens, what were those shapes?—little white tables, and waitresses who looked first at her and then at him; and there was a bill that he would pay with a real two-shilling piece, and it was real, all real, he assured himself, fingering the coin in his pocket, real to everyone except to him and to her; even to him it began to seem real; and then—but it was too exciting to stand and think any longer, and he pulled the parasol out of the earth with a jerk and was impatient to find the place where one had tea with other people, like other people.

"Come along, Trissie; it's time we had our tea."

"Wherever *does* one have one's tea?" she asked with the oddest thrill of excitement in her voice, looking vaguely round and letting herself be drawn down the grass path, trailing her parasol; turning her head this way and that way forgetting her tea, wishing to go down there and then down there, remembering orchids and cranes among wild flowers, a Chinese pagoda and a crimson crested bird; but he bore her on.

Thus one couple after another with much the same irregular and aimless movement passed the flower-bed and were enveloped in layer after layer of green-blue vapour, in which at first their bodies had substance and a dash of colour, but later both substance and colour dissolved in the green-blue atmosphere. How hot it was! So hot that even the thrush chose to hop, like a mechanical bird, in the shadow of the flowers, with long pauses between one movement and the next; instead of rambling vaguely the white butterflies dance one above another, making with their white shifting flakes the outline of a shattered, marble column above the tallest flowers; the glass roofs of the palm house shone as if a whole market full of shiny green umbrellas had opened in the sun; and in the drone of the aeroplane the voice of the summer sky murmured its fierce soul. Yellow and black, pink and snow white, shapes of all these colours, men, women, and children were spotted for a second upon the horizon, and then, seeing the breadth of yellow that lay upon the grass, they wavered and sought shade beneath the trees, dissolving like drops of water in the yellow and green atmosphere, staining it faintly with red and blue. It seemed as if all gross and heavy bodies had sunk down in the heat motionless and lay huddled upon the ground, but their voices went wavering from them as if they were flames lolling from the thick waxen bodies of candles. Voices. Yes, voices. Wordless voices, breaking the silence suddenly with such depth of contentment, such passion of desire, or, in the voices of children, such freshness of surprise; breaking the silence? But there was no silence; all the time the motor omnibuses were turning their wheels and changing their gear; like a vast nest of Chinese boxes all of wrought steel turning ceaselessly one within another the city murmured; on the top of witch the voices cried aloud and the petals of myriads of flowers flashed their colours into the air.

Questions:

1. What is the setting of the story?
2. What relates the four pairs of people to each other?
3. What kind of tone is revealed through the description of the garden and the showing of people's dialogues?
4. What is the theme of the story?

赏　析:

Interpretations of "Kew Gardens" Through Different Approaches

Written in 1919, "Kew Gardens" is one of Virginia Woolf's most celebrated and most frequently anthologized short stories. Having already published two other traditional novels *The Voyage Out* in 1915 and *Night and Day* in 1919, Woolf developed a new writing style in "Kew Gardens" which, according to many critics, resembles impressionist art and emphasizes more on impressions, moments of meditation and feelings instead of conventional elements in traditional fiction. It is a transitional yet important piece followed later by similar short stories and novels, like the well-known *The Mark on the Wall* and *Mrs. Dalloway*, in which the typically lyrical style of her writing is fully developed. In this short essay, the short story is interpreted using different critical approaches including

Traditional Approach, Formalistic Approach and Psychological Approach.

1. Traditional Approach

"Kew Gardens" is set in the post-war London in July, in Britain's largest botanical garden, Kew. The story begins with a detailed description of the flower-bed in the garden and a snail in it who attempts to go cross a dead leaf, interwoven with the dialogues of four couples who passed it by. The story progresses with the constant shifting of viewpoint between the snail and the passers-by. In the beginning of the story, the reader present with an animated impressionistic painting of the flower-bed:

> From the oval-shaped flower-bed there rose perhaps a hundred stalks spreading into heart-shaped or tongue-shaped leaves half-way up and unfurling at the tip red or blue or yellow petals marked with spots of colour raised upon the surface... The light fell either upon the smooth, grey back of a pebble, or the shell of a snail with its brown, circular veins, or falling into a raindrop, it expanded with such intensity of red, blue and yellow the thin walls of water that one expected them to burst and disappear. ("Kew Gardens")

The detailed description and the massive use of nouns and adjectives of colour and shape give an unusual presentation of the garden, as if the reader were moving with the snail to witness the picturesque flower-bed in magnified proportion. While the accumulation of moving colours and lights evokes a painting of impressionist art, the use of shape words like "heart", "tongue" and "throat" links the natural world with the human world. The link is further perfected with naturalness by the shifting of viewpoint in the last sentence of the first paragraph:

> Then the breeze stirred rather more briskly overhead and the colour was flashed into the air above, into the eyes of the men and women who walk in Kew Gardens in July. ("Kew Gardens")

Although Woolf wrote in her diary that the story was "slight and short" and didn't expect the praise it had received from the critics, the story is mature in writing skills and close in structure. The shifting between the two worlds is dealt with skillfulness without much abruptness; and the seemingly sketchy and random couples are also chosen and arranged with purposes. There are married couples, mentally disturbed men, lower-class women and young lovers, all connected by the flower-bed or by each other.

The first couple is infatuated with their past: Simon with his old time lover Lily, to whom he proposed but was refused; Eleanor with a kiss twenty years ago which was the mother of all the kisses of her life. Their past, the choices they made when they were young, are the cause and source of the reality, the reality that they were walking with their children passing the flower-bed, the reality of their happiness (unhappiness):

> …doesn't one always think of the past, in a garden with men and women lying under the trees? Aren't they one's past, all that remains of it, those men and women, those ghosts lying under the trees… one's happiness, one's reality? ("Kew Gardens")

The second pair consists of a disordered old man with a "shaky method of walking", and a young man who "wore an expression of unnatural calm". The older reminds the reader of the veteran Septimus in *Mrs. Dalloway* with the similar mental problem. We can infer that the old man may be also traumatized after the Great War. He talks of spirits and various things which he might have experienced during the war, and looks like a neurotic.

The eccentricity of the second couple draws the third couple in sight, two lower-class women to follow behind them, talking about complicated things in their dialogue; neither of them understands each other.

Then comes the last pair, two young lovers both "in the prime of youth", talking between long pauses and uttering in "toneless and monotonous voices." They're not engaged with their past but the present, talking about meaningless things and nothing about future.

Some critics insist that Woolf tries to connect the human world with the natural world by interweaving them into a fusion, and then to reach a final balance in the end. However, considering the fact that the story takes place after World War I, and then Woolf was suffering from her own suicidal behaviors and her inclination to mental illness, it is more reasonable that what she focuses in the story is the problems arising in the modern life, especially the life after the world war. This can be concluded from three aspects:

a. The negative adjectives used in the text. When describing the human being and the garden, Woolf uses different kinds of negative adjectives like "irregular" (which occurred several times), "irresolute", "pointless" and "toneless". All these negative words reflect the uncertainty of modern life.

b. The characters are mostly engaged with their past or trivial things in the present. It seems that all they have in life is the past, and nobody talks about the future. Even the most promising young lovers in their youth, they hesitate whether they should have tea. Without the future or even the vision of it, people are bound to be pessimistic. Here Woolf creates a dramatic contrast between the past/history and the transient moment of meditation at present, much like she did in Mr. Dalloway, when the protagonist experienced all her life in a single day.

c. Almost all the four couples had difficulty in understanding each other. The husband and wife seem to be talking about reality, but they are actually dragged to their own past. They're more like talking to themselves. The mentally disordered old man and the two ladies followed him talks with vagueness like they're dreaming; while the young lovers barely wanted to talk at all. The monotonous voices and long pauses all shows that people don't understand each other well.

Compared to the natural world of the garden, where the snail tried to go across a dead leaf, hesitated and finally reached its goal, the human being walking by it is rather aimless and desperate. They finally melt in the hot weather of July with the garden into a noisy world of chaos.

2. Formalistic Approach: Defamiliarization in "Kew Gardens"

The Russian Formalist Shklovsky refutes in his famous essay "Art as Technique" that art/poetry should not equal images, least of all the images known to our common sense. By defying the Imagists' and the Symbolists' assertion that poets' task is to arrange the already existing images rather than creating them, he claims that "poetic imagery is a means of creating the strongest possible impression." The poet creates rather than repeat. Thus the primary thing in literature creation is to see everything different from the common sense, which he calls "a way of experiencing the artfulness of an object". From this motive he developed the central and the most important idea of Russian Formalism: defamiliarization. The term indicates that the Formalists puts great emphasize on the form of literary work rather than content:

> The purpose of art is to impart the sensation of things as they're perceived and not as they're know. The technique of art is to make objects "unfamiliar", to make forms difficult, to increase the difficulty and length of perception because the process of perception is an aesthetic end in itself and must be prolonged. ("Art as Technique", Shklofsky)

This requires the text of literary work to be more like poetry than prose. Thus to a piece like "Kew Gardens", with intense poetic imagery and lyrical lines, adopting a Formalistic Approach to interpret it appears natural and reasonable. Actually, Woolf herself bears almost the similar modern thoughts in writing:

> …if a writer were a freeman and not a slave, if he could write what he chose, not what he must, if he could base his work upon feeling and not upon conviction, there would be no plot, no comedy, no tragedy, no love interest or catastrophe in the accepted style, and perhaps not a single button sewn on as the Bond Street tailors would have it… (*Modern Fiction*, Woolf)

Woolf is obviously aware that any writer who's shackled by literary convention would only end up repeating what has been already said and written, which could not be called creation. In "Kew Gardens" she conforms to her ideal with a brilliant new writing style and unique viewpoint.

Woolf defamiliarizes a common flower-bed in the garden by repeating and stacking colours, and by using particular human organs to describe the shape of flowers and plants. "Red or blue or yellow" is used several times to describe the petals, lights and the snail's shell. It is not so much that their connotative meaning appeals us, which is not important according to the formalists, and would not be discussed here, but rather the mere repetition of them creates an unusual vision and rhythmic resonance in the reader. And words like "heart-shaped", "tongue-shaped" and "throat" which would hardly appear in the daily speech or even in other literature, evokes no less visual sensation.

Apart from specific words she uses in the text, there're not a few sentences and passages also sparkling with strange beauty:

> The ponderous woman looked through the pattern of falling words at the flower standing cool, firm and upright in the earth, with a curious expression. She saw them as a sleeper waking from a heavy sleep sees a brass candlestick reflecting the light in an unfamiliar way, and closes his eyes and opens them, and seeing the brass candlestick again, finally starts broad awake and stares at the candlestick with all his powers. ("Kew Gardens")

"Falling words" is a vivid and brilliant way to visualize the triviality and obscurity of the talk, while in the second sentence, the woman's curiosity at the flower-bed is presented lively and efficiently with an analog.

From an overall standpoint, the two separate lines of the story intwine each other: the incident happened in the natural world is a continuous and complete one. The snail meets a difficult in achieving its goal; it hesitated and finds a solution at the end; problem solved, it reached the end; while the human world is presented to the reader like fragment. Four couples come into sight; snapshots of their dialogues/ monologues are taken with obscurity, with no obvious aim. The contradiction defamiliarizes both worlds, which neither of them could offer when presented alone.

In the ending paragraph the two worlds melt into a chaotic wholeness; the silent natural world and the hot noisy human world are finally brought together, making up the reality:

> Thus one couple after another with much the same irregular and aimless movement passed the flower-bed and were enveloped in layer after layer of green-blue vapour, in which at first their bodies had substance and a dash of colour, but later both substance and colour dissolved in the green-blue atmosphere...Wordless voices, breaking the silence suddenly with such depth of contentment, such passion of desire... ("Kew Gardens")

The relation between form and content gradually comes clear: either the integrated continuous life of the natural world or the fragmented "irregular and aimless" life of the human world serves as an instrument of constructing the structure and the artistic uniqueness of the story—the form.

3. Psychological Approach

As Freud has illustrated in "Creative Writers and Daydreaming", the writing process bears the resemblance to dreaming. A piece of literary work can be seen as a verbalized dream with art techniques, which releases the tension of the writer's fantasy. In Woolf's dream, "Kew Gardens", a pictorial representation of her unconsciousness is depicted under consciousness.

It is easy to start by designating the two different worlds: the nature and the human, respectively to consciousness and unconsciousness. The four fragments of human life represent the unconsciousness: disordered, obscure and illogical. The people in the story also appear to be in a state of daydreaming: the infatuated state of the first couple, the neurotic monologue of the old man, the meaningless murmur of the third woman and the illegible dialogue between the two young lovers, all these looks as if they're taking place in a dream state. In dreams we often leap from one image or one scene from another, without much logical association. The following event may be completely different from the previous one, and the people in them may not be related at all. Nevertheless, these imagistic fragments have a thematic centre beyond impressions, they all reflect the unconsciousness of the dreamer—the writer in this case.

According to Freud, every dream is a wish fulfillment of the dreamer's fantasy. In "Kew Gardens", Woolf tries to escape from the problematic life of post-war London to a natural world of continuity and integrity. The war has traumatized people's lives so much that they either linger on their past or wondering about the happiness and reality, or even fall into madness. The reality is full of uncertainty. The future is gloomy and distant. Dreading this chaotic mixture she longs the tranquil, balanced natural life in the garden, the life symbolized by the snail. This life is in Woolf's conscious—more important in her ego.

The interweaving process of the two lives poses a contradiction that clarifies Woolf's desire for the better one, however in the last paragraph, her daydreaming is shattered by the blending of the two worlds—the sudden noise that broke into the dream, which actually exist all the way through in the reality:

> Breaking the silence? But there was no silence; all the time the motor omnibuses were turning their wheels and changing their gear; like a vast nest of Chinese boxes all of wrought steel turning ceaselessly the voices cried aloud and the petals of myriads of flowers flashed their colours into the air. ("Kew Gardens")

Finally Woolf's awakes from the dream and realizes that her ideal (her ego) is defeated not by the dark force of unconsciousness but by reality, in which life is still in a noisy chaotic disorder. Her fantasy can only be fulfilled in writings like this, or continued in her other stories like *Mrs. Dalloway*.

References:

[1] Dolley, Christopher, ed. *The Penguin Book of English Short Stories*. Beijing: Foreign Languages Press, 1989.

[2] Wordsworth Classics. *Introduction to Mrs. Dalloway*. [S.l]: Wordsworth Editions Limited, 1996.

[3] 朱刚. 二十世纪西方文艺批评理论. 上海：上海外语教育出版社，2001.

(姚依东)

Chapter 4　Point of View

第四章　叙述视角

My task which I am trying to achieve is, by the power of the written word, to make you hear, to make you feel—it is above all, to make you see.

Joseph Coward

简要介绍：

Point of view refers to the way a story is told, that is, who tells the story and how much this person is allowed to tell. It is the mode established by an author by means of which the reader's view of the plot, characters and setting is controlled. From 18th century till now, novelists have developed many different ways to present a story, the chief division between points of view is usually between the third-person narratives and the first-person narratives. The classification below is widely accepted, which establishes a general division between the third-person narratives, including omniscient point of view, limited omniscient point of view and objective point of view, and the first-person narratives, including I-agent point of view and I-witness point of view.

1. Third-person Points of View

1) Omniscient Point of View

In this mode of narration, the narrator knows everything that needs to be known about the outer reality the characters live in: their appearance, their actions, their observations and the events they experience; and the inner world of the characters: their thoughts, their feelings, and their motives. He is free to move from character to character to report what they say, what they do and what they think. In addition, the narrator is allowed to make comments and to evaluate actions and motives of the characters. Yet the narrator is invisible, and does not participate in the events of the story himself. Many great English works of the 18th and 19th century are written in this way, for examples, works by Henry Fielding, Jane Austin, Charles Dickens, W. M. Thackeray, George Eliot, Thomas Hardy, etc.

Since all is arranged carefully and intentionally, the description of the feeling, thought and observation seems reasonable, logical and coherent. And the detailed and vivid depiction seems to be identical to our society and our daily life. But if we notify the fact that all the information is offered and arranged by the narrator only, we would ask the following question: is the narrator reliable? If the narrator offers us some false information, then all the readers may understand the story wrongly. Obviously, omniscient narrator possesses too many rights in narrating the story, he can consciously limit the information to his special intention, and he can mislead readers and even lie to readers. Omniscient point of view is certainly authoritative and subjective.

2) Limited Omniscient Point of View

In this mode of narration, the narrator tells the story in the third person, and limits the account to what he/she (a character in the story) observes, experiences, thinks, feels and perceives. The reader has access to the thoughts and feelings and perceptions of the character revealed by the narrator, but neither the reader nor the narrator (character) has access to the inner lives of any other characters in the story. Sometimes, the story could be narrated from several different perspectives by shifting the narrative points of view through one character to another. Thus, the reader could understand the story from various different perspectives. The most intense use of this point of view can be seen in stream of consciousness narration, in which the reader is presented only the continuous current of thought, memory, feelings, and associations, which constitute a narrator's total awareness. This narration, developed by modern writers, is therefore typically used in the works of James Joyce, Virginia Woolf and William Faulkner.

Generally speaking, the narration is reliable, but there is one point we should pay attention to: the story is completely restricted to one character's experience only, as a result, readers are likely to accept the limited description completely and spontaneously while neglecting all other possible perspectives.

3) Objective Point of View

In this mode of narration, the narrator remains unnamed and unidentified. The story is narrated from an external point of view, focusing on the exterior facts only, that is, the outer reality of the characters, the setting, and the events as they are developing in the story, with no reference to the inner world of characters. In other words, the narrator shows what happens without directly stating anything about the character's thought, feelings or motives, and he does not have the privilege to make any comment either. Hemingway's "Hills Like White Elephants" is a good example.

The reliability of the objective narrator is higher, since the narrator tells the story from a neutral and objective point of view. But the story is still manipulated by the narrator, who selects what is worth, while deleting all else. And the diction adopted by the narrator may also control the reader's understanding. But on the whole, this narration is much more reliable than any other narrative modes.

2. First-person Points of View

1) I-agent Point of View

In this mode of narration, the narration is limited to the inner world of the narrator "I", and outer reality which the narrator "I" observes and understands. All the other characters are depicted through the observing eyes of "I", and their inner world (their thoughts, feelings, experiences, etc.) could not be penetrated, though it could be guessed by "I". The most important fact is that the narrator "I" plays the role as a protagonist in the story, therefore the story is narrated from a personal subjective perspective. Daniel Defoe's *Moll Flanders*, Charlotte Bronte's *Jane Eyre*, Charles Dickens' *Great Expectations*, and Mark Twain's *The Adventures of Huckleberry Finn* are all good examples.

Compared with the previous narrative ways, it is the most unreliable point of view. The fact that we see the story through the eyes of "I", the main character in the story, indicates that we could not see the whole story, we are likely to accept the narrator's subjective understanding or even prejudice while neglecting all the other objective facts. Therefore, it is necessary that we shall be aware that the story might be told not only subjective but also partial and limited.

2) I-witness point of view

In this mode of narration, the narration is limited to the observation of the narrator "I", who plays the role as a minor character or only as an observer. As a participant, the narrator plays the role as a guide, telling us what is going on in detail. As an observer, he uses the following words frequently in describing the events he witnesses: "see", "guess", "find", "feel", "realize", "witness", "assure", etc. And the narrator tells the story from both the internal and external points of view. As a bystander, the narrator keeps a distance with what happens, but as a character inside, the narrator participates in the story more or less. Marlow in Joseph Conrad's *Heart of Darkness*, and Ishmael in Merman Melville's *Moby Dick* are good examples.

It seems that the narrator tries his best to tell the story objectively by keeping a distance from the event, but his account is mostly subjective, because his knowledge about the inner world of the characters are extremely limited, and his description is always partial since he could not tell us the whole story.

简　析：

关于"叙述视角"，我们需要注意的是：

1）叙述视角规定了讲故事的方式，因此，从某种程度上说，它限定了情节的发展，人物的塑造和背景的选择。它涉及的最主要的问题是：谁来讲故事？他讲什么？（或者他知道多少？）

2）文学作品的叙事视角大致可分为两种：第三人称叙事视角和第一人称叙事视角。前者可以进一步细分为全知视角、有限视角和客观视角三种，后者可以进一步细分为第一人称主人公叙事视角和第一人称见证人叙事视角。第三人称叙事视角与第一人称叙事视角的最大区别在于：前者的叙述者往往游离于故事之外，读者一般通过叙述者的眼光来观察和了解世界；而后者的叙述者则用故事内的人物的眼光来观察和了解世界。

3）全知、有限和客观三种视角的区别在于：全知视角让读者通过叙述者的眼光不仅观察了整个故事的外部世界，而且通过叙事者的讲述和总结知晓了所有人物的思想、知觉和情感；第三人称有限视角让读者通过叙述者的眼光看到了某个人物所能看到的外在世界并了解该人物的思想、知觉和情感，而不是整个故事的外在世界和所有人物的内心世界。客观视角通过叙述者的眼光向读者展示了整个故事的外部世界，却无法进入任何人物的内心世界。需要指出的是，现代作家笔下的第三人称有限视角与传统的有限视角有所不同，现代叙述者尽量用人物的眼光直接展示人物的思想和情感（比如意识流），而不再通过某个人物的视角间接讲述、总结和解释人物的思想和情感，因此这种现代的第三人称有限视角已经类似于第一人称主人公叙事视角，只是人称不同。

4）第一人称主人公叙事视角和第一人称见证人叙事视角的区别在于：第一人称主人公叙述视角用故事主人公第一人称视角回顾和讲述了"我"自己的经历、思想、知觉和情感；第一人称见证人叙述视角则用故事中某个次要人物第一人称视角回顾和讲述了"我"所看到的主人公的故事，虽然"我"可以对主人公的经历、思想、情感可以猜测、评论，但是"我"无法进入主人公的内心世界。

作　品：

ERNEST HEMINGWAY

[1898—1961]

Hills Like White Elephants

The hills across the valley of the Ebro[1] were long and white. On this side there was no shade and no trees and the station was between two lines of rails in the sun. Close against the side of the station there was the warm shadow of the building and a curtain, made of strings of bamboo beads, hung across the open door into the bar, to keep out flies. The American and the girl with him sat at a table in the shade, outside the building. It was very hot and the express from Barcelona would come in forty minutes. It stopped at this junction for two minutes and went on to Madrid.

"What should we drink?" the girl asked. She had taken off her hat and put it on the table.

"It's pretty hot," the man said.

"Let's drink beer."

"Dos cervezas," the man said into the curtain.

"Big ones?" a woman asked from the doorway.

"Yes. Two big ones."

The woman brought two glasses of beer and two felt pads. She put the felt pads and the beer glasses on the table and looked at the man and the girl. The girl was looking off at the line of hills. They were white in the sun and the country was brown and dry.

"They look like white elephants," she said.

"I've never seen one," the man drank his beer.

"No, you wouldn't have."

"I might have," the man said. "Just because you say I wouldn't have doesn't prove anything."

The girl looked at the bead curtain. "They've painted something on it," she said. "What does it say?"

1　西班牙北部的一条河流。

"Anis del Toro. It's a drink."

"Could we try it?"

The man called "Listen" through the curtain. The woman came out from the bar.

"Four reales[1]."

"We want two Anis del Toro."

"With water?"

"Do you want it with water?"

"I don't know," the girl said. "Is it good with water?"

"It's all right."

"You want them with water?" asked the woman.

"Yes, with water."

"It tastes like licorice," the girl said and put the glass down.

"That's the way with everything."

"Yes," said the girl. "Everything tastes of licorice. Especially all the things you've waited so long for, like absinthe."

"Oh, cut it out."

"You started it," the girl said. "I was being amused. I was having a fine time."

"Well, let's try and have a fine time."

"All right. I was trying. I said the mountains looked like white elephants. Wasn't that bright? "

"That was bright."

"I wanted to try this new drink. That's all we do, isn't it—look at things and try new drinks?"

"I guess so."

The girl looked across at the hills.

"They're lovely hills," she said. "They don't really look like white elephants. I just meant the coloring of their skin through the trees."

"Should we have another drink?"

"All right."

The warm wind blew the bead curtain against the table.

"The beer's nice and cool," the man said.

"It's lovely," the girl said.

"It's really an awfully simple operation, Jig," the man said. "It's not really an

---

1 西班牙硬币。

operation at all."

The girl looked at the ground the table legs rested on.

"I know you wouldn't mind it, Jig. It's really not anything. It's just to let the air in."

The girl did not say anything.

"I'll go with you and I'll stay with you all the time. They just let the air in and then it's all perfectly natural."

"Then what will we do afterward?"

"We'll be fine afterward. Just like we were before."

"What makes you think so?"

"That's the only thing that bothers us. It's the only thing that's made us unhappy."

The girl looked at the bead curtain, put her hand out and took hold of two of the strings of beads.

"And you think then we'll be all right and be happy."

"I know we will. You don't have to be afraid. I've known lots of people that have done it."

"So have I," said the girl. "And afterward they were all so happy."

"Well," the man said, "if you don't want to you don't have to. I wouldn't have you do it if you didn't want to. But I know it's perfectly simple."

"And you really want to?"

"I think it's the best thing to do. But I don't want you to do it if you don't really want to."

"And if I do it you'll be happy and things will be like they were and you'll love me?"

"I love you now. You know I love you."

"I know. But if I do it, then it will be nice again if I say things are like white elephants, and you'll like it?"

"I'll love it. I love it now but I just can't think about it. You know how I get when I worry."

"If I do it you won't ever worry?"

"I won't worry about that because it's perfectly simple."

"Then I'll do it. Because I don't care about me."

"What do you mean?"

"I don't care about me."

"Well, I care about you."

"Oh, yes. But I don't care about me. And I'll do it and then everything will be fine."

"I don't want you to do it if you feel that way."

The girl stood up and walked to the end of the station. Across, on the other side, were fields of grain and trees along the banks of the Ebro. Far away, beyond the river, were mountains. The shadow of a cloud moved across the field of grain and she saw the river through the trees.

"And we could have all this," she said. "And we could have everything and every day we make it more impossible."

"What did you say?"

"I said we could have everything."

"We can have everything."

"No, we can't."

"We can have the whole world."

"No, we can't."

"We can go everywhere."

"No, we can't. It isn't ours any more."

"It's ours."

"No, it isn't. And once they take it away, you never get it back."

"But they haven't taken it away."

"We'll wait and see."

"Come on back in the shade," he said. "You mustn't feel that way."

"I don't feel any way," the girl said. "I just know things."

"I don't want you to do anything that you don't want to do—"

"Nor that isn't good for me," she said. "I know. Could we have another beer?"

"All right. But you've got to realize—"

"I realize," the girl said. "Can't we maybe stop talking?"

They sat down at the table and the girl looked across at the hills on the dry side of the valley and the man looked at her and at the table.

"You've got to realize," he said, "that I don't want you to do it if you don't want to. I'm perfectly willing to go through with it if it means anything to you."

"Doesn't it mean anything to you? We could get along."

"Of course it does. But I don't want anybody but you. I don't want any one else. And I know it's perfectly simple."

"Yes, you know it's perfectly simple."

"It's all right for you to say that, but I do know it."

"Would you do something for me now?"

"I'd do anything for you."

"Would you please please please please please please please stop talking?"

He did not say anything but looked at the bags against the wall of the station. There were labels on them from all the hotels where they had spent nights.

"But I don't want you to," he said, "I don't care anything about it."

"I'll scream," the girl said.

The woman came out through the curtains with two glasses of beer and put them down on the damp felt pads. "The train comes in five minutes," she said.

"What did she say?" asked the girl.

"That the train is coming in five minutes."

The girl smiled brightly at the woman, to thank her.

"I'd better take the bags over to the other side of the station," the man said. She smiled at him.

"All right. Then come back and we'll finish the beer."

He picked up the two heavy bags and carried them around the station to the other tracks. He looked up the tracks but could not see the train. Coming back, he walked through the barroom, where people waiting for the train were drinking. He drank an Anis at the bar and looked at the people. They were all waiting reasonably for the train. He went out through the bead curtain. She was sitting at the table and smiled at him.

"Do you feel better?" he asked.

"I feel fine," she said. "There's nothing wrong with me. I feel fine."

Questions:

1. From what point of view is the story narrated? What will the story be like if you use other points of view? What qualities of the conversation make up for the lack of descriptions of appearance, gestures, information of the past lives of the characters?

2. What do you know about the characters from their conversation?

3. How important is setting in the story?

4. What arouses the quarrel? Has the quarrel been resolved at the end of the story?

5. What do you think of the ending of the story? What kind of the ending will you offer?

赏　析：

Three Approaches to "Hills Like White Elephants"

1. A Summary of the Story

An American man and "a girl" sit drinking beer in a bar by a train station in northern Spain, making self-consciously ironic, brittle small talk. The woman comments that the hills look like white elephants. Eventually, the two discuss an operation, and the man earnestly reassures the woman that it is "awfully simple... not really an operation at all... all perfectly natural". The woman is unconvinced, questioning, "What will we do afterward," but she says she will have the operation because "I don't care about me". A few moments later, however, she avers that they "could" have everything and go anywhere, suddenly as earnest as he had been earlier. When the man agrees that they "can" do these things, however, the woman now says no, they can't, her change in verb tense suggesting that the possible lives they once could have pursued and produced are now irrevocably out of reach. When the man says that he will go along with whatever she wants, the woman asks him to "please please please please please please please stop talking", or she will scream. The train arrives during this impasse, and once the bags are loaded, the woman, smiling brightly, insists she feels fine.

2. Historical-Biographical Approach

This approach sees a literary work chiefly, if not exclusively, as a reflection of its author's life and times or the life and times of the characters in the work.[1] The short story "Hills Like White Elephants" has a lot to do with Hemingway's personal life and his times.

Hemingway is a well-known representative writer for the "Lost Generation". In 1918, during World War I, Hemingway drove an ambulance for the American Red Cross. He was wounded on July 8 on the Italian front near Fossalta di Piave and had an affair with nurse Agnes von Kurowsky as he was convalescing after over 200 pieces of shrapnel were removed from his legs. (These experiences are the biographical basis for his first novel, *A Farewell to Arms*.[2]) He joined with those who saw the almost total destructive power of World War I. What kind of world had humans managed to create for themselves? Does such a world even make sense? If it makes no sense, as many had come to believe, why would anyone want to be a part of it? Hemingway struggles with these questions in his stories and leaves them unresolved. This short story focuses on two people, as they debate a life-changing event. Each seems exasperated with the situation and at times with each other. This is a

---

1　Guerin, W. L. *A Handbook of Critical Approaches to Literature*. Beijing: Foreign Language Teaching and Research Press, 2004: 22.

2　http://rio.atlantic.net/~gagne/hem/time.html.

fine example of "Lost Generation" writing. The characters are superficial people, wandering Europe in search of something that in reality is nothing. Jig observes that all they do is see new places and try new drinks. Their decision about the operation will surely determine their future, whether they remain together or apart. If they choose one path, the couple will be embracing that represented by the distant and fertile side of the valley with its greenness and the promise of rain. If they choose the other path, barrenness. The choice is not all that simple. Which one to choose? This is as complicated as the situation the "Lost Generation" were faced.

The short story has a lot to do with how the author lived. Hemingway married four times. The time period the story mostly relates to is when he was married to Hadley and having an affair with Pauline. The story shows problems within a relationship and a lack of communication between a couple. While Hemingway was writing this story, he wrote a letter to F. Scott Fitzgerald about Pauline. He wrote about sitting in the shade and talking with her while waiting at a station. In the story, "the American and the girl with him sat at a table in the shade, outside the building", the girl comments on the hills in the background, how they look like white elephants. Her boyfriend just ignores her and every time she talks about the hills, he changes the subject. According to James Mellow, "Another oddity is that in the earliest manuscript fragment relating to the story, written in 1925, is that Hemingway who remarks to Hadley, 'Look at those god-damn white mountains,' and she answers, 'They are the most mysterious things I have ever seen'". [3] This shows how Hemingway came up with the idea of the white elephants.

Another part of the story that relates to his life is the setting. While Hemingway was in Spain, the setting of the story, he found out that Hadley was pregnant for the second time. The story might have shown his true feelings about the pregnancy. In the story, the boyfriend is moody and wants the girl to do what he wants. This could be the same way Hemingway felt towards Hadley and towards the end of their marriage. Another relationship between the two is the way Hemingway dealt with women. He married four times, and one can imagine that he had his share of trouble in finding the right woman. The man in the story has trouble communicating with his girlfriend, which creates a problem in their relationship. Basically, he wants her to do what he wants and won't have it any other way.[4] In the story, Ernest Hemingway uses his own experiences for the make up of the story. His writing deals with how he probably acted and felt in the presence of the women he cared about. Therefore, Hemingway's personal life and experiences is the biographical basis of this fictional life.

3. Formalistic Approach

This approach examines the relationships between a text's ideas and its form, between what a

---

3　Mellow, James. *Hemingway: A Life Without Consequence*. Boston: Houghton Mifflin Company, 1992: 348.
4　www.123HelpMe.com.

text says and the way it says it. Working with imagery, narrative structure, point of view, and other techniques on close reading of the text, we seek to determine the function and appropriateness of these to the self-contained work and find the organic unity. What strikes me most in "Hills Like White Elephants" is Hemingway's objective point of view and symbolic way of writing.

The short story is told objectively, with little emotion, as if it were simply being reported. Hemingway completely removes himself from the story and offers little help to the reader in understanding what is behind the story, giving only a few moments of action where much is left unsaid, only hinted at. He only uses dialogues to convey the meaning of the story. Though the author doesn't explore the characters' minds at all, yet the dialogue does convey everything that we conclude about the characters. Every detail counts as we reconstruct the story behind the story.

The story starts with a description of the landscape, which is rather depressing, as we have a railway station in the middle of the desert with no shade. Why does the author choose this setting? Actually, the landscape itself is quite symbolic. The scene invites us to think about infertility and emptiness of the couple's future. Besides, the railway station with the two lines of rails lies in the middle of nowhere. The "American" and the "girl" are just like two lines; they run together but are separated. We do not know whether they will continue their relationship parallelly or go to the opposite direction. This comes to the important theme: choice. We have to make a lot of decisions throughout life. Which one to choose? This is the question facing the couple. After the introduction, the whole story is a long continuous dialogue, which is rarely interrupted. The dialogues are made up of the characters' ambiguous and short sentences. Yet we can conceive a lot from the seemingly simple dialogues.

The girl always looked across at the hills. "They're lovely hills," she said. "They don't really look like white elephants." Hills stand for life and fertility. They are lovely in the girl's eyes. Obviously, she wants the lovely unborn baby, and doesn't want to do the "simple operation"—abortion. In English idiom, a white elephant is an item that is worthless to one person but priceless to another. In this case, the baby is worthless to the man, but in the girl's eyes, it is priceless. Throughout the story we see signs that the American does not want to keep the baby. In his eyes, the unborn child is a kind of burden just like the white elephants. "I wanted to try this new drink. That's all we do." Such kind of reply is really heartbroken to the girl. How selfish and irresponsible the man is! When she looks across the river and sees fields of fertile grain and the river, contrasted to the barren sterility of the hills like white elephants, of course, she desires the beauty, loveliness, and fertility of the fields of grain, but she knows that she has to be content with the barren sterility of an imminent abortion. The man tries every means possible to persuade her to do the operation. He repeatedly says, "It's really an awfully simple operation" which involves only a doctor allowing "a little air in". From the calm and objective depiction of the couple's dialogues, we can sense the subtleness of their relationship and their inner heart. This is the power of Hemingway's writing, which is an expression of his "iceberg" theory.

4. Feminist Approach

In the patriarchal culture, women were marginalized and silenced. They belonged to the invulnerable group and were dominated by men. This short story deals with the relationship between men and women. Through the subtle dialogues, we can see that the girl becomes more and more independent and mature, from subordinating herself completely to the man's will to having her own thinking.

Everyone needs a mate in whom we can trust, on whom we can count, with whom we can share our thoughts, happiness, sadness, dreams and of course our whole life. However, we cannot find all this between the couple in this short story. Their dialogues do not show any harmony. At first, the girl is quite dependent on the man and does what the man tells her to do. She wants to have the lovely baby, at the same time she's afraid of losing the man and being left alone. Therefore, she is too weak and coward to make her own decisions. However, the way the man tried to convince the girl about the insignificance of the abortion is really disgusting. "It's really not anything. It's just to lead the air in... They just let the air in and then it's all perfectly natural... That is the only thing that bothers us. It's the only thing that's made us unhappy... If you don't want to, you don't have to. I wouldn't have you do it, if you didn't want to. But I know it's perfectly simple." How hypocritical and irresponsible! We can observe that the man wraps his recommends into the gown of free choice. But the answer is already in his words. Gradually, she realizes that there is no point in their talking about the baby, because the man is unable to understand her feelings, so she gives it up. But her feelings remain unspoken. Her unspoken words tell us everything about their relationship. Unspoken words are "more talkative" in this case. Their relationship is as empty as the landscape where their dialogue takes place.

The man is using his logic in order to be as persuasive as possible. Without a baby anchoring them down, they can continue to travel; they can "have everything." However, the girl contradicts him and, at that moment, seems suddenly strong and more in control of the situation. With or without the abortion, things will never be the same. She also realizes that she is not loved, at least not unconditionally. During the very short exchanges between the man and the girl, she changes from someone who is almost completely dependent upon the man to someone who is more sure of herself and more aware of what to expect from him. At the end of their conversation, she takes control of herself and of the situation. She no longer acts in her former childlike way. She tells the man to please shut up: "Would you please please please please please please please stop talking?" The word "please" is repeated seven times, indicating that she is overwhelmingly tired of his hypocrisy and his continual talking on the same subject. This shows the girl goes a step further to voice her opinions and speak her mind about her stance upon the pregnancy. Maybe in the end she still has the abortion (which the story does not tell), yet this scene shows the girl is not as subordinate and dependent as before. At the end of the story, she was sitting at the table and smiled at him. "Do you feel better?" he asked. "I feel fine," she said. "There's nothing wrong with me. I feel fine." From her "smile", we can sense her loneliness, agony, distress and despair... She wakes up from her beautiful childish dream.

The short story also touches upon an important issue between men and women. That is, the relationship of sex and love. From this story, we can still see the stereotype that man pays more attention to sex while woman attaches more importance to love. When the man repeatedly says, "It's really an awfully simple operation." The girl remains silent. She can't understand why a man who loves her can be so indifferent to her and their child. "That's the only thing that bothers us. It's the only thing that's made us unhappy." That's the very reason he insists on abortion at the risk of the girl's life. He just wants to seek pleasure. Seeing his selfishness, she's so disappointed that she "looked at the bead curtain, put her hand out and took hold of two of the string of beads", without any words. To some feminists, this kind of man is just like "an animal". So Women are fighting against oppression, repression and want more expression, trying to strike a balance with men.

5. Conclusion

Great literary works will inevitably invite multiple interpretations, so that the richness of literature can be sensed. This chapter provides an example of interpreting a literary work from different approaches.

References:

[1] Guerin, W. L. *A Handbook of Critical Approaches to Literature*. Beijing: Foreign Language Teaching and Research Press, 2004.

[2] Mellow, James. *Hemingway: A Life Without Consequence*. Boston: Houghton Mifflin Company, 1992.

[3] 丁丽军. 《白象似的群山》与"冰山原则"——海明威小说艺术特色探析. 南昌航空工业学院学报，2003，3.

[4] 方文开，李祖明. 《白象似的群山》解读. 荆州师范学院学报，2002，1.

[5] 甘文平. "梦"的建构、消解与幻灭——《白象似的群山》与《雨里的猫》的主题比较. 四川外语学院学报，2002，2.

[6] 霍冬克. 从《白象似的群山》看海明威小说创作的艺术风格. 丹东师专学报，2002，3.

[7] 刘建成. 海明威《白象似的山峦》叙事技巧和主题. 乌鲁木齐职业大学学报，2003，3.

[8] 上官燕. 海明威笔下之另类反英雄——评《白象似的群山》和《雨里的猫》中男性形象. 三峡大学学报，2003，4.

(王金)

Chapter 5   Irony

第五章   反讽

> There are several kinds of stories, but only one
> difficult—the humorous.
>
> Mark Twain

简要介绍：

Irony is a device that reveals discrepancy or incongruity between one thing and what it seems to be, which is one of the enduring themes in literature that reality is always different from what it appears to be. The contrast may be between what is said and what is meant, or between what happens and what is expected to happen. The novelist uses irony to dissemble or hide what is actually the case, not in order to deceive, but to achieve special rhetorical or artistic effects so as to suggest the complexity of life.

Irony could generally be divided into several kinds. **Verbal irony** refers to a statement in which what a speaker implies differs sharply from what the speaker expresses, in other words, what is said is opposite to what is meant. Through ironic statement, an explicit expression of one attitude or evaluation is always intended to be indicative of an opposite attitude or evaluation, which, however, is usually not aggressive but subtle and restrained. **Situational irony** exists when there is a discrepancy between appearance and reality, or between what is expected to happen and what actually happens, or between what is and what would seem appropriate. **Structural irony** exists when the author introduces a structure, which sustains a discrepancy between meaning and evaluation throughout the work. One common literary structure is the invention of a naive hero, or a naive narrator, whose naïve interpretation leads the reader to the true implication of the author. **Dramatic irony** involves a discrepancy between what a character believes or says and what the reader and the author know to be true. **Cosmic irony** involves a discrepancy between the protagonist's false hope for life and his actual frustrating destiny.

As a literary device, irony has many effects. Firstly, irony helps achieve an effect of compression in describing the complexity of life. Secondly, irony allows readers to get deep insight into plot, characters and setting, and helps their quest for theme. Thirdly, irony makes a story more striking, effective and memorable.

简　析：

关于"反讽"，我们需要注意的是：

1）反讽是小说的基调，正是因为反讽的使用，才使小说成为最适合反映生活的复杂性的文学体裁。反讽的主要特征是外表和本质之间的不一致，甚至截然相反。这种不一致可以表现在语言层面，也可以表现在情节层面，还可以表现在人物层面。它的主要作用是：使语言超越它原有的意义。

2）言辞反讽主要表现在小说的措辞上面，它通过语词与上下文语境之间的不和谐，使该语词体现出与本身词义相反的意义。这种反讽的主要作用是以一种含混的方式向读者传递真实的情感和思想。

3）情景反讽和结构反讽主要表现在小说的情节和结构的安排上：前者使情节的发展总是出乎人们的意料，或者表象与现实之间，或者事实与真相之间，或者期望与结果之间，总是不一致；后者用特别的结构设计，比如安排一个天真的人物来担任主角或故事叙述人，使读者从他可笑、幼稚的言行中体会出作者的深层思想。

4）戏剧反讽和命运反讽主要表现在人物身上，前者让读者预先知道人物所不知道的信息，使人物的表现显得可笑、可悲；后者则让人物对自身命运的期望与他真实的命运遭遇截然相反。

作　品：

KATE CHOPIN
[1851—1904]

The Story of an Hour

Knowing that Mrs. Mallard was afflicted with a heart trouble, great care was taken to break to her as gently as possible the news of her husband's death.

It was her sister Josephine who told her, in broken sentences; veiled hints that revealed in half concealing. Her husband's friend Richards was there, too, near her.

It was he who had been in the newspaper office when intelligence of the railroad disaster was received, with Brently Mallard's name leading the list of "killed". He had only taken the time to assure himself of its truth by a second telegram, and had hastened to forestall any less careful, less tender friend in bearing the sad message.

She did not hear the story as many women have heard the same, with a paralyzed inability to accept its significance. She wept at once, with sudden, wild abandonment, in her sister's arms. When the storm of grief had spent itself she went away to her room alone. She would have no one follow her.

There stood, facing the open window, a comfortable, roomy armchair. Into this she sank, pressed down by a physical exhaustion that haunted her body and seemed to reach into her soul.

She could see in the open square before her house the tops of trees that were all aquiver with the new spring life. The delicious breath of rain was in the air. In the street below a peddler was crying his wares. The notes of a distant song which some one was singing reached her faintly, and countless sparrows were twittering in the eaves.

There were patches of blue sky showing here and there through the clouds that had met and piled one above the other in the west facing her window.

She sat with her head thrown back upon the cushion of the chair, quite motionless, except when a sob came up into her throat and shook her, as a child who has cried itself to sleep continues to sob in its dreams.

She was young, with a fair, calm face, whose lines bespoke repression and even a certain strength. But now there was a dull stare in her eyes, whose gaze was fixed away off yonder on one of those patches of blue sky. It was not a glance of reflection, but rather indicated a suspension of intelligent thought.

There was something coming to her and she was waiting for it, fearfully. What was it? She did not know; it was too subtle and elusive to name. But she felt it, creeping out of the sky, reaching toward her through the sounds, the scents, the color that filled the air.

Now her bosom rose and fell tumultuously. She was beginning to recognize this thing that was approaching to possess her, and she was striving to beat it back with her will—as powerless as her two white slender hands would have been.

When she abandoned herself a little whispered word escaped her slightly parted lips. She said it over and over under her breath: "Free, free, free!" The vacant stare and the look of terror that had followed it went from her eyes. They stayed keen and bright. Her pulses beat fast, and the coursing blood warmed and relaxed every inch of her body.

She did not stop to ask if it were or were not a monstrous joy that held her. A clear and exalted perception enabled her to dismiss the suggestion as trivial.

She knew that she would weep again when she saw the kind, tender hands folded in death; the face that had never looked save with love upon her, fixed and gray and dead. But she saw beyond that bitter moment a long procession of years to come that would belong to her absolutely. And she opened and spread her arms out to them in welcome.

There would be no one to live for her during those coming years; she would live for herself. There would be no powerful will bending hers in that blind persistence with which men and women believe they have a right to impose a private will upon a fellow-creature. A kind intention or a cruel intention made the act seem no less a crime as she looked upon it in that brief moment of illumination.

And yet she had loved him—sometimes. Often she had not. What did it matter! What could love, the unsolved mystery, count for in face of this possession of self-assertion which she suddenly recognized as the strongest impulse of her being!

"Free! Body and soul free!" she kept whispering.

Josephine was kneeling before the closed door with her lips to the keyhole, imploring for admission. "Louise, open the door! I beg, open the door—you will make yourself ill. What are you doing, Louise? For heaven's sake open the door."

"Go away. I am not making myself ill." No; she was drinking in a very elixir of life through that open window.

Her fancy was running riot along those days ahead of her. Spring days, and summer days, and all sorts of days that would be her own. She breathed a quick prayer that life might be long. It was only yesterday she had thought with a shudder that life might be long.

She arose at length and opened the door to her sister's importunities. There was a feverish triumph in her eyes, and she carried herself unwittingly like a goddess of Victory. She clasped her sister's waist, and together they descended the stairs. Richards stood waiting for them at the bottom.

Some one was opening the front door with a latchkey. It was Brently Mallard who entered, a little travel-stained, composedly carrying his grip-sack and umbrella. He had been far from the scene of accident, and did not even know there had been one. He stood amazed at Josephine's piercing cry; at Richards' quick motion to screen him from the view of his wife.

But Richards was too late.

When the doctors came they said she had died of heart disease—of joy that kills.

Questions:

1. Why does Mrs. Mallard plunge into joy when she knows her husband's death?
2. Is Mrs. Mallard glad to be free of her actual marriage or of any marriage or of any relationship that might smother her personal will? What is she really longing for?
3. What kind of irony is used in the story? Is it effective?
4. What is the theme of the story?

赏　析：

Three Approaches to "The Story of an Hour"

1. Tension and Irony: A Formalist View on "The Story of an Hour"

Noted for a talented local-colorist, Kate Chopin has also been considered a skilled practitioner of humorous techniques in short story writing. She excelled at mixing literary devices such as irony and tension into her exquisite depiction of typical southern environment. This abstracted novelette epitomizes Chopin's sophisticated mastery of tension and irony—a formalist technique that provides an eternal artistic impact to literary work. She covered up her critique in a mask of irony and paradox, avoiding any blunt hint at "women's self-awareness". So when the publication of *The Awakening* received flurries of outrage, she picked up her usual flippant tone in defense of the novel:

"Having a group of people at my disposal, thought it might be entertaining (to myself) to show then together and see what would happen. I never dreamed of Mrs. Potellier making such a mess of things and working out her own damnation as she did. If I had had the slightest intimation of such a thing I would have excluded her from the company. But when I found out what she was up to, the play was half over and it was then too late."

She used humor to create the pretense that she had little control over her own creation and thereby to disarm her critics. Meanwhile her appealing purports to the conventional prejudices that repulsed women's quest for independence and self-assertion.

Tension in Plotting

Formalism expounds "tension" in the principle of the arch. The arch stands because the force of gravity pulls several stones down while pushing them against the keystones. [1] When it applies to the literary writing, what formalism calls the quality of tension takes shape. Tension is the resolution of two opposites, often in irony and paradox. Here goes my key issue: how does Kate Chopin put up the literary arch and how and what two resisting factors help enhance the work's ironic impact?

Allen Tate asserts tension in poetry is the "full, organized body of all the extension and intension". [2] It goes the same with a good novelette. For tension in a short story could never be revealed more markedly in the plot than elsewhere. A plot is the "author's dramatic manipulation of the events of his tale for the maximum artistic effect". According to the formalist view, what makes the plot move is a continual resolution of opposing forces, the conflict of tension.

"The Story of an Hour" is a tale about a wife's joyful expectation of freedom from her husband's suffocating love when she learns the news of his accidental death and her fatal dismay when he returns home alive. The plotting is so arranged as to be the shape of three linked "Z" where Chopin has designed three implicit subtle suspenses. The first is a scene of news-breaking where Louise Mallard's response comes beyond our expectation; the second scene explores in the heroine's "dramatic monologue" where we are surprised even more to the mystique of Mrs. Mallard's psychological changes; and the story's sardonic tone culminates at the last brief part. When the plot reaches "Richards was too late", we have a feeling as if all the lights on stage suddenly put out before the curtain falls down. And then there appeared a silent line of words on that darkened screen: "(the doctors said) she died of heart disease—of joy that kills". The literary tension finds its way in repetitions of twists and turns that end up in the heroine's tragic death.

In each of these suspenses, we discover extension and intension, or two opposing forces between the lines. Extension lies in what we might speculate from the seeming events; intension in what hides behind the story which arouses our curiosity and awaits our exploration. What a kind of woman is Louise Mallard? How on earth does she deal with her husband's death? How can we account for her abnormal and "amoral" performance? Well, surely "answers to them are not of my business," a formalist critic would claim. Anyway tension in a narrative genre arrives at its own destination by virtue of these seeming contradictions of extension and intension. It's also based on those confusions that arose such questions I've mentioned above.

Irony of Fate

Irony of fate is also named situational irony. It foregrounds the context "when there is an incongruity between appearance and reality, between expectation and fulfillment, or between what is and what would seem appropriate". [3] "The Story of an Hour" undoubtedly falls in this category. Chopin's tone is composed but not without any playfulness on Louise's fragility and Richards' pretension. On a whole, tragedy of the Mallards shows irony of fate so as to arouse people's serious thinking and critique on status of the housewife.

Mrs. Mallard serves as an embodiment of irony of fate in this story. Her moods change step by step, from "she did not hear the news as many women have heard the same" to "she kept whispering freedom", from "she carried herself unwittingly like a goddess of Victory" to "Richards was too late to screen Mr. Mallard from his wife". Aside from the obvious distance between what she expects and what she deserves, there's another incongruity in her. How could Louise Mallard's awakening self-awareness be so vulnerable that she finally fell into a humiliating defeat? I consider it not only the true fact of Chopin's time but also meeting the demand of dramatic conflict. In fact, double identities coexist in this heroine. When the story begins in the very first sentence, the author reminds us of Mrs. Mallard's heart trouble. Her sister Josephine and the family friend Mr. Richards trouble themselves, "in broken sentence and veiled hints" to "break to her as gently as possible the news of her husband's death". The heroine has well known for her physic weakness, emotional and dependent. She is surrounded by care and concern in every minute. Nevertheless, long restraint of passion for life and longing for individuality and freedom come to as the husband's control would perish once for all. The other identity of Mrs. Mallard desires independence and freedom. She exults at "the new spring life"; she is eager to retrieve self-assertion, even at the price of losing "the unsolved mystery of love". "What does love counts for in face of this possession of self-assertion." There are also intangible combats of these two contradictionary forces. For all her internal struggles and later determination, she never escapes the Irony of Fate.

To sum up, opposing factors in character as well as the plot have achieved the ironic impact that Kate Chopin dedicated to create.

Dramatic Irony in Mr. Richards

Dramatic irony expresses a disparity between what a character behaves and what the reader understands to be true. (4) It can be an effective way for the author to have a character unwittingly reveal his true colors.

As the key person to strain the story's thread, Mr. Richards contributes a lot to the development of plotting. As far as irony is concerned, this character underlies a consistent undertone of irony throughout the story. Kate Chopin employed dramatic irony in portrayal of Mr. Richards to disclose the theme. This figure directs the reader's attention to two significant acts in respective outset and outcome. "He had only taken the time" to check the truth of the news and "had hastened to forestall any less careful, less tender friend in bearing the sad message". His seeming discretion and exaggeration in the ending scene show us a sketch of pretension and moralism. Yet dramatic irony is revealed in that Mr. Richards assumes himself as one gentleman tender, considerate and sympathetic with a friend's mishap. His efforts and good intention didn't work well, or rather wound up in vain. At first he was forestalled by the rash Josephine, shortly after which he was too late to screen the returned husband. His self-importance in mask of "great care" turns out to be "painted lily". While Mr.

Richards poses an air of a savior, he becomes something of a clown with all his exaggeration and pretension. However, the real blunder Mr. Richards committed is not so much that he didn't prepare Louise for any explosive change as he failed to realize the interpersonal understanding and communication in coming to one's rescue. Small wonder most readers would feel the author's implicit deride and jeer at Mr. Richards. It is where dramatic irony of a character finds its way.

"The Story of an Hour" has tension and irony as its major characteristic. This typical formalist technique promotes forcefully the compact structure, well-knitted plotting and distinctive characters of the story. Most of all it has made the writing a high-degreed consistency of irony.

2. Superego versus Ego: Psychoanalysis on "The Story of an Hour"

Unlike formalist critics who interest themselves in constructing the literary structure and techniques, psychoanalytic approach probes into a winding maze of human psychic recess. They discover in "The Story of an Hour" an allegory of the tragedy resulting from the imbalanced ego. As the title of the novelette suggests, the author displays what has happened to Mrs. Mallard in an hour's time. Chopin devoted a majority of the writing space to demonstrating the heroine's riotous psychological state. In just one hour, the human psyche undergoes dramatic ups and downs, from the first grief and desolation to gradual exultation and to last despair and disillusionment.

Closed Room as the Superego Castle

Mrs. Mallard retired into her own upstairs room when all of her mental storm broke out. Some details deserve meticulous psychoanalysis. "She went away to her room alone and there stood, facing the open window, a comfortable and roomy armchair." This closed room is a symbol of her inner world. This room on another level is a well fortified castle built not only by her husband but also her repressive superego. In fact, their "great care" and "kind intention" equal in her eyes nothing less than confinement and supervision. Feminists of the twentieth century would state, beneath that care is an unremitting supervising face of Mr. Mallard that "never looked save love upon her" and out of the kind intention stands a "powerful will" bending hers in that blind persistence that keeps man or woman a right to impose a private will on a fellow-creature. After all was still a formidable castle of social conventions, new historians might add. Yet descendants of Freud think differently. In their view, her husband's control, her relatives' relentless care, and the conventional ideologies about family, all of these were actually amplified or foregrounded in Louise's mental world. To speak explicitly, if Mrs. Mallard should blame her depression on anybody, it is her inordinately repressive nerves being the main killer. "She was young, with a fair, calm face, whose lines bespoke repression and even a certain strength." Superego kept reminding herself of being a passive, devoted, and independent housewife, while she was all along trying against her own will to repress women's true emotion and desire for self-assertion. Mrs. Mallard closed herself in a room alone where nobody heard her whispering. Her problem, as a matter of fact, is in want of communication and recognition. We could safely surmise that even though she lived her own life since then, her fate would probably follow the shoes of Miss Emily under Faulkner's pen, becoming a queer person for her surroundings. Tragedies happen after they wait you a long time.

Heart Trouble as Vulnerable Ego

Even in the closed upstairs room Mrs. Mallard can always face toward an open window. It is the only link which ties her fancy and the immense alluring outside world. This creak on the superego keeps open toward freedom—patches of blue sky and piles carefree clouds, toward the living impulse—delicious breath of rain and countless sparrows twittering in the eves, toward the creating enthusiasm and passion—notes of a distant song and cry of a peddler. "Her breast rose tumultuously" and "her fancy ran riot". But don't forget in clinic pathology they are premonitions of heart trouble attack. Awakening unconsciousness began rimming with vigor and passion, in Freudian terminology the libidinal force. Considering Mrs. Mallard's reaction to the dead/living husband is also the choice of heart not of mind, heart trouble is a metaphor of her vulnerable ego, which follows id in search of a primordial pleasure principle. The author painted Mrs. Mallard's ecstasy at that moment: "What did it (love) matter! What could love, the unsolved mystery, count for in face of this possession of self-assertion which she suddenly recognized as the strongest impulse of her being!"

Combats among Superego/Ego/Id

But I would not reach a simple conclusion that Mr. Mallard must have to die accidentally to emancipate her wife. For in the immense iceberg of the unconscious, superego/ego and id form more complicated relationships. On this case, collapse of superego defense-line awakens the fidgeting id; however, none of these three waxes and wanes in order. We see clearly strenuous struggles of id/ego/superego. Id/ego tries to break through the surround of superego: "There was something coming to her, and she was waiting for it, fearfully." Superego/ego all the same tries to cast back away id: "She did not stop to ask if it were or were not a monstrous joy that held her... She was striving to beat it back with her will (will is superego)." Patriarchal consciousness succumbs to feminist unconsciousness. When id takes the upper hand Louise's eyes is burning with "a feverish triumph". She chooses to dismiss her love and sympathy toward her husband, more important, her role as a responsible wife.

Discovering her husband back again, Mrs. Mallard lost her ego in the embarrassment of superego vs. id. Had either one taken possession of her consciousness, there was an incompatible gap for her to fill in. And that's too hard for her at the moment. If superego, she couldn't stand up against the reprimand of her superego for wild fancy and monstrous joy at her own husband's death. And if id, she couldn't bear the fatal disillusionment that God-know gloomy long days submissive to a powerful will. It was on this reason that I'm convinced Mrs. Mallard dies of the cornered and

imbalanced ego. Some critical emphases on the heroine's despair or self guilt or both, or rather the view of betrayal of morality and its tragic price, in my opinion, have been tinged with the traditional morality and physiological approach. In psychoanalytic thinking, the story with its psychological allegory demonstrates to us that freedom, independence or happiness can't do without balanced ego.

3. Dilemma of Married Women in the 19th Century: A Culture Study

"She wanted something to happen—something, anything, she did not know what." A century has lapsed since Kate Chopin's last novel stroke American society like a bolt from the blue. Even today we can feel that remote but distinct life's impulse and anxious expectation from the depth of heart of numerous women whose voices had once been muffled and ignored. This haunting idea of married women's independence and freedom ran through most of Chopin's works. In this short story, there's one very similar paragraph out crying women's depression and persistence:

"There was something coming to her and she was waiting for it, fearfully. What was it? She did not know; it was too subtle and elusive to name. But she felt it, creeping out of the sky, reaching toward her through the sounds, the scents, the color that filled the air."

Uncovering Chopin's sensitive, acute linguistic veil, we'll see a Vigorous naked beating heart, with its name "awakening self-awareness" inscribed on it. However, all through this short story, neither the author nor Mrs. Mallard spells out such a "subtle and elusive" concept. Although literary device has an unwritten rule that justifies the writer's right to beat round the corner for lasting artistic impact, my focus is on how Mrs. Mallard can't escape a dilemma of married women. What, with the contemporary social conventions about family and the possible innate sensitivity, the way of women's self-discovery is so strenuous that it becomes either a temporal dream (as the story is also entitled the dream of an hour) or leads to a tragic death. The story somewhat reveals a dilemma of Chopin herself. She covered up her critique in a mask of irony and paradox, avoiding any blunt hint at "women's self-awareness".

Women's Imprisonment inside Home: Cultural and Historical Root

The image of Mrs. Mallard crystallizes a generation of women confined inside home in particular the 19th century American South or Victorian England. The contemporary moral view held that a wife should be subjective "body and soul" to a family mastered by the husband. Family is the blessing sanctuary of morality. For Louise Mallard, marital life is no less than living for some one whose powerful will, out of a kind intention or a cruel one, bends hers "in that blind persistence with which men and women believe they have a right to impose a private will upon a fellow-creature". And her link with the external world might be no more than a window open toward "patches of blue sky". Chopin's exquisite depiction of the landscape naturally associates our imagination with prisoners behind the bar. Many a feminist has likened domestic isolation/servitude to women's imprisonment.

We have good cause to be grateful to the slave. In striving to strike his irons off, we found most surely, that we were manacled ourselves. (Abby Kelley) (5)

I now fully understand the practical difficulties most women had to contend with. The general discontent I felt with women's portion as wife, mother, housekeeper, physician, and spiritual guide… impressed me with the strong feeling that some active measures should be taken."(Elizabeth Cady Stanton, *Eight Years and More*, 1898) (6)

"Physician" and "spiritual guide" has pointed to women's importance in preserving virtual codes in the industrialized American society. Men in Chopin's time were prone to tighten women' connection to family and domesticity, because men unwittingly projected their cherishing for the diminishing social moral codes onto women's role as a model wife: pure and devoted. One monograph on women's studies in America reports that American traditional ideologies of womanhood developed with the division of labor inside and outside the family:

In the early 19th century, as 'productive labor' moved increasingly out of the home, and ideological framework developed that historian Barbara Welter(1966) has called the 'cult of true womanhood'. It was at that time that women came to be viewed as delicate, frail, asexual, and the keepers of the home fires to which men could return after a harrowing day in the work. (7)

In order to isolate the middle-class wife from the public competition as well as from cruel progress of urbanization, housewives were kept inside the house, also trapped in a dilemma of the all-considerate love and control of the husband.

The separation between domestic life and production, and the consequent identification of men with the external world of work and women with the internal world of feeling, was intensified and exaggerated through the absolute exclusion of middle-class women from any form of labor. This came about not simply to confine women to the home and so safeguard their chastity… It came about largely in order to protect the home and family as ideals. (8)

This reality turns especially grave in the late-nineteenth-century American South. The 1860's Civil War crushed southern agrarian ideal, after which rapid industrial expansion caused a more acute conflict between the northern big-city bosses (the uprising bourgeoisie) and declining southern aristocracy of plantation. Industrial growth called for a flood of foreign immigrants whose participation added more multiple and tumultuous factors to the nation. Besides, the South was afflicted by grave economic problems caused by lack of slave labor forces. It was complicated by the White Counterrevolution. (9) A prevailing tension between the whites and blacks has since then fermented the Southern violence. All of these impelled the South to a strong sense of family and persistence on purity of Southern womanhood. Family and the wife have been loaded with too many cultural implications in the eye of Southerners.

"Women in the South do not have to earn a living. The men put them on pedestals; in other words, men elevate women's importance. Men serve women like gallant gentlemen. Men go out, work hard and earn a living while their wives stay at home and take care of culture." [10]

The southern wife, like Mrs. Mallard, thereby firmly set in this miserable and discriminating land, must have to experience a tear road to pursue independence and individuality.

Women's Awakening Self-awareness

Kate Chopin had all her novelettes in two collections, *At Folk* in 1894 and *A Night in Acadie* in 1897, at her 40s when she had been widowed for a dozen years. At the age of five, Kate Chopin lost her father in a work-related railroad accident; thereon she was raised by three generations of women. Chopin spent her youth in prestigious Sacred Heart Academy of St. Louis, a pro-North city. Early life experience cultivated her intelligence and independent thinking. Chopin was a thoughtful writer. Known as a peculiar local-colorist, she gave a great deal of thought to important issues. "She was involved in the idea of an independent woman and encouraged not to become a 'useless' wife. Chopin also challenged Catholicism's implicit authoritarianism, which admonished women to be submissive to their husbands." [11] Her usage of humor and satire easily found a way to critique manifestations of late-nineteenth-century American society as ostentatious philanthropy, social pretentiousness, as well as aspects of Southern culture. This short story is a representative writing of her lifelong concerns.

"The Story of an Hour" was published during the second wave of Women's Liberation Movement, which Elaine Showalter labeled the "feminist" phase (1880—1920) when women writers advocated minority rights and protested. Dating far back to the Enlightenment, Mary Wollstonecraft wrote in 1792 *A Vindication of the Rights of Men*, arguing that autocratic and patriarchal power relations between the sexes are as unjust and indefensible as those between monarch and subject. [12] In the early 19th century liberalism was widely adopted by feminist activists. This thought defended women's equal liberty, independence and revered faculties of reason as liberals sought to abolish "artificial constraints of law and social institutions that stem from people's irrational prejudices". "Their struggles involved the tearing down of barriers that kept women the freedom to develop as individuals, including laws that barred married women from holding property or that kept women from holding certain kinds of jobs or voting." [13] By the middle of that century, feminism combined with Marxist thought on capitalist family drew more attention on the hapless status of the average housewife. Discontent of Suffragettes extended to economic and ideological aspects. Meanwhile, another influential approach from European Freudian psychoanalysis irritated American Suffragists by male dominance in terms of sexuality. In 1890 Women's Christian Temperance Union and Suffrage groups merged to form the

National American Woman Suffrage Association. [14]

Kate Chopin created her story in such a social background which tended to reduce women to men's copy version. She bestowed Mrs. Mallard with the time's vigor and confusion. But her keen insight even surpassed her contemporary age, for Mrs. Mallard's search for self-assertion and resistance against patriarchy. To put another way, Kate Chopin with her typical womanish humanitarianism suggests that woman should be treated as an individual on an individual level, not as a special class or interest of group. In this sense, Louise Mallard's "whispering" and "fancy" have got a distant resonance in Betty Friedan's and Kate Millett's or Elaine Showalter's writings—women's returning to the "female" phase. Out of such daring attempt to portray the true female emotion and will, Chopin's rather disreputable novel *The Awakening* could be as popular among modern readers as notorious among Chopin's own days. Louise Mallard's awakening is likewise inexcusable to the judgment of Mr. Mallard, her sister and Mr. Richards. Strictly speaking, her awakening is more of a kind of intoxication or day-dream than sobriety. "She was drinking in a very elixir of life through that open window." Her untimely death implies not only Chopin's critique about the social conventions but also a wide embarrassing situation facing married women. So far as the southern women are concerned, women's revolt means a new identification of womanhood in culture. Women hoped to break off the imprisonment of family but they couldn't stand up with that formidable pressure from both society and their own doubts and fears. That's what I call the dilemma of women in a particular historical period of the late-nineteenth-century American south. What is the way out after those Mrs. Mallards awoke? Kate Chopin didn't look for a solution so that the answer was left to generations of feminist descendants.

Notes:

(1) (2) Guerin, Wilfred L., ed. *A Handbook of Critical Approaches to Literature*. Beijing: Foreign Language Teaching and Research Press, 2004: 90.

(3) (4) 叶华年等. 英语短篇小说导读：结构与理解（Introduction to English Short Stories: Structure and Interpretation）. 上海：华东师范大学出版社，1999: 193.

(5) (6) (9) (14) Garraty, John. *A Short History of the American Nation*. 4th ed. New York: Harper & Row, Publishers, 1985: 198-199, 281, 456.

(7) (12) (13) Sapiro, Virginia. *Women in American Society: An Introduction to Women's Studies*. [S.l.]: Mayfield Publishing Company, 1986: 50, 57.

(8) (10) (11) Stubbs, Patricia. *Woman & Fiction: Feminism & the Novel 1880—1920*. [S.l.]: The Harvester Press Ltd., 1979: 5, 35, 78.

（刘鎏）

Chapter 6   Theme

第六章   主题

> Beauty, love… actually, I think, all the time that I write, I am writing about love or its absence…
>
> Toni Morrison

简要介绍：

Theme is the central idea or insight of a story, whether explicit or implicit, which a literary work is designed to make persuasive to the reader. It is the unifying generalization about life stated or implied by the story, for which the plot, characters, setting, point of view, irony and other elements of the story are organized. Therefore, theme is what gives a story its unity, it is the soul of a literary work.

We express the theme not by summarizing the plot or by reducing it to its subject but by a one-sentence statement generalizing our understanding of a certain subject. The theme is different from the subject. Many stories share identical subjects, such as love, death, loneliness, disillusionment, alienation, but each story makes its own statement about one certain subject, which reveals its understanding of and insight into this subject. This statement is the theme. If we say that the subject of Washington Irving's "Rip Van Winkle" is "identity", then the theme of the story may be that "one's identity depends on recognition by the others".

Sometime, the theme of a story is explicitly stated by the author or a character in the story, but mostly the theme is implied, for the most important task of the writer is to reveal life instead of explaining or commenting it like philosophers or essayists. The function of the writer is not to state the theme but to vivify it, therefore, the writer is likely to refrain from interpreting it or making remarks about it. Good writings are not for the purpose of illustrating themes, but bring alive fragments of human life. Themes arise naturally in the process of writing. As a result, while we are determining what the theme of the story is, we should ask two essential questions: what view of life it supports, and what insight into life it reveals.

The following are some principles and strategies we may keep in mind while we are seeking the theme.

Some principles:

1. The theme should be expressed in a sentence.

2. The theme should be stated as an insight into life.

3. The theme is the central and unifying concept of a story, it can account for all the major details of the story. If some important incidents are contradictory with the theme, the theme may be partial and incomplete.

4. There is no single theme of a story. Different readers may have different understandings of the story, for the story is to present a view of life, and people's responses to life are different. But it does not mean that any interpretation is valid. To be valid, the statement of the theme must be responsive to the major details of the story.

Some strategies:

1. Pay attention to the title of the story.

2. Write down some important statements by the author and the characters, especially the protagonist.

3. Look for the details that repeated several times, and make sure whether they are of any symbolic meaning.

4. Pay special attention to some contradictory parts, there may be secrets beneath.

5. Comparison and contrast may be good ways to discover the theme.

简　析：

关于"主题"，我们需要注意的是：

1）主题是从作品对生活的再现或表达中提炼出来的核心观点。不论主题是明晰的，还是隐含的，它都是有机统一情节、人物、背景、叙述视角和反讽等作品要素的枢纽。

2）主题往往用一句精练的话语来表达。它既不同于话题（subject），也不同于情节——话题是对作品内容的一种笼统而简单的概括，比如爱、死亡、信仰等；情节是对作品有机结构的一种具体而细致的描述，比如"爱米丽在绝望中杀死了她的情人以便将爱永远留在身边"。主题是对包含在作品中的生命感悟的完整表达，比如"当爱情因为过度的欲望而违背人性的时候，它的结果只能是悲剧"。

3）提炼主题并不是一件容易的事，因为主题是不确定的。它以读者自己的经历和自己对世界和生活的理解为依据，深入感悟作品之后产生的一种共鸣。

作　品：

TILLIE OLSEN
[1913—　]

I Stand Here Ironing

I stand here ironing, and what you asked me moves tormented back and forth with the iron.

"I wish you would manage the time to come in and talk with me about your daughter. I'm sure you can help me understand her. She's a youngster who needs help and whom I'm deeply interested in helping."

"Who needs help"… Even if I came, what good would it do? You think because I am her mother I have a key, or that in some way you could use me as a key? She has lived for nineteen years. There is all that life that has happened outside of me, beyond me.

And when is there time to remember, to sift, to weigh, to estimate, to total? I will start and there will be an interruption and I will have to gather it all together again. Or I will become engulfed with all I did or did not do, with what should have been and what cannot be helped.

She was a beautiful baby. The first and only one of our five that was beautiful at birth. You do not guess how new and uneasy her tenancy in her now-loveliness. You did not know her all those years she was thought homely, or see her poring over her baby pictures, making me tell her over and over how beautiful she had been—and would be, I would tell her—and was now, to the seeing eye. But the seeing eyes were few or non-existent. Including mine.

I nursed her. They feel that's important nowadays. I nursed all the children, but with her, with all the fierce rigidity of first motherhood, I did like the books then said. Though her cries battered me to trembling and my breasts ached with swollenness, I waited till the clock decreed.

Why do I put that first? I do not even know if it matters, or if it explains anything.

She was a beautiful baby. She blew shining bubbles of sound. She loved motion, loved light, loved color and music and textures. She would lie on the floor in her blue overalls patting the surface so hard in ecstasy her hands and feet would blur. She was a miracle to me, but when she was eight months old I had to leave her daytimes with the woman downstairs to whom she was no miracle at all, for I worked or looked for work and for Emily's father, who "could no longer endure" (he wrote in his good-bye note) "sharing want with us."

I was nineteen. It was the pre-relief, pre-WPA world of the depression. I would start running as soon as I got off the streetcar, running up the stairs, the place smelling sour, and awake or asleep to startle awake, when she saw me she would break into a clogged weeping that could not be comforted, a weeping I can hear yet.

After a while I found a job hashing at night so I could be with her days, and it was better. But it came to where I had to bring her to his family and leave her.

It took a long time to raise the money for her fare back. Then she got chicken pox and I had to wait longer. When she finally came, I hardly knew her, walking quick and nervous like her father, looking like her father, thin, and dressed in a shoddy red that yellowed her skin and glared at the pockmarks. All the baby loveliness gone.

She was two. Old enough for nursery school they said, and I did not know then what I know now—the fatigue of the long day, and the lacerations of group life in the kinds of nurseries that are only parking places for children.

Except that it would have made no difference if I had known. It was the only place there was. It was the only way we could be together, the only way I could hold a job.

And even without knowing, I knew. I knew the teacher that was evil because all these years it has curdled into my memory, the little boy hunched in the corner, her rasp, "Why aren't you outside, because Alvin hits you? That's no reason, go out, scaredy." I knew Emily hated it even if she did not clutch and implore "don't go Mommy" like the other children, mornings.

She always had a reason why we should stay home. Momma, you look sick, Momma. I feel sick. Momma, the teachers aren't there today, they're sick. Momma, we can't go, there was a fire there last night. Momma, it's a holiday today, no school, they told me.

But never a direct protest, never rebellion. I think of our others in their three-, four-year-oldness—the explosions, the tempers, the denunciations, the demands—and I feel suddenly ill. I put the iron down. What in me demanded that goodness in her? And what was the cost, the cost to her of such goodness?

The old man living in the back once said in his gentle way: "You should smile at Emily more when you look at her." What *was* in my face when I looked at her? I loved her. There were all the acts of love.

It was only with the others I remembered what he said, and it was the face of joy, and not of care of tightness or worry I turned to them—too late for Emily. She does not smile easily, let alone almost always as her brothers and sisters do. Her face is closed and somber, but when she wants, how fluid. You must have seen it in her pantomimes, you spoke of her rare gift for comedy on the stage that rouses a laughter out of the audience so dear they applaud and applaud and do not want to let her go.

Where does it come from, that comedy? There was none of it in her when she came back home that second time, after I had had to send her away again. She had a new daddy now to learn to love, and I think perhaps it was a better time.

Except when we left her alone nights, telling ourselves she was old enough.

"Can't you go some other time, Mommy, like tomorrow?" she would ask. "Will it be just a little while you'll be gone? Do you promise?"

The time we came back, the front door open, the clock on the floor in the hall. She rigid awake. "It wasn't just a little while. I didn't cry. Three times I called you, just three times, and then I ran downstairs to open the door so you could come faster. The clock talked loud. I threw it away, it scared me what it talked."

She said the clock talked loud again that night I went to the hospital to have Susan. She was delirious with the fever that comes before red measles, but she was fully conscious all the week I was gone and the week after we were home when she could not come near the new baby or me.

She did not get well. She stayed skeleton thin, not wanting to eat, and night after night she had nightmares. She would call for me, and I would rouse from exhaustion to sleepily call back: "You're all right, darling, go to sleep, it's just a dream," and if she still called, in a sterner voice, "now go to sleep, Emily, there's nothing to hurt you." Twice, only twice, when I had to get up for Susan anyhow, I went in to sit with her.

Now when it is too late (as if she would let me hold and comfort her like I do the others) I get up and go to her at once at her moan or restless stirring. "Are you awake, Emily? Can I get you something?" And the answer is always the same: "No, I'm all right, go back to sleep, Mother."

They persuaded me at the clinic to send her away to a convalescent home in the country where "she can have the kind of food and care you can't manage for her, and you'll be free to concentrate on the new baby." They still send children to that place. I see pictures on the society page of sleek young women planning affairs to raise money for it, or dancing at the affairs, or decorating Easter eggs or filling Christmas stockings for the children.

They never have a picture of the children so I do not know if the girls still wear those gigantic red bows and the ravaged looks on the every other Sunday when parents can come to visit "unless otherwise notified"—as we were notified the first six weeks.

Oh it is a handsome place, green lawns and tall trees and fluted flower beds. High up on the balconies of each cottage the children stand, the girls in their red bows and white dresses, the boys in white suits and giant red ties. The parents stand below shrieking up to be heard and the children shriek down to be heard, and between them the invisible wall "Not To Be Contaminated by Parental Germs or Physical Affection."

There was a tiny girl who always stood hand in hand with Emily. Her parents never came. One visit she was gone. "They moved her to Rose Cottage," Emily shouted in explanation. "They don't like you to love anybody here."

She wrote once a week, the labored writing of a seven-year-old. "I am fine. How is the baby? If I write my letter nicely I will have a star. Love." There never was a star. We wrote every other day, letters she could never hold or keep but only hear read—once. "We simply do not have room for children to keep any personal possessions," they patiently explained when we pieced one Sunday's shrieking together to plead how much it would mean to Emily, who loved so to keep things, to be allowed to keep her letters and cards.

Each visit she looked frailer. "She isn't eating," they told us.

(They had runny eggs for breakfast or mush with lumps, Emily said later, I'd hold it in my mouth and not swallow. Nothing ever tasted good, just when they had chicken.)

It took us eight months to get her released home, and only the fact that she gained back so little of her seven lost pounds convinced the social worker.

I used to try to hold and love her after she came back, but her body would stay stiff, and after a while she'd push away. She ate little. Food sickened her, and I think much of life too. Oh she had physical lightness and brightness, twinkling by on skates, bouncing like a ball up and down up and down over the jump rope, skimming over the hill; but these were momentary.

She fretted about her appearance, thin and dark and foreign-looking at a time when every little girl was supposed to look or thought she should look a chubby blonde replica of Shirley Temple. The doorbell sometimes rang for her, but no one seemed to come and play in the house or be a best friend. Maybe because we moved so much.

There was a boy she loved painfully through two school semesters. Months later she told me how she had taken pennies from my purse to buy him candy. "Licorice was his favorite and I brought him some every day, but he still liked Jennifer better'n me. Why, Mommy?" The kind of question for which there is no answer.

School was a worry to her. She was not glib or quick in a world where glibness and quickness were easily confused with ability to learn. To her overworked and exasperated teachers she was an overconscientious "slow learner" who kept trying to catch up and was absent entirely too often.

I let her be absent, though sometimes the illness was imaginary. How different from my now-strictness about attendance with the others. I wasn't working. We had a new baby, I was home anyhow. Sometimes, after Susan grew old enough, I would keep her home from school, too, to have them all together.

Mostly Emily had asthma, and her breathing, harsh and labored, would fill the house with a curiously tranquil sound. I would bring the two old dresser mirrors and her boxes of collections to her bed. She would select beads and single earrings, bottle tops and shells, dried flowers and pebbles, old postcards and scraps, all sorts of oddments; then she and Susan would play Kingdom, setting up landscapes and furniture, peopling them with action.

Those were the only times of peaceful companionship between her and Susan. I have edged away from it, that poisonous feeling between them, that terrible balancing of hurts and needs I had to do between the two, and did so badly, those earlier years.

Oh there are conflicts between the others too, each one human, needing, demanding, hurting, taking—but only between Emily and Susan, no, Emily toward Susan that corroding resentment. It seems so obvious on the surface, yet it is not obvious. Susan, the second child, Susan, golden- and curly-haired and chubby, quick and articulate and assured, everything in appearance and manner Emily was not; Susan, not able to resist Emily's precious things, losing or sometimes clumsily breaking them; Susan telling jokes and riddle to company for applause while Emily sat silent (to say to me later: that was *my* riddle, Mother, I told it to Susan); Susan, who for all the five years' difference in age was just a year behind Emily in developing physically.

I am glad for that slow physical development that widened the difference between her and her contemporaries, though she suffered over it. She was too vulnerable for that terrible world of youthful competition, of preening and parading, of constant measuring of yourself against every other, of envy, "If I had that copper hair", "If I had that skin..." She tormented herself enough about not looking like the others, there was enough of the unsureness, the having to be conscious of words before you speak, the constant caring—what are they thinking of me? Without having it all magnified by the merciless physical drives.

Ronnie is calling. He is wet and I change him. It is rare there is such a cry now. That time of motherhood is almost behind me when the ear is not one's own but must always be racked and listening for the child cry, the child call. We sit for a while and I hold him, looking out over the city spread in charcoal with its soft aisles of light. "Shoogily", he breathes and curls closer. I carry him back to bed, asleep. Shoogily. A funny word, a family word, inherited from Emily, invented by her to say: comfort.

In this and other ways she leaves her seal, I say aloud. And startle at my saying it. What do I mean? What did I start to gather together, to try and make coherent? I was at the terrible, growing years. War years. I do not remember them well. I was working, there were four smaller ones now, there was not time for her. She had to help be a mother, and housekeeper, and shopper. She had to set her seal. Mornings of crisis and near hysteria trying to get lunches packed, hair combed, coats and shoes found, everyone to school or Child Care on time, the baby ready for transportation. And always the paper scribbled on by a smaller one, the book looked at by Susan then mislaid, the homework not done. Running out to that huge school where she was one, she was lost, she was a drop; suffering over her unpreparedness, stammering and unsure in her classes.

There was so little time left at night after the kids were bedded down. She would struggle over books, always eating (it was in those years she developed her enormous appetite that is legendary in our family) and I would be ironing, or preparing food for the next day, or writing V-mail to Bill, or tending the baby. Sometimes, to make me laugh, or out of her despair, she would imitate happenings or types at school.

I think I said once: "Why don't you do something like this in the school amateur show?" one morning she phoned me at work, hardly understandable through the weeping: "Mother, I did it. I won, I won; they gave me first prize; they clapped and clapped and wouldn't let me go."

Now suddenly she was Somebody, and as imprisoned in her difference as she had been in her anonymity.

She began to be asked to perform at other high schools, even in colleges, then at city and statewide affairs. The first one we went to, I only recognized her that first moment when thin, shy, she almost drowned herself into the curtains. Then: Was this Emily? The control, the command, the convulsing and deadly clowning, the spell, then the roaring, stamping audience, unwilling to let this rare and precious laughter out of their lives.

Afterwards: You ought to do something about her with a gift like that—but without money or knowing how, what does one do? We have left it all to her, and the gift has as often eddied inside, clogged and clotted, as been used and growing.

She is coming. She runs up the stairs two at a time with her light graceful step, and I know she is happy tonight. Whatever it was that occasioned your call did not happen today.

"Aren't you ever going to finish the ironing, Mother? Whistler painted his mother in a rocker. I'd have to paint mine standing over an ironing board." This is one of her communicative nights and she tells me everything and nothing as she fixed herself a plate of food out of the icebox.

She is so lovely. Why did you want me to come in at all? Why were you concerned? She will find her way.

She stars up the stairs to bed. "Don't get *me* up with the rest in the morning." "But I thought you were having midterms." "Oh, those," she comes back in, kisses me, and says quite lightly, "in a couple of years when we'll all be atom-dead they won't matter a bit."

She has said it before. She *believes* it. But because I have been dredging the past, and all that compounds a human being is so heavy and meaningful in me, I cannot endure it tonight.

I will never total it all. I will never come in to say: she was a child seldom smiled at. Her father left me before she was a year old. I had to work her first six years when there was work, or I sent her home and to his relatives. There were years she had care she hated. She was dark and thin and foreign-looking in a world where the prestige went to blondeness and curly hair and dimples, she was slow where glibness was prized. She was a child of anxious, not proud, love. We were poor and could not afford for her the soil of easy growth. I was a young mother, I was a distracted mother. There were the other children pushing up, demanding. Her younger sister seemed all that she was not. There were years she did not let me touch her. She kept too much in herself, her life was such she had to keep too much in herself. My wisdom came too late. She has much to her and probably little will come of it. She is a child of her age, of depression, of war, of fear.

Let her be. So all that is in her will not bloom—but in how many does it? There is still enough left to live by. Only help her to know—help make it so there is cause for her to know—that she is more than this dress on the ironing board, helpless before the iron.

Questions:

1. How much do you know about Emily from her mother's stream of consciousness? What does the mother really want to say?
2. What does "they" refer to? What is the relationship between mother, daughter, and "they"?
3. How important is the old man who tells the mother to learn to smile to her daughter? What does "smile" mean to mother and daughter in their life?
4. How do you understand the ending of the story?
5. What do you think is the theme of the story? Why?

赏　析：

解读《我站在这儿熨烫》

内容提要： 本文在充分解读蒂莉·奥尔森在论文集《沉默》中关于母性涵义的理论的基础上，用精神分析理论剖析了蒂莉·奥尔森的小说《我站在这儿熨烫》，说明这个发生在 20 世纪美国经济萧条时期的自传性故事实际上是"人类的天性、欲望和永不枯竭的潜力"与"抑制、压迫、扭曲、扼杀这一切的生活现实"碰撞和冲突的真实再现。

关键词： 母性　生活现实　人类天性　自我　欲望

　　《我站在这儿熨烫》是美国当代女作家蒂莉·奥尔森在文坛沉寂多年后复出的第

一篇小说。操持家务、赚钱养家、哺育子女，这样繁重琐碎的工作耗费了奥尔森整整二十年的写作光阴，同时也在不断地加深着她对母亲角色、女性地位、社会责任这一系列问题的认识和思考。"二十年来我孕育子女，养育他们，同时还得外出工作，创作的基本条件都无法满足。但是写作，写作的欲望，就像'呼吸的空气一样重要，只要我依然活着'。"（Olsen, p.19）正是这样的创作激情、文化积淀和反思能力最终促使奥尔森重拾纸笔，并将艺术视角投向同她一样挣扎在美国主流文化之外的边缘人物：疲惫不堪的母亲、失意落寞的少女、孤苦无依的弃儿、漂泊不定的浪子…… 在所有的小说中，体现在女性身上的"母性"是奥尔森着墨最多、思考得最为深入的一个问题。"她"不仅是奥尔森小说创作中的灵魂，也是奥尔森女性问题研讨的中心。我们可以在《我站在这儿熨烫》、《告诉我一个谜》、《哦，是的》等多部中短篇小说中看到"她"形象而生动的影子，我们也可以在《母亲对女儿，女儿对母亲》、《沉默》等论文集中读到关于"她"的问题的严肃而深入的思考。

我们应该如何理解"母性"？"母性"是如何影响女性的生活？奥尔森在她的论文集《沉默》（*Silences*, 1979）一书中这样概括她对母性的理解："母性的内涵，包括……人类的天性、欲望和永不枯竭的潜力，以及抑制、压迫、扭曲、扼杀这一切的生活现实。"（Olsen, p.202）本文将在充分解读奥尔森对"母性"的理解的基础上，用精神分析理论剖析奥尔森复出后创作的第一篇小说《我站在这儿熨烫》。

母性与生活现实

《我站在这儿熨烫》并不是传统意义上的那种小说，它没有跌宕起伏的故事情节，没有扣人心弦的疑团悬念，也没有个性鲜明的主要人物，它只是一位心力交瘁的母亲对她女儿十九年来的成长历程的回忆。回忆是以某种对话式的内心独白表现的，对话的双方是母亲和女儿的某位不在场的老师。对话的起因是正在熨烫衣服的母亲接到了女儿的老师的电话，要求她抽时间到学校去谈谈她女儿的情况。"我希望你能挤出点时间来我这儿一趟，我们来谈谈你的女儿。我想你可以帮我了解她。她还年轻，需要帮助，而且我也很想帮她。"老师的话在母亲的耳边回响，于是母亲一边继续熨衣，一边开始与想象中的老师进行对话。正因为是对话，而不是单向度的回忆，于是，我们不仅听到了母亲心目中的女儿的成长故事，还听到了母亲不断为自己所作的辩解，母亲的内疚和思考，母亲对女儿的信心和希望，于是，想象中的对话的中心从女儿扩展到了母亲，从回忆扩展到思考。母亲想要做的是好好回想一下，在女儿的成长过程中，"哪些是我曾经做过的，哪些是未能做到的，哪些是本该做好的，哪些是无可挽回的"。

母亲的内心独白是从自我辩解开始的："即使我去了，又有什么用呢？你以为我是她母亲，我就一定有办法，或者你就可以从我身上找到办法？她已经十九岁了。这十九年来，她一直游离在我的体外，生活在我无法企及的地方。"这样的辩解紧接着老师的话语，显然母亲已经感受到了老师话语中对女儿的担忧、关心和希望，以及对母亲的某种质备。于是母亲急切地表达了她对女儿的现状的无奈，想以此逃脱她内心的愧疚。然而，母亲对女儿的内疚心理却在无意识中主宰了母亲整个内心独白。母亲的意识流虽然断断续续，零零碎碎，不时地被外界的干扰打断，然而这些看似不经意的片断却始终围绕着女儿不断受到的伤害展开的，围绕着女儿的"天性、欲望和永不枯竭的潜力"如何一次一次受到"抑制、压迫、扭曲、扼杀"而展开的。透过这些片段，我们和母亲一起感受了女儿艾米莉从一个"非常可爱"的女婴成长为一个自我封闭的少女的痛苦历程。

艾米莉出生在 20 世纪 30 年代美国经济萧条时期。呱呱落地的女孩活泼可爱："她出生时非常可爱。是五个孩子中第一个也是唯一的一个一落地就容貌秀丽的宝宝。"年仅十九的母亲，初为人母，得不到任何的指导和帮助，只有盲目地追随育儿手册上所谓的指导。手册上倡导整点按时喂养婴儿，于是"尽管她的哭声使我心疼得颤抖，尽管双乳胀得肿痛，我还是固执地等到时钟敲响的那一刻才给她喂奶"。这是母亲记忆中艾米莉遭受的第一次痛苦，是由母亲的无知造成的，不过母亲不确定这"对她的成长是否有影响"。

女儿才八个月大时，女儿的父亲就无情地遗弃了她们。年轻的母亲举目无亲，彷徨无依。没有任何社会机构或政府部门向贫困交加的母女伸出援助之手。为了生存，视女儿为奇迹的母亲"只能白天把她托付给住在楼下的一个女人照看，那女人根本就不把她当回事儿"。而母亲自己则不得不外出工作挣钱。这次母女分离的结果是，女儿从"非常可爱"的婴儿变成了一见母亲就"抽抽搭搭地哭个不停，怎么哄也哄不好"的孩子。

紧接着，母亲迫于生计，又不得不把女儿送往她父亲的家寄养。等到她终于攒够了钱接女儿回来时，女儿"婴儿时期的那份可爱已经荡然无存"。她变得消瘦、孤僻、瑟缩、怯懦。这次的分离给艾米莉的身心造成了严重的伤害，更给母女二人之间的关系留下了一道疏远和隔阂的阴影。

那时，艾米莉刚好两岁，在旁人的劝说下，母亲将她送进了托儿所。然而，母亲不知道，那个时代的托儿所，仅仅是一些"儿童寄存处"，严厉暴躁的老师和你争我抢的群体生活折磨着弱小的艾米莉，使她日夜惊恐不安。但"这是她唯一可去的地方。这是我们能在一起而我又能继续工作的唯一方法"。年幼的艾米莉不得不努力去适应这一切：托儿所、新爸爸、晚上一个人留在家里、做了噩梦尽量不喊妈妈……处于生活重压之下的母亲开始意识到女儿个性上的压抑，和与她的日益疏远。母亲心酸地发现女儿遇事"从不直接反对，或公开抗议"；女儿不断地向她表示她的懂事，"我没有哭。我就是喊了你三次，只有三次"。"两次，她只叫两次"，女儿逐渐变得自我封闭，对于母亲的问候与关心，"她的回答总是千篇一律：'不用，我没事儿，去睡吧，妈妈。'"

当母亲学会褪下满脸的忧虑，而把笑脸迎向艾米莉时，已经太迟了，"她不苟言笑，更不用说像她的弟弟妹妹一样成天乐呵呵了"。

　　染上风疹的艾米莉始终没有完全康复，她骨瘦如柴，食欲不振。毫无经验的母亲又一次听从了他人的意见，将她送到了康复中心。这些由富人出资的所谓的慈善机构被宣扬得有如天堂，报纸上刊登着大幅的为孩子们募捐筹款、组织活动的照片，但是"他们从不刊登关于孩子们的照片"，所以人们无从知晓那里的孩子不得不与自己的亲人隔离，每日吞咽着"黏糊糊的鸡蛋做早餐，或是结成块状的玉米粥"，只能在阳台上声嘶力竭地与前来探望他们的父母对话，不能爱自己的朋友，甚至不能保留父母寄来的信件。康复中心的生活使艾米莉的健康每况愈下，她的个性也愈发内向。这一次的经历几乎扭曲了艾米莉的天性，扼杀了她的爱的能力，她开始拒绝母亲的爱："我经常有意去拥抱她，以此表达我的爱意，可她的身子总是绷得紧紧的，只一会儿就把我推开。"她的生活态度完全变了，她不仅厌食，也厌倦生活。她为自己的相貌平平而自卑，为笨嘴拙舌而懊恼，为妹妹各方各面胜过自己而心怀敌意。她沉默寡言，形单影只，在家庭和学校都郁郁不得志。

　　毫无疑问，是现实生活使母女二人饱受肉体和精神上的伤害。战争、经济危机、不健全的婴幼儿护理体系和机构，以及面对选择和挑战的时候那些所谓的权威声音，这一切一起造成了"无可挽回"的过去。然而，在这一过程中，存在于母性中的那一种被动地适应和接受现实的倾向使母亲在无意中扮演了对女儿直接实施伤害的可悲的角色。小说中，母亲的一切行动似乎都是在无形的"他们"引领下进行的："他们"教导母亲整点哺乳孩子，"他们"建议母亲送两岁的女儿进托儿所，"他们"劝说母亲把女儿隔离在康复中心，"他们"不许孩子们保留属于自己的东西……而在每一次给女儿造成伤害后母亲都以"我不知道"、"我不了解"、"我没有意识到"、"即使我了解这些也于事无补"、"我能做什么呢"、"又有什么用"等等理由来表示她对现实生活的无奈和被动。而正是母亲这种被动的观念、态度和决定使母亲丧失了为女儿营造一个安全和爱的空间和环境的能力，在不自觉中将自己弱小的孩子直接置身于与社会期待和现实生活的不协调之中，使孩子在自我形成的过程中受到了严重的伤害。

　　根据拉康的理论，我们可以将幼儿建构"我"的镜像阶段理解为"一个认同"，在这个过程中，"我"处于某种原始形式，"之后通过和他者的认同辩证法，'我'被具体对象化了"。（Lacan, p.2）即"我"要成为我自己必须经过在他者的介入之下与外部的镜像认同的过程，也就是说，在"我"的形成过程中，一定存在着主体、镜像和第三人称他者的目光，幼儿作为主体只有通过在微笑着欢迎自己的镜像的成人的目光中进行确认，才能接受它。而在艾米莉成长的过程中，本应该担当介于她和她的"镜像"之间的第三者充满爱和微笑的目光的母亲却由于忙于生计和缺乏经验而缺席了，艾米莉看到的、感受到的都是现实对她的否定。作为弱小的个体，艾米莉因无法承受这些压力而不断从积极抗争（啼哭）到消极抵抗（压抑天性：听话、懂事），直至完全进入自我封闭的状态（扭曲、扼杀天性：孤僻、冷漠、仇恨）。

母性与天性

然而，虽然小说人物的经历是痛苦的，小说的基调却并不悲观。严峻的现实生活一次又一次的挑战，压抑着母亲，也伤害着女儿，更给母女二人的关系蒙上了一层无法摆脱的阴影。身处逆境，母女二人也曾失落、彷徨，然而"母性"的天性促使她们不再一味地退缩和逃避，而是以各自的方式，勇敢地向生活喊出了"不"字。

"母性"中"爱"的天性是不可能被生活完全埋没的。被丈夫遗弃之后，年轻的母亲曾经在生活的压力中迷失自己，尽管她以自己柔嫩的肩膀挑起生活的重担，尽自己最大的努力为女儿遮风挡雨，然而她却将焦虑、苦恼和担忧误作为自己生活的主色调，在忙忙碌碌中丢失了对自己和对艾米莉的微笑和信心。艾米莉的压抑和慈祥老人的提醒使母亲很快意识到了问题的症结所在。尽管对艾米莉来说有些迟了，但母亲终于学会在现实生活的苦难中展露自己的笑脸，用笑脸面对自己的儿女，用拥抱安慰经历创伤的儿女。她再次结婚、生儿育女，为自己和艾米莉重新建立了一个完整健全的家庭。虽然数次与艾米莉分离，她总是千方百计接她回来，用母爱弥补过失，呵护孩子孤僻自闭的心灵。她深信"一切都在好转"，相信女儿在生活各处留下了自己的印记："舒舒。这是个有趣的词汇，是我们家传的词汇，是艾米莉发明的，意思是：舒服。她就是用这样那样的方法在生活中刻下了她的印记。"她尽量为艾米莉提供一个自由成长的空间和环境：在艾米莉无法承受学校的压力的时候，她"任由她缺课"；为调解艾米莉和苏珊之间的敌意，她创造交流和和解的机会；为帮助和鼓励艾米莉克服自卑，树立信心，她建议擅长模仿的艾米莉去"学校的业余表演中露一手"。她深信女儿"是如此的可爱……她会找到自己的方向"。总之，她努力用她的爱改变艾米莉原先形成的那个虚假和扭曲的自我，尽量用微笑和赞赏激发艾米莉对生活的欲望，使她认识和发挥自身无穷的潜力。

而艾米莉，在母亲微笑的目光下，也终于开始逐渐摆脱幼年时形成的封闭的自我原型，努力在与他者的交往和联系中寻找和建构新的自我。她专注地翻看自己的婴儿照，在母亲一遍一遍肯定的语气中感受自己的可爱与漂亮；她用自己的方式，尝试着结交异性朋友；她以自己的勤奋，努力去博得老师和同学的认可；她努力与漂亮的妹妹苏珊建立起和谐共处的关系，不再因为被苏珊夺走了自己想象中的理想形象而妒忌、愤怒乃至心怀敌意。虽然她依然为各式各样的小事烦恼，但是她终于找到了自我表达的方式。在母亲的建议下，艾米莉在学校的业余表演中崭露头角，充分展现了她表演哑剧的天赋。这位一向默默无闻的"笨学生"一下子成了学校的风云人物，每次表演都能引起轰动。不善言辞的艾米莉学会了通过自己的手势和形体动作展露丰富多彩的内心世界，不苟言笑的艾米莉能够在台上赢得观众"一阵接一阵的笑声，一浪又一浪的掌声"。这是一种特殊的言说和交流方式，正如亚当·杰沃斯基在《沉默的力量》(*The Power of Silence*, 1993) 中所说，"哑剧中的沉默其实是一个表现人生百态的容器"，"是表演的特殊境界"。(Jaworski, p.146) 这种言说形式抛弃了传统意义上的权威性语言，用独特的方式使"笨嘴拙舌"的艾米莉发出了自己的声音，实现了自己的存在价值，并得到了大家的认可和喜爱。

母女之间的隔阂也在爱的融化下消失了。"妈！惠斯勒画了一幅他母亲坐在摇椅里的画。我得画一幅你站在熨衣板前的画。"艾米莉无心的戏谑在作者笔下有意地传达这样一个事实：男孩们描绘的母亲通常是静态的。在传统的文艺作品中，母亲往往只是一幅画面，一个意象，一个被描绘的静止客体，而不是一个活生生的施动者。虽然母亲的日常工作渺小琐碎得不能作为文学和艺术的对象，但艾米莉已经开始意识到母亲这种熨衣、做饭的日常生活，母亲那些简单朴实的言语和笑容对她的重要性。他们作为爱的传达方式曾如此有力地帮助她重建了她的自我，他们已经深深融入她的生活和生命中，成为了一个不可分割的整体。这样行动着的、爱着的母亲，才是真实的有生命力的。

小说的结尾，母亲感慨着"她不该只像熨板上的这件裙子一样，无助地等待被熨烫的命运"。对艾米莉来说，孤独自闭的童年时代和失意落寞的少女时期都已"无可挽回"，但是她有爱她的母亲可以帮她解开自我封闭的想象，学会倾听自己的心声，挖掘自己的潜力，创造自己的未来。而母亲，也在追忆生活的往事同时，也逐渐因为爱而感悟到了自身内在的欲望和潜力，开始点燃自己生命的光亮。小说似乎想说明，当主体在只承认实用功能的社会里，面对强大的社会联结体，遭受极度的个人焦虑时，唯有爱才能解除现实对主体的欲望和潜能的束缚，回归正常的心理。这一点也是精神分析学家拉康的结论。他在自己最有影响力的论文《镜像期：精神分析实践中所揭示的'我'的功能构成》的结尾中说："神经症和心理症所引发的痛苦对我们来说是心灵激情的磨难，就像精神分析天平的横杆一样，当我们计算它对整个社会造成的威胁的倾斜时，它向我们提供了扑灭社会激情的标志。在这种自然与文化的交接处……唯独精神分析学认识到了想象的奴役这一死结，爱必须再一次解开或割断这一死结。"(Lacan, p.7)

《我站在这儿熨烫》是奥尔森最具自传性质的作品。像小说中的母亲一样，她在十九岁时成了单身母亲；经历过贫穷和分离，再次组建了家庭并有了更多的孩子；她不得不一边工作一边料理家务抚育子女；她的大女儿卡拉，也"有一段并不轻松的成长经历"，(Olsen, p.20) 但同时又颇具舞蹈天赋。对此，奥尔森这样解释："故事的基调和我的经历有些相似，然而共同点不在于具体的情节，而在于母亲的心情。"(Olsen, p.21) "她站在这儿熨烫，而我是站在这儿写作"(Olsen, p.23)，这可能是小说中的母亲与小说作者奥尔森之间最大的区别。奥尔森的小说几乎都是在夜深人静时孩子们都入睡以后在熨衣板前写就的。数十年来，她一直在寻求着家务、工作和写作三者之间的平衡，或者说，她一直在寻求着社会责任、家庭责任与主体欲望之间的平衡，思考着"母性"的内涵与本质，以及母性本质与生活现实交织碰撞的真实状态。传统和社会给母亲的定位常常使母亲在生活中丧失属于自己的生存空间和时间，就如奥尔森在《沉默》一书中所描绘的，"母亲的角色意味着随时被打扰，时时操心，刻刻仔细……母亲要习惯的是打扰，而不是沉思；是中断，而不是连续；是突发状况，而不是一成不变"（Olsen, p.19）。过于沉重的社会责任与家庭责任常常使母亲忽视甚至扼杀自己和家人，尤其是孩子的内在欲望，给自己和家人造成心灵的伤害。个人的经历使奥尔森感觉到了现实责任与人类天性之间的矛盾和冲突，然而，面对这个人类永恒的难题，奥尔森也只能给出模糊的答案。不过，她始终在探索和思考这个问题，她同她笔下的人物一样，身处逆境而不轻言放弃，这是她仅靠寥寥数篇作品就在美国文学史上留下一席之地的主要原因之一。

参考书目：

[1] 陈晓兰. 女性主义批评与文学诠释. 兰州：敦煌文艺出版社，1999.

[2] Fyre, Joanne S. *Tillie Olsen: A Study of the Short Fiction.* New York: Twayne Publishers, 1995.

[3] Jaworski, Adam. *The Power of Silence.* London: Sage Publications, 1993.

[4] Lacan, Jacques. *Ecrits: A Selection.* Trans. Alan Sheridan. [S.l.]: Tavistock Publications, 1977.

[5] Olsen, Tillie. *Silences.* New York: Dell Publishing Co., Inc., 1979.

（高奋　沈燕艳　发表于《外国文学》2004 年第 3 期）

Chapter 7   Stories for Further Reading

第七章   延伸阅读小说选

WILLIAM FAULKNER
[1897—1962]

A Rose for Emily

I

When Miss Emily Grierson died, our whole town went to her funeral: the men through a sort of respectful affection for a fallen monument, the women mostly out of curiosity to see the inside of her house, which no one save an old manservant—a combined gardener and cook—had seen in at least ten years.

It was a big, squarish frame house that had once been white, decorated with cupolas and spires and scrolled balconies in the heavily lightsome style of the seventies, set on what had once been our most select street. But garages and cotton gins had encroached and obliterated even the august names of that neighborhood; only Miss Emily's house was left, lifting its stubborn and coquettish decay above the cotton wagons and the gasoline pumps—an eyesore among eyesores. And now Miss Emily had gone to join the representatives of those august names where they lay in the cedar-bemused cemetery among the ranked and anonymous graves of Union and Confederate soldiers who fell at the battle of Jefferson.

Alive, Miss Emily had been a tradition, a duty, and a care; a sort of hereditary obligation upon the town, dating from that day in 1894 when Colonel Sartoris, the mayor—he who fathered the edict that no Negro woman should appear on the streets without an apron—remitted her taxes, the dispensation dating from the death of her father on into perpetuity. Not that Miss Emily would have accepted charity. Colonel Sartoris invented an involved tale to the effect that Miss Emily's father had loaned money to the town, which the town, as a matter of business, preferred this way of repaying. Only a man of Colonel Sartoris' generation and thought could have invented it, and only a woman could have believed it.

When the next generation, with its more modern ideas, became mayors and aldermen, this arrangement created some little dissatisfaction. On the first of the year they mailed her a tax notice. February came, and there was no reply. They wrote her a formal letter, asking her to call at the sheriff's office at her convenience. A week later the mayor wrote her himself, offering to call or to send his car for her, and received in reply a note on paper of an archaic shape, in a thin, flowing calligraphy in faded ink, to the effect that she no longer went out at all. The tax notice was also enclosed, without comment.

They called a special meeting of the Board of Aldermen. A deputation waited upon her, knocked at the door through which no visitor had passed since she ceased giving china-painting lessons eight or ten years earlier. They were admitted by the old Negro into a dim hall from which a stairway mounted into still more shadow. It smelled of dust and disuse—a close, dank smell. The Negro led them into the parlor. It was furnished in heavy, leather-covered furniture. When the Negro opened the blinds of one window, they could see that the leather was cracked; and when they sat down, a faint dust rose sluggishly about their thighs, spinning with slow motes in the single sun-ray. On a tarnished gilt easel before the fireplace stood a crayon portrait of Miss Emily's father.

They rose when she entered—a small, fat woman in black, with a thin gold chain descending to her waist and vanishing into her belt, leaning on an ebony cane with a tarnished gold head. Her skeleton was small and spare; perhaps that was why what would have been merely plumpness in another was obesity in her. She looked bloated, like a body long submerged in motionless water, and of that pallid hue. Her eyes, lost in the fatty ridges of her face, looked like two small pieces of coal pressed into a lump of dough as they moved from one face to another while the visitors stated their errand.

She did not ask them to sit. She just stood in the door and listened quietly until the spokesman came to a stumbling halt. Then they could hear the invisible watch ticking at the end of the gold chain.

Her voice was dry and cold. "I have no taxes in Jefferson. Colonel Sartoris explained it to me. Perhaps one of you can gain access to the city records and satisfy yourselves."

"But we have. We are the city authorities, Miss Emily. Didn't you get a notice from the sheriff, signed by him?"

"I received a paper, yes," Miss Emily said. "Perhaps he considers himself the sheriff… I have no taxes in Jefferson."

"But there is nothing on the books to show that, you see. We must go by the—"

"See Colonel Sartoris. I have no taxes in Jefferson."

"But, Miss Emily—"

"See Colonel Sartoris." (Colonel Sartoris had been dead almost ten years.) "I have no taxes in Jefferson. Tobe!" The Negro appeared. "Show these gentlemen out."

II

So she vanquished them, horse and foot, just as she had vanquished their fathers thirty years before about the smell.

That was two years after her father's death and a short time after her sweetheart—the one we believed would marry her—had deserted her. After her father's death she went out very little; after her sweetheart went away, people hardly saw her at all. A few of the ladies had the temerity to call, but were not received, and the only sign of life about the place was the Negro man—a young man then—going in and out with a market basket.

"Just as if a man—any man—could keep a kitchen properly," the ladies said; so they were not surprised when the smell developed. It was another link between the gross, teeming world and the high and mighty Griersons.

A neighbor, a woman, complained to the mayor, Judge Stevens, eighty years old.

"But what will you have me do about it, madam?" he said.

"Why, send her word to stop it," the woman said. "Isn't there a law?"

"I'm sure that won't be necessary," Judge Stevens said. "It's probably just a snake or a rat that nigger of hers killed in the yard. I'll speak to him about it."

The next day he received two more complaints, one from a man who came in diffident deprecation. "We really must do something about it, Judge. I'd be the last one in the world to bother Miss Emily, but we've got to do something." That night the Board of Aldermen met—three graybeards and one younger man, a member of the rising generation.

"It's simple enough," he said. "Send her word to have her place cleaned up. Give her a certain time to do it in, and if she don't…"

"Dammit, sir," Judge Stevens said, "will you accuse a lady to her face of smelling bad?"

So the next night, after midnight, four men crossed Miss Emily's lawn and slunk about the house like burglars, sniffing along the base of the brickwork and at the cellar openings while one of them performed a regular sowing motion with his hand out of a sack slung from his shoulder. They broke open the cellar door and sprinkled lime there, and in all the outbuildings. As they recrossed the lawn, a window that had been dark was lighted and Miss Emily sat in it, the light behind her, and her upright torso motionless as that of an idol. They crept quietly across the lawn and into the shadow of the locusts that lined the street. After a week or two the smell went away.

That was when people had begun to feel really sorry for her. People in our town, remembering how old lady Wyatt, her great-aunt, had gone completely crazy at last, believed that the Griersons held themselves a little too high for what they really were. None of the young men were quite good enough for Miss Emily and such. We had long thought of them as a tableau, Miss Emily a slender figure in white in the background, her father a spraddled silhouette in the foreground, his back to her and clutching a horsewhip, the two of them framed by the backflung front door. So when she got to be thirty and was still single, we were not pleased exactly, but vindicated; even with insanity in the family she wouldn't have turned down all of her chances if they had really materialized.

When her father died, it got about that the house was all that was left to her; and in a way, people were glad. At last they could pity Miss Emily. Being left alone, and a pauper, she had become humanized. Now she too would know the old thrill and the old despair of a penny more or less.

The day after his death all the ladies prepared to call at the house and offer condolence and aid, as is our custom. Miss Emily met them at the door, dressed as usual and with no trace of grief on her face. She told them that her father was not dead. She did that for three days, with the ministers calling on her, and the doctors, trying to persuade her to let them dispose of the body. Just as they were about to resort to law and force, she broke down, and they buried her father quickly.

We did not say she was crazy then. We believed she had to do that. We remembered all the young men her father had driven away, and we knew that with nothing left, she would have to cling to that which had robbed her, as people will.

III

She was sick for a long time. When we saw her again, her hair was cut short, making her look like a girl, with a vague resemblance to those angels in colored church windows—sort of tragic and serene.

The town had just let the contracts for paving the sidewalks, and in the summer after her father's death they began the work. The construction company came with niggers and mules and machinery, and a foreman named Homer Barron, a Yankee—a big, dark, ready man, with a big voice and eyes lighter than his face. The little boys would follow in groups to hear him cuss the niggers, and the niggers singing in time to the rise and fall of picks. Pretty soon he knew everybody in town. Whenever you heard a lot of laughing anywhere about the square, Homer Barron would be in the center of the group. Presently we began to see him and Miss Emily on Sunday afternoons driving in the yellow-wheeled buggy and the matched team of bays from the livery stable.

At first we were glad that Miss Emily would have an interest, because the ladies all said, "Of course a Grierson would not think seriously of a Northerner, a day laborer." But there were still others, older people, who said that even grief could not cause a real lady to forget *noblesse oblige*—without calling it *noblesse oblige*. They just said, "Poor Emily. Her kinsfolk should come to her." She had some kin in Alabama; but years ago her father had fallen out with them over the estate of old lady Wyatt, the crazy woman, and there was no communication between the two families. They had not even been represented at the funeral.

And as soon as the old people said, "Poor Emily," the whispering began. "Do you suppose it's really so?" they said to one another. "Of course it is. What else could..." This behind their hands; rustling of craned silk and satin behind jalousies closed upon the sun of Sunday afternoon as the thin, swift clop-clop-clop of the matched team passed: "Poor Emily."

She carried her head high enough—even when we believed that she was fallen. It was as if she demanded more than ever the recognition of her dignity as the last Grierson; as if it had wanted that touch of earthiness to reaffirm her imperviousness.

Like when she bought the rat poison, the arsenic. That was over a year after they had begun to say "Poor Emily," and while the two female cousins were visiting her.

"I want some poison," she said to the druggist. She was over thirty then, still a slight woman, though thinner than usual, with cold, haughty black eyes in a face the flesh of which was strained across the temples and about the eyesockets as you imagine a lighthouse-keeper's face ought to look. "I want some poison," she said.

"Yes, Miss Emily. What kind? For rats and such? I'd recom—"

"I want the best you have. I don't care what kind."

The druggist named several. "They'll kill anything up to an elephant. But what you want is—"

"Arsenic," Miss Emily said. "Is that a good one?"

"Is... arsenic? Yes, ma'am. But what you want—"

"I want arsenic."

The druggist looked down at her. She looked back at him, erect, her face like a strained flag. "Why, of course," the druggist said. "If that's what you want. But the law requires you to tell what you are going to use it for."

Miss Emily just stared at him, her head tilted back in order to look him eye for eye, until he looked away and went and got the arsenic and wrapped it up. The Negro delivery boy brought her the package; the druggist didn't come back. When she opened the package at home there was written on the box, under the skull and bones: "For rats."

IV

So the next day we all said, "She will kill herself"; and we said it would be the best thing. When she had first begun to be seen with Homer Barron, we had said, "She will marry him." Then we said, "She will persuade him yet," because Homer himself had remarked—he liked men, and it was known that he drank with the younger men in the Elks' Club—that he was not a marrying man. Later we said, "Poor Emily" behind the jalousies as they passed on Sunday afternoon in the glittering buggy, Miss Emily with her head high and Homer Barron with his hat cocked and a cigar in his teeth, reins and whip in a yellow glove.

Then some of the ladies began to say that it was a disgrace to the town and a bad example to the young people. The men did not want to interfere, but at last the ladies forced the Baptist minister—Miss Emily's people were Episcopal—to call upon her. He would never divulge what happened during that interview, but he refused to go back again. The next Sunday they again drove about the streets, and the following day the minister's wife wrote to Miss Emily's relations in Alabama.

So she had blood-kin under her roof again and we sat back to watch developments. At first nothing happened. Then we were sure that they were to be married. We learned that Miss Emily had been to the jeweler's and ordered a man's toilet set in silver, with the letters H. B. on each piece. Two days later we learned that she had bought a complete outfit of men's clothing, including a nightshirt, and we said, "They are married." We were really glad. We were glad because the two female cousins were even more Grierson than Miss Emily had ever been.

So we were not surprised when Homer Barron—the streets had been finished some time since—was gone. We were a little disappointed that there was not a public blowing-off, but we believed that he had gone on to prepare for Miss Emily's coming, or to give her a chance to get rid of the cousins. (By that time it was a cabal, and we were all Miss Emily's allies to help circumvent the cousins.) Sure enough, after another week they departed. And, as we had expected all along, within three days Homer Barron was back in town. A neighbor saw the Negro man admit him at the kitchen door at dusk one evening.

And that was the last we saw of Homer Barron. And of Miss Emily for some time. The Negro man went in and out with the market basket, but the front door remained closed. Now and then we would see her at a window for a moment, as the men did that night when they sprinkled the lime, but for almost six months she did not appear on the streets. Then we knew that this was to be expected too; as if that quality of her father which had thwarted her woman's life so many times had been too virulent and too furious to die.

When we next saw Miss Emily, she had grown fat and her hair was turning gray. During the next few years it grew grayer and grayer until it attained an even pepper-and-salt iron-gray, when it ceased turning. Up to the day of her death at seventy-four it was still that vigorous iron-gray, like the hair of an active man.

From that time on her front door remained closed, save during a period of six or seven years, when she was about forty, during which she gave lessons in china-painting. She fitted up a studio in one of the downstairs rooms, where the daughters and granddaughters of Colonel Sartoris' contemporaries were sent to her with the same regularity and in the same spirit that they were sent to church on

Sundays with a twenty-five-cent piece for the collection plate. Meanwhile her taxes had been remitted.

Then the newer generation became the backbone and the spirit of the town, and the painting pupils grew up and fell away and did not send their children to her with boxes of color and tedious brushes and pictures cut from the ladies' magazines. The front door closed upon the last one and remained closed for good. When the town got free postal delivery, Miss Emily alone refused to let them fasten the metal numbers above her door and attach a mailbox to it. She would not listen to them.

Daily, monthly, yearly we watched the Negro grow grayer and more stooped, going in and out with the market basket. Each December we sent her a tax notice, which would be returned by the post office a week later, unclaimed. Now and then we would see her in one of the downstairs windows—she had evidently shut up the top floor of the house—like the carven torso of an idol in a niche, looking or not looking at us, we could never tell which. Thus she passed from generation to generation—dear, inescapable, impervious, tranquil, and perverse.

And so she died. Fell ill in the house filled with dust and shadows, with only a doddering Negro man to wait on her. We did not even know she was sick; we had long since given up trying to get any information from the Negro. He talked to no one, probably not even to her, for his voice had grown harsh and rusty, as if from disuse.

She died in one of the downstairs rooms, in a heavy walnut bed with a curtain, her gray head propped on a pillow yellow and moldy with age and lack of sunlight.

V

The Negro met the first of the ladies at the front door and let them in, with their hushed, sibilant voices and their quick, curious glances, and then he disappeared. He walked right through the house and out the back and was not seen again.

The two female cousins came at once. They held the funeral on the second day, with the town coming to look at Miss Emily beneath a mass of bought flowers, with the crayon face of her father musing profoundly above the bier and the ladies sibilant and macabre; and the very old men—some in their brushed Confederate uniforms—on the porch and the lawn, talking of Miss Emily as if she had been a contemporary of theirs, believing that they had danced with her and courted her perhaps, confusing time with its mathematical progression, as the old do, to whom all the past is not a diminishing road but, instead, a huge meadow which no winter ever quite touches, divided from them now by the narrow bottleneck of the most recent decade of years.

Already we knew that there was one room in that region above stairs which no one had seen in forty years, and which would have to be forced. They waited until Miss Emily was decently in the ground before they opened it.

The violence of breaking down the door seemed to fill this room with pervading dust. A thin, acrid pall as of the tomb seemed to lie everywhere upon this room decked and furnished as for a bridal: upon the valance curtains of faded rose color, upon the rose-shaded lights, upon the dressing table, upon the delicate array of crystal and the man's toilet things backed with tarnished silver, silver so tarnished that the monogram was obscured. Among them lay a collar and tie, as if they had just been removed, which, lifted, left upon the surface a pale crescent in the dust. Upon a chair hung the suit, carefully folded; beneath it the two mute shoes and the discarded socks.

The man himself lay in the bed.

For a long while we just stood there, looking down at the profound and fleshless grin. The body had apparently once lain in the attitude of an embrace, but now the long sleep that outlasts love, that conquers even the grimace of love, had cuckolded him. What was left of him, rotted beneath what was left of the nightshirt, had become inextricable from the bed in which he lay; and upon him and upon the pillow beside him lay that even coating of the patient and biding dust.

Then we noticed that in the second pillow was the indentation of a head. One of us lifted something from it, and leaning forward, that faint and invisible dust dry and acrid in the nostrils, we saw a long strand of iron-gray hair.

ALICE WALKER
[1944—   ]

Everyday Use

For your grandmamma

I will wait for her in the yard that Maggie and I made so clean and wavy yesterday afternoon. A yard like this is more comfortable than most people know. It is not just a yard. It is like an extended living room. When the hard clay is swept clean as a floor and the fine sand around the edges lined with tiny, irregular grooves, anyone can come and sit and look up into the elm tree and wait for the breezes that never come inside the house.

Maggie will be nervous until after her sister goes: she will stand hopelessly in corners, homely and ashamed of the burn scars down her arms and legs, eyeing her sister with a mixture of envy and awe. She thinks her sister has held life always in the palm of one hand, that "no" is a word the world never learned to say to her.

You've no doubt seen those TV shows where the child who has "made it" is confronted, as a surprise, by her own mother and father, tottering in weakly from backstage. (A pleasant surprise, of course: What would they do if parent and child came on the show only to curse out and insult each other?) On TV mother and child embrace and smile into each other's faces. Sometimes the mother and father weep, the child wraps them in her arms and leans across the table to tell how she would not have made it without their help. I have seen these programs.

Sometimes I dream a dream in which Dee and I are suddenly brought together on a TV program of this sort. Out of a dark and soft-seated limousine I am ushered into a bright room filled with many people. There I meet a smiling, gray, sporty man like Johnny Carson who shakes my hand and tells me what a fine girl I have. Then we are on the stage and Dee is embracing me with tears in her eyes. She pins on my dress a large orchid, even though she has told me once that she thinks orchids are tacky flowers.

In real life I am a large, big-boned woman with rough, man-working hands. In the winter I wear flannel nightgowns to bed and overalls during the day. I can kill and clean a hog as mercilessly as a man. My fat keeps me hot in zero weather. I can work outside all day, breaking ice to get water for washing; I can eat pork liver cooked over the open fire minutes after it comes steaming from the hog. One winter I knocked a bull calf straight in the brain between the eyes with a sledge hammer and had the meat hung up to chill before nightfall. But of course all this does not show on television. I am the way my daughter would want me to be: a hundred pounds lighter, my skin like an uncooked barley pancake. My hair glistens in the hot bright lights. Johnny Carson has much to do to keep up with my quick and witty tongue.

But that is a mistake. I know even before I wake up. Who ever knew a Johnson with a quick tongue? Who can even imagine me looking a strange white man in the eye? It seems to me I have talked to them always with one foot raised in flight, with my head fumed in whichever way is farthest from them. Dee, though. She would always look anyone in the eye. Hesitation was no part of her nature.

"How do I look, Mama?" Maggie says, showing just enough of her thin body enveloped in pink skirt and red blouse for me to know she's there, almost hidden by the door.

"Come out into the yard," I say.

Have you ever seen a lame animal, perhaps a dog run over by some careless person rich enough to own a car, sidle up to someone who is ignorant enough to be kind to him? That is the way my Maggie walks. She has been like this, chin on chest, eyes on ground, feet in shuffle, ever since the fire that burned the other house to the ground.

Dee is lighter than Maggie, with nicer hair and a fuller figure. She's a woman now, though sometimes I forget. How long ago was it that the other house burned? Ten, twelve years? Sometimes I can still hear the flames and feel Maggie's arms sticking to me, her hair smoking and her dress falling off her in little black papery flakes. Her eyes seemed stretched open, blazed open by the flames reflected in them. And Dee. I see her standing off under the sweet gum tree she used to dig gum out of; a look of concentration on her face as she watched the last dingy gray board of the house fall in toward the red-hot brick chimney. Why don't you do a dance around the ashes? I'd wanted to ask her. She had hated the house that much.

I used to think she hated Maggie, too. But that was before we raised money, the church and me, to send her to Augusta to school. She used to read to us without pity; forcing words, lies, other folks' habits, whole lives upon us two, sitting trapped and ignorant underneath her voice. She washed us in a river of make-believe, burned us with a lot of knowledge we didn't necessarily need to know. Pressed us to her with the serious way she read, to shove us away at just the moment, like dimwits, we seemed about to understand.

Dee wanted nice things. A yellow organdy dress to wear to her graduation from high school; black pumps to match a green suit she'd made from an old suit somebody gave me. She was determined to stare down any disaster in her efforts.

Her eyelids would not flicker for minutes at a time. Often I fought off the temptation to shake her. At sixteen she had a style of her own: and knew what style was.

I never had an education myself. After second grade the school was closed down. Don't ask my why: in 1927 colored asked fewer questions than they do now. Sometimes Maggie reads to me. She stumbles along good-naturedly but can't see well. She knows she is not bright. Like good looks and money, quickness passed her by. She will marry John Thomas (who has mossy teeth in an earnest face) and then I'll be free to sit here and I guess just sing church songs to myself. Although I never was a good singer. Never could carry a tune. I was always better at a man's job. I used to love to milk till I was hooked in the side in '49. Cows are soothing and slow and don't bother you, unless you try to milk them the wrong way.

I have deliberately turned my back on the house. It is three rooms, just like the one that burned, except the roof is tin; they don't make shingle roofs any more. There are no real windows, just some holes cut in the sides, like the portholes in a ship, but not round and not square, with rawhide holding the shutters up on the outside. This house is in a pasture, too, like the other one. No doubt when Dee sees it she will want to tear it down. She wrote me once that no matter where we "choose" to live, she will manage to come see us. But she will never bring her friends. Maggie and I thought about this and Maggie asked me, "Mama, when did Dee ever have any friends?"

She had a few. Furtive boys in pink shirts hanging about on washday after school. Nervous girls who never laughed. Impressed with her they worshiped the well-turned phrase, the cute shape, the scalding humor that erupted like bubbles in lye. She read to them.

When she was courting Jimmy T she didn't have much time to pay to us, but turned all her faultfinding power on him. He flew to marry a cheap city girl from a family of ignorant flashy people. She hardly had time to recompose herself.

When she comes I will meet—but there they are!

Maggie attempts to make a dash for the house, in her shuffling way, but I stay her with my hand. "Come back here," I say. And she stops and tries to dig a well in the sand with her toe.

It is hard to see them clearly through the strong sun. But even the first glimpse of leg out of the car tells me it is Dee. Her feet were always neat-looking, as if God himself had shaped them with a certain style. From the other side of the car comes a short, stocky man. Hair is all over his head a foot long and hanging from his chin like a kinky mule tail. I hear Maggie suck in her breath. "Uhnnnh," is what it sounds like. Like when you see the wriggling end of a snake just in front of your foot on the road. "Uhnnnh."

Dee next. A dress down to the ground, in this hot weather. A dress so loud it hurts my eyes. There are yellows and oranges enough to throw back the light of the sun. I feel my whole face warming from the heat waves it throws out. Earrings gold, too, and hanging down to her shoulders. Bracelets dangling and making noises when she moves her arm up to shake the folds of the dress out of her armpits. The dress is loose and flows, and as she walks closer, I like it. I hear Maggie go "Uhnnnh" again. It is her sister's hair. It stands straight up like the wool on a sheep. It is black as night and around the edges are two long pigtails that rope about like small lizards disappearing behind her ears.

"Wa-su-zo-Tean-o!" she says, coming on in that gliding way the dress makes her move. The short stocky fellow with the hair to his navel is all grinning and he follows up with "Asalamalakim, my mother and sister!" He moves to hug Maggie but she falls back, right up against the back of my chair. I feel her trembling there and when I look up I see the perspiration falling off her chin.

"Don't get up," says Dee. Since I am stout it takes something of a push. You can see me trying to move a second or two before I make it. She turns, showing white heels through her sandals, and goes back to the car. Out she peeks next with a Polaroid. She stoops down quickly and lines up picture after picture of me sitting there in front of the house with Maggie cowering behind me. She never takes a shot without making sure the house is included. When a cow comes nibbling around the edge of the yard she snaps it and me and Maggie and the house. Then she puts the Polaroid in the back seat of the car, and comes up and kisses me on the forehead.

Meanwhile Asalamalakim is going through motions with Maggie's hand. Maggie's hand is as limp as a fish, and probably as cold, despite the sweat, and she keeps trying to pull it back. It looks like Asalamalakim wants to shake hands but wants to do it fancy. Or maybe he don't know how people shake hands. Anyhow, he soon gives up on Maggie.

"Well," I say. "Dee."

"No, Mama," she says. "Not 'Dee,' Wangero Leewanika Kemanjo!"

"What happened to 'Dee'?" I wanted to know.

"She's dead," Wangero said. "I couldn't bear it any longer, being named after the people who oppress me."

"You know as well as me you was named after your aunt Dicie," I said. Dicie is my sister. She named Dee. We called her "Big Dee" after Dee was born.

"But who was she named after?" asked Wangero.

"I guess after Grandma Dee," I said.

"And who was she named after?" asked Wangero.

"Her mother," I said, and saw Wangero was getting tired. "That's about as far back as I can trace it," I said. Though, in fact, I probably could have carried it back beyond the Civil War through the branches.

"Well," said Asalamalakim, "there you are."

"Uhnnnh," I heard Maggie say.

"There I was not," I said, "before 'Dicie' cropped up in our family, so why should I try to trace it that far back?"

He just stood there grinning, looking down on me like somebody inspecting a Model A car. Every once in a while he and Wangero sent eye signals over my head.

"How do you pronounce this name?" I asked.

"You don't have to call me by it if you don't want to," said Wangero.

"Why shouldn't I?" I asked. "If that's what you want us to call you, we'll call you."

"I know it might sound awkward at first," said Wangero.

"I'll get used to it," I said. "Ream it out again."

Well, soon we got the name out of the way. Asalamalakim had a name twice as long and three times as hard. After I tripped over it two or three times he told me to just call him Hakim-a-barber. I wanted to ask him was he a barber, but I didn't really think he was, so I didn't ask.

"You must belong to those beef-cattle peoples down the road," I said. They said "Asalamalakim" when they met you, too, but they didn't shake hands. Always too busy: feeding the cattle, fixing the fences, putting up salt-lick shelters, throwing down hay. When the white folks poisoned some of the herd the men stayed up all night with rifles in their hands. I walked a mile and a half just to see the sight.

Hakim-a-barber said, "I accept some of their doctrines, but farming and raising cattle is not my style." (They didn't tell me, and I didn't ask, whether Wangero (Dee) had really gone and married him.)

We sat down to eat and right away he said he didn't eat collards and pork was unclean. Wangero, though, went on through the chitlins and corn bread, the greens and everything else. She talked a blue streak over the sweet potatoes. Everything delighted her. Even the fact that we still used the benches her daddy made for the table when we couldn't afford to buy chairs.

"Oh, Mama!" she cried. Then turned to Hakim-a-barber. "I never knew how lovely these benches are. You can feel the rump prints," she said, running her hands underneath her and along the bench. Then she gave a sigh and her hand closed over Grandma Dee's butter dish. "That's it!" she said. "I knew there was something I wanted to ask you if I could have." She jumped up from the table and went over in the corner where the churn stood, the milk in it crabber by now. She looked at the churn and looked at it.

"This churn top is what I need," she said. "Didn't Uncle Buddy whittle it out of a tree you all used to have?"

"Yes," I said.

"Un huh," she said happily. "And I want the dasher, too."

"Uncle Buddy whittle that, too?" asked the barber.

Dee (Wangero) looked up at me.

"Aunt Dee's first husband whittled the dash," said Maggie so low you almost couldn't hear her. "His name was Henry, but they called him Stash."

"Maggie's brain is like an elephant's," Wangero said, laughing. "I can use the churn top as a centerpiece for the alcove table," she said, sliding a plate over the churn, "and I'll think of something artistic to do with the dasher."

When she finished wrapping the dasher the handle stuck out. I took it for a moment in my hands. You didn't even have to look close to see where hands pushing the dasher up and down to make butter had left a kind of sink in the wood. In fact, there were a lot of small sinks; you could see where thumbs and fingers had sunk into the wood. It was beautiful light yellow wood, from a tree that grew in the yard where Big Dee and Stash had lived.

After dinner Dee (Wangero) went to the trunk at the foot of my bed and started rifling through it. Maggie hung back in the kitchen over the dishpan. Out came Wangero with two quilts. They had been pieced by Grandma Dee and then Big Dee and me had hung them on the quilt frames on the front porch and quilted them. One was in the Lone Star pattern. The other was Walk Around the Mountain. In both of them were scraps of dresses Grandma Dee had worn fifty and more years ago. Bits and pieces of Grandpa Jattell's Paisley shirts. And one teeny faded blue piece, about the size of a penny matchbox, that was from Great Grandpa Ezra's uniform that he wore in the Civil War.

"Mama," Wangro said sweet as a bird. "Can I have these old quilts?"

I heard something fall in the kitchen, and a minute later the kitchen door slammed.

"Why don't you take one or two of the others?" I asked. "These old things was just done by me and Big Dee from some tops your grandma pieced before she died."

"No," said Wangero. "I don't want those. They are stitched around the borders by machine."

"That'll make them last better," I said.

"That's not the point," said Wangero. "These are all pieces of dresses Grandma used to wear. She did all this stitching by hand. Imagine!" She held the quilts securely in her arms, stroking them.

"Some of the pieces, like those lavender ones, come from old clothes her mother handed down to her," I said, moving up to touch the quilts. Dee (Wangero) moved back just enough so that I couldn't reach the quilts. They already belonged to her.

"Imagine!" she breathed again, clutching them closely to her bosom.

"The truth is," I said, "I promised to give them quilts to Maggie, for when she marries John Thomas."

She gasped like a bee had stung her.

"Maggie can't appreciate these quilts!" she said. "She'd probably be backward enough to put them to everyday use."

"I reckon she would," I said. "God knows I been saving 'em for long enough with nobody using 'em. I hope she will!" I didn't want to bring up how I had offered Dee (Wangero) a quilt when she went away to college. Then she had told me they were old-fashioned, out of style.

"But they're *priceless*!" she was saying now, furiously; for she has a temper. "Maggie would put them on the bed and in five years they'd be in rags. Less than that!"

"She can always make some more," I said. "Maggie knows how to quilt."

Dee (Wangero) looked at me with hatred. "You just will not understand. The point is these quilts, *these* quilts!"

"Well," I said, stumped. "What would *you* do with them?"

"Hang them," she said. As if that was the only thing you *could* do with quilts.

Maggie by now was standing in the door. I could almost hear the sound her feet made as they scraped over each other.

"She can have them, Mama," she said, like somebody used to never winning anything, or having anything reserved for her. "I can 'member Grandma Dee without the quilts."

I looked at her hard. She had filled her bottom lip with checkerberry snuff and it gave her face a kind of dopey, hangdog look. It was Grandma Dee and Big Dee who taught her how to quilt herself. She stood there with her scarred hands hidden in the folds of her skirt. She looked at her sister with something like fear but she wasn't mad at her. This was Maggie's portion. This was the way she knew God to work.

When I looked at her like that something hit me in the top of my head and ran down to the soles of my feet. Just like when I'm in church and the spirit of God touches me and I get happy and shout. I did something I never done before: hugged Maggie to me, then dragged her on into the room, snatched the quilts out of Miss Wangero's hands and dumped them into Maggie's lap. Maggie just sat there on my bed with her mouth open.

"Take one or two of the others," I said to Dee.

But she turned without a word and went out to Hakim-a-barber.

"You just don't understand," she said, as Maggie and I came out to the car.

"What don't I understand?" I wanted to know.

"Your heritage," she said. And then she turned to Maggie, kissed her, and said, "You ought to try to make something of yourself, too, Maggie. It's really a new day for us. But from the way you and Mama still live you'd never know it."

She put on some sunglasses that hid everything above the tip of her nose and chin.

Maggie smiled; maybe at the sunglasses. But a real smile, not scared. After we watched the car dust settle I asked Maggie to bring me a dip of snuff. And then the two of us sat there just enjoying, until it was time to go in the house and go to bed.

Section 2 Reading Poetry
第二部分　阅读诗歌

一切语言起源于诗。

海德格尔

简要介绍：

世界有了语言，也就有了诗歌；只要世界上有语言，就会有诗歌。诗歌是人们表达情感和思想的最好途径：从人类祖先的祭奠仪式到现代社会的轻歌曼舞，富有节奏和韵律的诗歌一直是人们表达内心的喜悦、哀伤、恐惧、困惑和敬畏的传统方式，也是人们传诵和记载思想、文化、历史的特殊方式。

诗歌是抒情的，它述说的是人们灵魂深处的渴求和欲望，记载的是每一个时代无以言说的精神。诗歌是超越理性的，它用意象、隐喻、象征、节奏、韵律等等冲破语言的牢笼，表达出无限的情感和想象。因此，诗歌是人类最为原初的语言，也是永恒的语言。

阅读诗歌是一个感悟和欣赏语言的过程。在这个过程中，我们需要了解一些关于诗歌阅读的技巧和方法。但是，更为重要的是我们要对语词表达情感和想象的过程产生兴趣，对诗歌所表达的情感和思想产生共鸣。在我们开始讨论本章有关诗歌的一些基本知识之前，我们不妨先来阅读一首诗歌，感受一下其中的乐趣，享受一下诗歌语词的魅力。

作 品:

Catch

Robert Francis

Two boys uncoached are tossing a poem together,
Overhand, underhand, backhand, sleight of hand, every hand,
Teasing with attitudes, latitudes, interludes, altitudes,
High, make him fly off the ground for it, low, make him stoop,
Make him scoop it up, make him as-almost-as-possible miss it,
Fast, let him sting from it, now, now fool him slowly,
Anything, everything tricky, risky, nonchalant,
Anything under the sun to outwit the prosy,
Over the tree and the long sweet cadence down,
Over his head, make him scramble to pick up the meaning,
And now, like a posy, a pretty one plump in his hands.

赏 析:

请你阅读下面的一段关于这首诗歌的复述:

"**Paraphrase**: A poet's relationship to a reader is similar to a game of catch. The poem, like a ball, should be pitched in a variety of ways to challenge and create interest. Boredom and predictability must be avoided if the game is to be engaging and satisfying."[1]

对比这首诗和它的"复述",你会发现,"复述"虽然比较准确地用散文的方式概括了这首诗的基本思想,却丢失了诗歌语言带给我们的乐趣和韵味。其实,诗的乐趣和韵味就隐藏在诗歌不合常规的、跳跃的词的后面,是无法用几句话来阐释的,当然,诗的乐趣和韵味更多的是隐藏在作者和读者丰富的想象之中,就像这首诗中的两个男孩。

让我们可以一起来细细品味这首诗。两个男孩(不妨说,这两个男孩分别指称"作者"和"读者")未经培训就开始饶有趣味地扔抛"一首诗"。这样不规范的表达手法,让我们不由自主地想用"一只球"替代"一首诗"。后面诗句证实了我们的联想。虽

---

1 Meyer, Michael. *The Compact Bedford Introduction to Literature*. 5th ed. Boston: Bedford/St. Martin's, 2000: 537.

然整首诗从未出现过"球"这一词，然而，诗人形象的语词和描写记录的似乎就是抛球的过程以及该过程中的乐趣。是的，我们的确可以感受到诗人试图以描写抛球的具体过程来形象说明写诗或读诗的抽象过程的用意，可以感受到诗人通过形象、生动的词语传递的想法；创作和阅读诗歌就如抛球一样充满了挑战和乐趣。

再一次阅读这首诗，我们感觉到了更多的意味。如果说诗的头三行描写的是两个男孩随心所欲地用各种手法、各种姿态逗弄这只球/诗，那么在后面的诗行里，我们吃惊地发现，两个男孩忽然只剩下了一个"他"（him），而这个"他"（不妨说，"他"是"读者"的指代词）被代表诗歌的"它"（it）狠狠地作弄了一番。是"它"使"他"上蹿下跳，还几乎抓不住"它"；"它"之所以用尽心计逗弄"他"，却是为了超越平常，让"他"在优美的旋律跌落之前，奋力抓住"它"特殊的意味（meaning）；最后"他"惊喜地发现，"它"就躺在"他"的手中，像一束蓬松的紫罗兰。是"他"写了诗，还是诗写了"他"？是"他"读了诗，还是诗读了"他"？这并不是不可理喻的问题，在很多时候，我们会发现，我们无法完全左右我们的写作和阅读。在我们遍地寻觅却无法获得合适的表达方式，在我们苦苦思索却依然对面前的诗歌不得其解的时候，其实"它"（不管它是什么）正在树的枝头上冲着我们狡猾地微笑。当我们千辛万苦，终于逮住"它"的时候，我们会由衷地感到一阵发自内心的喜悦，因为"它"是如此美丽，因为这时的"它"已经不是那首静止的诗，"它"已经融入了我们自己的情感和感悟。

我们从诗歌中获得的，是我们自己认为最重要和最珍贵的东西。我们从诗歌中读出的是我们所能看到和感觉到的世界，和我们如此熟悉和陌生的自我。诗人之所以在两个男孩后面加了一个形容词"未经培训"（uncoached），其实是想告诉我们所有的读者，写作诗歌和阅读诗歌更需要的是一种自然的流露和丰富的想象，这是无法培训的。

Questions：

> In this section, we will discuss these questions in the following chapters:
>
> 1. What is poetry?
>
> 2. What are diction and syntax? How do they help convey meaning of poetry?
>
> 3. What are speaker and tone? How do they constitute emotion of poetry?
>
> 4. What are image, metaphor and allusion? What are their functions in enriching themes of the poem?
>
> 5. What are rhythm and rhyme? How do they express meaning through form?
>
> 6. What are basic types of poetry?

Chapter 8   What Is Poetry?

第八章   诗歌是什么?

Poetry is the record of the best and happiest moments
of the happiest and best minds.

P. B. Shelley (1827)

简要介绍:

诗歌是什么? 这是最不好回答的一个问题, 却又是诗人和批评家思考最多的一个问题。既然我们要阅读诗歌, 我们同样需要了解这一问题。让我们看看批评家、诗人和诗歌本身是如何诠释诗歌的。

批评家的界定

Poetry, language sung, chanted, spoken, or written according to some pattern of recurrence that emphasizes the relationships between words on the basis of sound as well as sense: this pattern is almost always a rhythm or metre, which may be supplemented by rhyme or alliteration or both. The demands of verbal patterning usually make poetry a more condensed medium than prose or everyday speech, often involving variations in syntax, the use of special words and phrases (poetic diction) peculiar to poets, and a more frequent and more elaborate use of figures of speech, principally metaphor or simile. All cultures have their poetry, using it for various purposes from sacred ritual to obscene insult, but it is generally employed in those utterances and writings that call for heightened intensity of emotion, dignity of expression, or subtlety of meditation. Poetry is valued for combining pleasures of sound with freshness of ideas, whether these be solemn or comical. Some critics make an evaluative distinction between poetry, which is elevated or inspired, and verse, which is merely clever or mechanical. The three major categories of poetry are narrative, dramatic, and lyric, the last being the most extensive.[1]

简　析：

批评家对诗歌的界定是最权威、最全面、最清楚的，但却是最缺乏诗意的。上面对诗歌的界定引自牛津英语百科分类词典系列中的《牛津文学术语词典》。该定义分别从诗歌的语言形态、文化作用和文学体裁的独特性几个方面对诗歌进行了比较全面的描述。

1）诗歌有其特殊的语言形式，可以用唱、诵、说、写来表达。其语音的主要特征是重复，主要表现方式有：节奏、音步、押韵、头韵等；其语词的主要特征是简约，通过运用独特的句法、措辞、修辞来实现。

2）诗歌是文化的产物，其用途广泛，但主要用于再现丰富的情感和精妙的思想。

3）诗歌不同于散文，是声音的愉悦和意义的新奇的结合体，高雅而富有激情。诗歌通常有三种主要类型，即叙事诗、戏剧诗、抒情诗，其中抒情诗的运用最为广泛。

显然，批评家对诗歌的界定是从评论的视角出发的，他们喜欢将诗歌视为一种独立的整体，以诗歌不同于其他的文体这样的假设为出发点，然后从内部和外部对它的形式、作用和特殊性作全面的概括。这种界定最大的优势在于它的确定性，而最大的弱点在于它的限定性。这是一种概念性的界定。

诗人的界定

Definition by Sir Philip Sidney (1585)

Poesy therefore is an art of imitation...to speak metaphorically, a speaking picture: with this end, to teach and delight.

Definition by Samuel Johnson (1765)

The end of writing is to instruct; the end of poetry is to instruct by pleasing.

Definition by William Enfield (1796)

...poetry (is) the immediate offspring of a vigorous imagination and quick sensibility... the language of fancy and passion.

Definition by William Wordsworth (1802)

Poetry is the spontaneous overflow of powerful feelings: it takes its origin from emotion recollected in tranquillity.

---

1 Baldick, Chris. *Oxford Concise Dictionary of Literary Terms*. 上海：上海外语教育出版社，2000: 172-173.

Definition by P. B. Shelley (1827)

Poetry is the record of the best and happiest moments of the happiest and best minds.

Definition by S. T. Coleridge (1827)

…prose—words in their best order; poetry—the best words in the best order.

简　析：

　　与批评家的视角不同，诗人对诗歌的界定似乎总是从创作的视角出发的。他们关注的焦点是诗歌与诗歌的创作对象——生活的关系，诗歌与诗歌的阅读对象——读者的关系，诗歌与诗歌的创作者——诗人之间的关系，或者诗歌与其他文学体裁的区别。于是，就有了上面这许多丰富多彩的界定。可以看出，Sir Philip Sidney 的界定是从诗歌与生活的关系和诗歌对社会的作用这样的角度入手的，它传达的是诗歌模仿生活的观点；Samuel Johnson 强调了诗歌的教育作用，特别突出了诗歌的愉悦效果；William Enfield 和 William Wordsworth 作为欧洲浪漫主义运动的代言人，着重指出了人的想象和情感在诗歌中的主导地位；P. B. Shelley 和 S. T. Coleridge 同为欧洲浪漫主义文学的重要诗人，特别关注的是诗歌语言本身的美、悦和纯。虽然，诗人对诗歌的界定是有所侧重的，似乎缺乏科学性和全面性，但是他们的界定却富有诗意和韵味，鲜活而灵动，最能深入心扉。这是一种形象性的描写。

诗歌本身的诠释

Poem

William Carlos Williams

As the cat
climbed over
the top of

the jamcloset
first the right
forefoot

carefully

then the hind
stepped down

into the pit of
the empty
flowerpot

简　析：

　　如果说批评家和诗人有关诗歌的界定已经帮助我们在诗歌的丛林里开拓了一条小径，那么这首以"诗歌"为标题的诗却似乎又将这条小径遮蔽了起来了。它似乎不仅没有向我们揭示诗歌的奥妙，而且还用厚厚的浓雾包围了诗歌。这首诗歌似乎是拒绝阐释的，除了能感悟到猫的敏捷和小心翼翼的动作，看不出猫和诗歌到底有什么关系。不过，且慢，如果我们将这首诗转化为散文的形式，然后再与原诗进行对比，两者又有什么不同呢？

　　As the cat climbed over the top of the jamcloset, first the right forefoot carefully then the hind stepped down into the pit of the empty flowerpot.

　　诗和散文的确是不同的。诗通过分行和分节，不仅在视觉和听觉上使语词充满了节奏感和音乐感，而且突出了原来埋没在散文语句中的意象，使每一诗行都有了生动而形象的图画，而这每一幅图像都给读者留出了无限的想象和联想的空间。看来，William Carlos Williams 是在用诗的语言和诗的形式直接展示诗的奥秘，只能意会，无法言说。这是一种图像化的勾勒。

Questions:

1. How do you understand poetry?
2. Will you express your understanding of poetry in the form of a short statement or a poem?

Chapter 9　Diction and Syntax

第九章　措辞和句法

> Prose—words in their best order; poetry—the best words in the best order.
>
> S. T. Coleridge

简要介绍：

　　在所有文学家中，诗人最关注作品的措辞（diction），即词语的选用，和句法(syntax)，即词与词之间的关系研究。这不仅因为相对于几十万字的小说和戏剧而言，短短数十行的诗歌几乎字字如珠玑，而且因为短小精悍的诗歌所表达的思想的深刻，情感的丰富和想象的浩瀚完全不逊色于篇幅长达几百页的小说和戏剧。要做到这一切，诗人精妙的措辞和别具一格的句法的运用就成为创作中关键的环节，而读者对诗歌中的措辞和句法的把握同样成为理解诗歌的关键。本章节将分两个部分分别探讨诗歌措辞和句法的特征以及他们传达意义的方式。

第一节　诗歌的措辞

> **Diction,** the choice of words used in a literary work.

简　析：

　　所谓"措辞"，即文学作品中语词的选用。作家的措辞各不相同，但通常带有某种鲜明的特征。常见的措辞可分为下面几种：

　　规范措辞（formal diction），即用词高雅、非个人化。比如英国著名诗人John Milton的"Paradise Lost"：

　　Of man's first disobedience, and the fruit

Of that forbidden tree whose mortal taste

Brought death into the world, and all our woe,

With loss of Eden, till one greater Man

Restore us, and regain the blissful seat...

诗歌的句法和措辞规范，所用的词，如："disobedience"、"mortal"、"woe"、"blissful"等较少出现在我们日常语中。

普通措辞（middle diction or common diction），即一般受过教育人们的书面用语。用词简单、普通，但不庸俗，比如英国诗人William Wordsworth的"I Wandered Lonely as a Cloud"。

非正式措辞（informal diction or colloquial diction），即用词口语化，或者选用的语词来自方言或俚语。比如美国诗人 Gwendolyn Brooks 在下面的诗歌中使用了黑人的方言。

We Real Cool

We real cool. We

Left school. We

Lurk late. We

Strike straight. We

Sing sin. We

Thin gin. We

Jazz June. We

Die soon.

(1917)

一般来说，18 世纪的英国新古典主义诗人比较崇尚规范措辞，他们给诗歌用词一个特定的名称"poetic diction"，特别指称那些不同于日常生活用语，只用于诗歌创作的词、词组和修辞。他们推崇欧洲文学史上著名诗人，比如 Roman Virgil、Edmund Spenser 和 John Milton，以模仿他们的措辞、风格和体裁为荣，坚持认为诗歌语言不同于日常用语。但是到了 19 世纪，英国浪漫主义诗人华兹华斯在《抒情歌谣集》（1800）的序言中批评了这种创作标准，认为 18 世纪诗歌措辞极其不自然，指出诗歌语言与散文语言并没有本质的区别，诗歌措辞的标准应该是使人的情感自然流露。整个 19 世纪，包括 20 世纪的大多数诗人不再人为地在诗歌措辞与日常语言之间划出界线。诗歌措辞的自然和流畅成为最基本的准则。

那么，接近生活用语的诗歌语言是如何超越日常交际语言，表达出丰富的意义的呢？

我们知道，任何语词同时包含两层意义，语词用于指称事物的本义（denotation）

和语词在特定语境中激发的引申和隐含意（connotation）。比如，英语中的"tree"，它的"denotation"是指"a very tall plant that has a wooden trunk, branches, and leaves, and lives for many years"，也就是我们在自然界中所能看到的"树"的总称。而人们根据自己的生活经验对"树"进行联想而产生的关于"树"的"connotation"则远远超出了"树"的本义，它可以指"生命"、"自然"、"美"、"神秘"、"创造力"等等不一而足。也就是说，"树"的引申和隐含意随着语境、时空、读者的经历的不同而不同。不同文化、时代、学历的人对"树"的理解不会完全相同，不同诗歌中的"树"的引申和隐含意也不可能完全相同。语词的丰富内涵为诗歌特殊魅力的形成提供了可能。更明确地说，日常用语和诗歌用词在使用过程中是各有侧重的。日常交际语言侧重的是信息的交流，它的基本要求是信息传送的正确性、确定性和有效性，因此日常语言更重视在语法和逻辑的语境中传达语词确定的本义；诗歌语言侧重的是情感和思想的传达，而情感和思想在很多时候是超越语法和逻辑的，因此诗歌往往在传达语词的本义的同时，借助联想将处于特殊语境中的语词的引申和隐含意激发出来，最终将无法言说的情感和感悟传递出来，显然诗歌语言更侧重构建、寻找和引发语词的引申和隐含意。

由此，我们可以说，优秀的诗歌是语词最好的表演场所，因为在这些诗歌中，诗人用词的精妙、雅致、深刻、精练可以说达到了极致。

作　品：

I Wandered Lonely as a Cloud

William Wordsworth

I wandered lonely as a cloud
That floats on high o'er vales and hills,
When all at once I saw a crowd,
A host, of golden daffodils;
Beside the lake, beneath the trees,
Fluttering and dancing in the breeze.

Continuous as the stars that shine
And twinkle on the Milky Way,
They stretched in never-ending line
Along the margin of a bay:

Ten thousand saw I at a glance,
Tossing their heads in sprightly dance.

The waves beside them danced; but they
Outdid the sparkling waves in glee:
A poet could not but be gay,
In such a jocund company:
I gazed—and gazed—but little thought
What wealth the show to me had brought:

For oft, when on my couch I lie
In vacant or in pensive mood,
They flash upon that inward eye
Which is the bliss of solitude;
And then my heart with pleasure fills,
And dances with the daffodils.

赏　析：

在第一诗节中，诗人用比喻的方式将"我"和"一片云"联系起来，特别在"我"和"一片云"之间放置了"lonely"一词。"lonely"的本义是"孤独"，这一词义衬托出"我"和"一片云"形单影只的孤寂状态，同时，使紧跟着"我"和"一片云"后面的两个动词"wandered"、"floats"在描绘"漫步"、"漂浮"这样一种轻松的动作的时候带上了一份感伤的情绪。而云朵高高（"high"）漂浮在群山和溪谷之上的意象更让人感觉到了导致孤独的那种空间距离。然而，诗人笔锋一转，让"我"猛然看见了一大片金灿灿的水仙花，正在湖的旁边（"beside"）和树的下面（"beneath"），随着风翩翩起舞。这里，诗人使用的两个动词"fluttering"（原意为鸟拍翅膀）和"dancing"（跳舞）立即使人感受到了水仙花欢快的律动。这时，我们如果比照一下这一节中的6行诗句，我们发现，这里的"我"与"水仙花"形成了鲜明的对比："I"、"a cloud"与"a crowd"、"a host"、"daffodils"之间的对比，"wandered"、"floats"与"fluttering"、"dancing"之间的对比，"o'er"与"beside"、"beneath"、"in"之间的对比。如果细致分析一下这些对比，我们也许可以感觉到一些东西，比如这种对比似乎是在单数与复数、物与物之间距离的远近等方面展开的。诗人想要述说什么呢？

在第二诗节中，诗人更为形象、具体地描绘了水仙花。诗人用形容词"continuous"、

"never-ending"，数量词 "ten thousand (at a glance)"，名词 "Milky Way"、"line"，动词 "stretched" 等等突现出水仙花的数量之多；用动词 "shine"、"twinkle" 和名词 "stars"、"Milky Way" 形容了水仙花的色彩之艳丽，与上一诗节中的 "golden" 形成呼应；用动词 "shine"、"twinkle"、"tossing"，名词 "dance"，以及形容词 "sprightly" 强调水仙花的舞动之欢快。这种真切的描绘似乎给我们一种感觉：诗人与水仙花的距离越来越近了。在这一诗节中，诗人将水仙花与天空中闪烁的星星作了对比，重点突出了水仙花的数量与美丽。

在第三诗节中，诗人在进一步描述水仙花的欢快的舞姿的同时，述说了 "我" 的心情的变化。诗人首先将欢乐的水仙花与舞动的浪花进行对比，指出水仙花比浪花更快乐；然后，诗人让 "我" 置身于这一快乐的伙伴中间，用 "gay" 一词直接点明了 "我" 由 "孤寂" 转入 "快乐" 的情绪的变化，用 "gazed"、"little thought" 等词语揭示了 "我" 当时的忘我境界。在这一诗节中，诗人不断重复着表示 "快乐" 的词，比如："danced"、"sparkling"、"glee"、"gay"、"jocund"；最后，以 "wealth" 一词为 "快乐" 作了定性。特别需要注意的是这一诗节中的介词 "in"，不仅暗示了 "我" 从原先孤独的游离状态转入一种与水仙花合为一体的状态，也暗示了我的 "快乐" 的源头："我" 与 "水仙化" 之间空间距离的消失。

最后的诗节是在第三诗节中的 "wealth" 一词的基础上展开的。诗人旨在说明水仙花为何对 "我" 如此之珍贵。该诗节的开头两行，诗人又让 "我" 陷入孤独的状态，但此时的孤独与诗歌开头时候的孤独完全不一样，因为 "我" 心灵中的水仙花随时可以闪现，抚慰 "我" 孤寂的灵魂；随时可以使 "我" 的心与水仙花一起翩翩起舞，充满欢愉。在这一诗节中，诗人用 "flash upon"、"bliss"、"pleasure"、"dances" 等词反复点明 "水仙花" 对 "我" 的重要意义。

如果现在再回过头来，重新读一遍诗歌，我们对诗歌隐含的主题大致可以作一个概括：只有当自然万物和谐相处的时候，这个世界才会有幸福。水仙花快活，因为她有湖水、树木、微风为伴（第一诗节）。水仙花幸福，因为有成千上万的花儿生活在湖湾之畔（第二诗节）。水仙花开心，还因为她有浪花为友。"我" 也开心，因为我有快乐的水仙花为伴（第三诗节）；"我" 不再孤独，因为水仙花就在我的心中（第四诗节）。

小　结：

（一）阅读诗歌的过程中，我们要特别关注诗歌中某些语词的本义与另外一些语词的引申义相连接时产生的语言张力。比如，水仙花（本义）并不会拍翅膀（fluttering）和跳舞（dancing），因此，这后面两个词所要表达的绝不会是它们的本义，而是诗歌通过这一特殊语境在读者心中激发的某种情感和想象（引申义）。

（二）在关注语词与语词之间不确定的空白点的基础上，反复阅读诗歌的上下文，从整体语境中获得某种比较确定的引申义，并努力将分布在各诗节中的引申义连接为一个合理的有机体。比如，综合分析诗歌中所有形容水仙花舞动的动词、形容词，所有表示数量从单数到复数的量词，所有表示从有距离到零距离的介词；等等。这种脱离语法和逻辑的词的分析可以帮助你发现隐藏在诗行后面的意义、想象和情感。

第二节   诗歌的句法

Syntax refers to the way in which words are ordered and connected into phrases, clauses and sentences.

简 析：

句法（syntax）研究的是词与词之间的关系。

诗歌除了用词的本义和引申义传达它的意义之外，另外一个传递意义的重要途径是句法。诗人对常规的词语、从句和句子的特殊处理可以使诗歌传递出奇特的情感和意味。比如，美国女诗人艾米莉·狄金森在一首诗歌中描写人发现蛇时的情形，她用了这样的诗句："His notice sudden is." 按照常规，句子应该是："His notice is sudden." 狄金森这一倒装的句法不仅使读者感受到人看见蛇的时候的那种突然的感觉，而且还让读者听到了蛇发出的"嘶嘶"声（hiss / is）。诗歌句法的独特性主要表现在倒装（inversion）、叠句（refrain）、标点符号（punctuation）的使用上。

倒装（inversion）

Inversion refers to the reversal of the normal order of words, which is used to preserve the rhyme scheme or the metre of a verse line, or to place special emphasis on particular words.

简 析：

在诗歌中，倒装的主要作用有两个：

1）有助于建构特定的音韵和格律；

2）打破规范的语法和句法，将意义的重心放置在某个特定的词上，使诗歌散发出特殊魅力和韵味

本节主要讨论倒装的第二个作用。我们不妨通过分析 William Wordsworth 的诗歌 "Composed upon Westminster Bridge" 来了解诗歌中的倒装。

作 品：

Composed upon Westminster Bridge, September 3, 1802

William Wordsworth

Earth has not anything to show more fair[1]:
Dull would he be of soul who could pass by
A sight so touching in its majesty[2];
This City now doth[3], like a garment[4], wear
The beauty of the morning; silent, bare,
Ships, towers, domes, theaters, and temples lie
Open unto the fields, and to the sky;
All bright and glittering in the smokeless air.
Never did sun more beautifully steep[5]
In his first splendor, valley, rock, or hill;
Ne'er saw I, never felt, a calm so deep!
The river glideth[6] at his own sweet will:
Dear God! the very houses seem asleep;
And all that mighty heart is lying still!

简 析：

在这首诗歌中，第二、第九和第十一诗行采用了倒装。

Dull would he be of soul who could pass by (第二诗行)

Never did sun more beautifully steep (第九诗行)

Ne'er saw I, never felt, a calm so deep! (第十一诗行)

常规的语序应该是：

He would be dull of soul who could pass by (第二诗行)

Sun did never steep more beautifully (第九诗行)

---

1 fair: beauty.
2 majesty: splendor.
3 doth: does.
4 garment: beautiful clothes.
5 steep: soak.
6 glideth: glides, flows.

I never saw, never felt, so deep a calm (第十一诗行)

对比常规语序与华兹华斯的诗行，华兹华斯的诗句通过倒装特别强调了"dull"、"never"等具有强烈情感意味的语词。相对于常规语序的直接、简单和求实的风格，倒装不仅增强了诗行的节奏，而且突出了诗歌中的说话人面对伦敦宁静、壮丽的晨景时所感受到的震撼和激动。

标点符号（punctuation）

另一个有助于建构诗歌特殊句法的途径是重视标点符号的使用，用标点符号来传达诗歌中说话人的情感，控制诗歌的进展速度（tempo）。

让我们阅读 Robert Hayden 的诗歌，特别关注诗歌中标点符号的运用。

作 品：

Those Winter Sundays

Robert Hayden

Sundays too my father got up early
and put his clothes on in the blueblack cold,
then with cracked hands that ached
from labor in the weekday weather made
banked fires blaze. No one ever thanked him.

I'd wake and hear the cold splintering[1], breaking.
When the rooms were warm, he'd call,
and slowly I would rise and dress,
fearing the chronic[2] angers of that house,

Speaking indifferently to him,
who had driven out the cold
and polished my good shoes as well.
What did I know, what did I know
Of love's austere[3] and lonely offices[4]?

---

1 splinter: break something such as wood into pieces.
2 chronic: a problem and difficulty that you cannot get rid of or that keeps coming back.
3 austere: plain and simple and without any decoration; strict and serious.
4 offices: duties and authority a person possesses, here refers to help given by my father who has authority.

简　析：

　　这首诗的句法相当规范，引人注目的是诗歌中标点符号的使用。

　　第一诗节使用了两个句号，前面的长句占据了四个半诗行的篇幅，只给后面的句子留出半个诗行的空间，这样不对称的长、短句安排，使得前面长句中描述的父亲的辛劳和对孩子无言的爱与后面短句孩子对这一切的漠视形成鲜明的对比。

　　第二、三两个诗节共有七个逗号、两个句号和一个问号，包含一个短句、一个跨越两个诗节的长句和一个问句。与第一诗节不同的是，这一次是短句后面跟长句，最后以问句结束。短句中"我"对寒冷的畏惧与长句中"我"对父亲沉默的爱的不理解、害怕和隔膜同样形成明显的对比。最后的问句通过重复"what did I know"，表达了"我"对没有能够早一点感知父亲平淡而普通的爱的表达方式的懊悔。

　　诗歌中所有描写父亲的动作的诗句，都用长句连贯成几个诗行，朗读起来流利而顺畅，尽可能多地将蕴涵着父亲的热情和爱心的动作都表现了出来，而所有描写"我"的冷漠和不懂事的诗句则十分短促和简练，长和短、热和冷似乎形成了一种对应关系。最后的问句恰如其分地表达了"我"的心境：懊悔，但并没有太多的自责。

叠句（refrain）

> **Refrain** refers to the repetition of a line, or part of a line, or a group of lines in the course of a poem, sometimes with slight changes, and usually at the end of each stanza.

简　析：

　　叠句曾在英国民谣和伊丽莎白时期的诗歌中大量采用，歌曲的词句中也有大量的叠句。叠句的采用可以给诗歌带来一种特别的美，也为词语突破规范句法的束缚提供了一种机会。让我们一起阅读美国作家艾伦·坡的诗歌，感受一种奇特的浪漫。

作　品：

Annabel Lee

Edgar Allan Poe

It was many and many a year ago,
  In a kingdom by the sea,
That a maiden there lived whom you may know

By the name of **Annabel Lee**;
And this maiden she lived with no other thought
　　Then to **love** and be **loved** by me.

She was a child and I was a child,
　　In this kingdom by the sea,
But we **loved** with a **love** that was more than **love**,
　　I and **my Annabel Lee**;
With a **love** that winged seraphs[1] of Heaven
　　Coveted[2] **her and me**.

And this was the reason that, long ago,
　　In this kingdom by the sea,
A wind blew out of a cloud by night
　　Chilling **my Annabel Lee**;
So that her highborn kinsmen came
　　And bore her away from me,
To shut her up in a sepulchre[3]
　　In this kingdom by the sea.

The angels, not half so happy in Heaven,
　　Went envying **her and me**;
Yes! That was the reason (as all men know,
　　In this kingdom by the sea)
That the wind came out of a cloud, chilling
　　And killing **my Annabel Lee**.

But our **love** it was stronger by far than the **love**
　　Of those who were older than we,
　　Of many far wiser than we;
And neither the angels in Heaven above,
　　Nor the demons under the sea,

1 seraphs: angels.
2 covet: desire eagerly to possess something.
3 sepulchre: tomb.

Can ever dissever my soul from the soul
Of the beautiful Annabel Lee:

For the moon never beams without bringing me dreams
Of the beautiful Annabel Lee;
And the stars never rise but I see the bright eyes
Of the beautiful Annabel Lee;
And so, all the night-tide, I lie down by the side,
Of my darling, my darling, my life and my bride,
In her sepulchre there by the sea,
In her tomb by the side of the sea.

赏　析：

　　这是一首措辞极为简单，意境却十分美丽的诗歌。诗歌意境的美与叠句的采用有着十分密切的关系。我们已经将诗歌中最主要的叠句（或叠词）用黑体表示了出来。可以看出，诗歌中主要的叠句（或叠词）有："In a kingdom by the sea"、"my Annabel Lee"、"her and me"、"Of the beautiful Annabel Lee"、"love"。这些叠句（或叠词）贯穿着整首诗歌，不仅突现了诗歌的爱情主题，而且将诗歌放置到一个超越时空和现实的童话的世界，将一个悲伤的爱情悲剧演绎成了一段凄美的爱情神话。

小　结：

　　（一）如果诗歌中有倒装的诗行，不妨多读几遍，思考诗人采用倒装手法的意图，也许这正是我们理解诗歌的一个突破口。

　　（二）阅读诗歌的时候，不妨留意一下诗歌的标点符号，如果标点符号的使用有什么特别的地方，那么它们可能在向读者传递着某种有助于理解的信息。

　　（三）遇到诗歌中的叠句，先通读全诗，看看诗歌中有几处出现了叠句/叠词，这些叠句/叠词有什么特征，在诗歌中营造了什么样的氛围，突出了什么样的主题词。或许它正是通向诗歌主题的通道。

Chapter 10   Speaker and Tone

第十章   说话人和基调

> (A poem is) heard as sung or spoken by a person in a
> scene—in character, in setting. By whom, where and when
> is the question. By a dreamer of the better world out in a
> storm in Autumn; by a lover under a window at night.
>
> Robert Frost

简要介绍：

在阅读一首诗歌的时候，我们总能听到一个说话人（speaker）的声音（voice）。诗歌中的说话人大约相当于小说中的叙述人（narrator）或戏剧中的人物（character），都是作者为了实现某种创作目标而设定的一个特定的视角。当然，相比较而言，诗歌中的说话人是最不引人注目的，但这并不是说我们可以忽视他/她的存在，因为我们正是通过说话人的声音，才感觉到诗歌的基调（tone），而诗歌的基调是读者感知诗歌中所表达的情感的最佳途径。

第一节   说话人 (Speaker)

Introduction: Speaker

> **Speaker:** While reading or perceiving a poem, we will soon be aware that the voice heard and the tone conveyed are both given by a fictitious person, who may either be the implied author or a fictitious character. He is the speaker in a poem.

诗歌是由诗人写成的，但是却是由一位虚构的说话人诉说的。这位虚构的说话人实践和体现着诗人的创作意图。诗歌中主要有两类说话人：

　　一类说话人在诗歌中往往以第一人称出现，这个"我"基本上就是作者的代言人，诉说着作者通过自身的体验获得的对世界和对人类的理解和感悟，因此这个"我"既代表着作者，又指称"人"这一集合体，"我"是非个性化的。抒情诗中的说话人大多属于这一类，这也就是为什么，曾有批评家这样断定："叙事要求读者判断其人物，抒情诗要求读者不要判断其说话者"[1]。

作　品：

Stopping by Woods on a Snowy Evening

Robert Frost

Whose woods these are I think I know.
His house is in the village though;
He will not see me stopping here
To watch his woods fill up with snow. (The First Stanza)

Ode to a Nightingale

John Keats

My heart aches, and a drowsy numbness pains
　My sense, as though of hemlock[2] I had drunk,
Or emptied some dull opiate to the drains
　One minute past, and Lethe-wards[3] had sunk:
'Tis not through envy of thy happy lot,
　But being too happy in thine happiness—
　　That thou, light winged Dryad[4] of the trees,
　　　In some melodious plot
Of beechen green, and shadows numberless，
　　Singest of summer in full-throated ease. (The First Stanza)

　　另一种说话人是完全虚构的人物，他在诗歌中扮演着一个特定的角色，就像小说和戏剧中的一个人物，因此他的叙述只能代表他自己，并不代表作者。这种说话人大多出现在叙事诗和戏剧诗之中，比如英国诗人Robert Browning的"My Last Duchess"

---

1 詹姆斯·费伦. 作为修辞的叙事. 陈永国译. 北京：北京大学出版社, 2002: 3.
2 hemlock: A poisonous herb.
3 Lethe-wards: Toward Lethe, the river of forgetfulness in Hades, the underworld, in classical mythology.
4 Dryad: In classical mythology, a wood nymph.

中的说话人"公爵"。

作 品：

My Last Duchess

Ferrara[1]

Robert Browning

That's my last Duchess painted on the wall,
Looking as if she were alive. I call
That piece a wonder, now; Fra Pandolf's[2] hands
Worked busily a day, and there she stands.
Will't please you sit and look at her? I said
"Fra Pandolf" by design, for never read
Strangers like you that pictured countenance[3],
The depth and passion of its earnest glance,
But to myself they turned (since none puts by
The curtain I have drawn for you, but I)
And seemed as they would ask me, if they durst[4],
How such a glance came there; so, not the first
Are you to turn and ask thus. Sir, 'twas not
Her husband's presence only, called that spot
Of joy into the Duchess' cheek; perhaps
Fra Pandolf chanced to say, "Her mantle[5] laps
Over my lady's wrist too much," or "Paint
Must never hope to reproduce the faint
Half-flush that dies along her throat." Such stuff
Was courtesy[6], she thought, and cause enough
For calling up that spot of joy. She had
A heart—how shall I say?—too soon made glad,
Too easily impressed; she liked whate'er
She looked on, and her looks went everywhere.

---

1 Ferrara: a city-state in Renaissance Italy.
2 Fra Pandolf's: The work of Brother Pandolf, an imaginary painter.
3 countenance: face.
4 durst: dared.
5 mantle: (old use) a piece of clothing without sleeves which was worn over other clothes 披风.
6 courtesy: polite behavior, or a polite action or remark.

Sir, 'twas all one! My favor at her breast,
The dropping of the daylight in the West,
The bough of cherries some officious[7] fool
Broke in the orchard for her, the white mule
She rode with round the terrace—all and each
Would draw from her alike the approving speech,
Or blush, at least. She thanked men—good! but thanked
Somehow—I know not how—as if she ranked
My gift of nine-hundred-year-old name
With anybody's gift. Who'd stoop to[8] blame
This sort of trifling? Even had you skill
In speech—which I have not—to make you will
Quiet clear to such an one, and say "Just this
Or that in you disgusts me; here you miss,
Or there exceed the mark"—and if she let
Herself be lessoned so, nor plainly set
Her wits to yours, forsooth[9], and made excuse—
E'en then would be some stooping; and I choose
Never to stoop. Oh sir, she smiled, no doubt,
Whene'er I passed her; but who passed without
Much the same smile? This grew; I gave commands;
Then all smiles stopped together. There she stands
As if alive. Will't please you rise? We'll meet
The company below, then. I repeat,
The Count your master's known munificence[10]
Is ample warrant that no just pretense[11]
Of mine for dowry[12] will be disallowed;
Though his fair daughter's self, as I avowed[13]
At starting, is my object. Nay, we'll go
Together down, sir. Notice Neptune[14], though,
Taming a sea-horse, thought a rarity,
Which Claus of Innsbruck[15] cast in bronze for me!

7 officious: overly eager to please.
8 stoop to: lower one's moral standard by doing something which is unpleasant, dishonest or unfair.
9 forsooth: in truth.
10 munificence: great generosity.
11 pretense: claim.
12 dowry: property that a woman brings to her husband at marriage.
13 avowed: swore.
14 Neptune: In Roman mythology, the god of the sea.
15 Claus of Innsbruck: An imaginary Austrian sculptor.

赏 析：

这段戏剧独白是公爵向前来提亲的使者作介绍的时候说的。在独白中，公爵得意洋洋地向提亲者展示了他那位刚去世的公爵夫人的画像，言辞极为优雅，语调却十分霸道。他在提到自己因为公爵夫人对所有人都笑容可掬而怒火中烧，下令处死公爵夫人的时候，竟轻描淡写地一句带过，很快转入另一个话题，开始向提亲使者提出对本次婚嫁的要求。公爵的一席温文尔雅的独白，揭示的却是他自己那颗伪善、冷酷、贪婪、毫无人性的心，勃朗宁的创作功底的确非同一般，而这种创作上的成功在一定程度上要归功于勃朗宁对说话人的选择，即：让说话人自己来揭示自己的本性，这当然是最真实和最有力的。此外，这种创作上的成功还要归功于勃朗宁在创作中对说话人的独白的特殊处理：说话人不可一世的傲慢话语始终与最基本的人性和常理相违背。比如，独白中公爵将公爵夫人对他人的微笑列为处死公爵夫人的罪证，足以显示出公爵的自私、专横和霸道，而公爵讲述下令杀死公爵夫人时那种轻松的语调则进一步映照出公爵灭绝人性的冷酷。

第二节 基调 (Tone)

Tone is a very vague critical term, which is broadly designating the mood or atmosphere of a work, and strictly refers to the author's attitude to the reader or to the subject-matter. It was defined by I. A. Richards as "the expression of a literary speaker's 'attitude to his listener'"[1], and by Mikhail Bakhtin as the one "oriented in two directions: with respect to the listener as ally or witness and with respect to the object of the utterance as the third, living participant whom the intonation scolds or caresses, denigrates or magnifies."[2]

"基调"这一术语的内涵就像它所指称的内容那样复杂和微妙，简单地说，它是指作者通过作品向读者传递的一种腔调或语气。我们不妨举例说明，如：小丽要完成一项有一定难度的工作，她原以为需要一天时间才能完成这项工作，结果半天不到她就完成工作了。她开心地告诉同伴："真高兴，只用三个小时就搞定了。"然后她决定去购买一张著名歌星演唱会门票，结果排了半天的队才买到门票，于是她叹息着对一起排队的人说："真高兴，只用三个小时就搞定了。"小丽的两句话从形式上看一模一样，然而他们传递的情感和意义并不相同。如果直接听小丽说这两句话，我们可以凭小丽说话的语气立即感觉到小丽的话所包含的不同含义和不同感情；但是，如果是在

---

1 Abrams, M. H. *A Glossary of Literary Terms*. 7th ed. Harcourt Brace College Publishers, 1999: 218.
2 Ibid.

文学作品中读到这两句话，那么我们就只能通过作品的语境和语言技巧来感受它们内在的含义和情感，也就是我们所说的"基调"。我们说"基调"是"复杂"的，那是因为它至少包含着两个层面的内涵，一方面，它是指作者向他的同谋者——读者传递的语气，作者期望读者能够通过它感受到作者隐含的情感和意图；另一方面，它是指作者在文学作品中通过说话人或各种创作技巧表达的腔调或语气，它同时也指作者对创作题材的态度。我们说"基调"是"微妙"的，那是因为在大多数作品中，作者不会直接用语言告诉读者作品的"基调"，而是希望读者通过措辞、句法、修辞、音韵、格律等创作技巧间接感悟到它。正因为它是一种超越语言的情感和意义的传递，因此它在文学作品的理解的过程中发挥着举足轻重的作用。

虽然，我们在概括诗歌的基调的时候，我们可以简练地用一些形容词来进行描述，比如欢快的、哀伤的、严肃的、轻松的、辛辣的、幽默的、讽刺的、赞赏的、感伤的、平静的、自负的、谦和的，等等。但是，进行概括的过程需要大量的分析和判断。要分析诗歌的基调，我们可以考虑从下面几个方面入手：

（一）考察作者对创作题材的语气和态度。比如英国诗人 William Wordsworth 在"I Wandered Lonely as a Cloud"非常肯定地表达了他对水仙花的赞赏和喜爱；而美国诗人 Gwendolyn Brooks 在"We Real Cool"中则直接用"we die soon"表达了他对诗中所描述的生活的批判。我们可以通过提出下列问题对作者的态度进行思考：

1. How does the author make his attitude clear?
2. Are there any common assumptions about religious views, political ideas, moral and behavioral standards?
3. Are there any commonly acceptable ideas?

（二）考察作者在作品中通过说话人或各种创作技巧表达的多种语气。比如，美国作家Edgar Allan Poe在"Annabel Lee"中，用叠句"In a kingdom by the sea"将爱的题材放入一个童话世界，用童话般美丽的语言讲述了一个短暂却永恒的爱的故事，表达了说话人对逝去的爱人的无限爱怜和思念。英国诗人Robert Browning在"My Last Duchess"中让说话人用自鸣得意的话语揭示了他自己的自私和丑恶，同时又我们从他狂妄的语词中感觉到了公爵夫人的优雅和可爱。正是通过这种鲜明的对比，作者表达了他对公爵的辛辣批判。我们可以通过提出下列问题来分析、判断作品的多种语气：

1. What is the basic situation in the work?
2. Are there any systematic references such as colors, sounds, noises, natural scenes, and so on that collectively reveal an attitude?
3. Do speech or dialect patterns indicate attitudes about the speaker or his living conditions?

4. Are there any unusual words or expressions that reveal a particular attitude?

5. Is the work ironic, or humorous, or funny?

6. How is the irony \ humor \ fun achieved?

（三）考察作者对读者的语气和态度。在写作过程中，作者始终清醒地意识到读者的存在，因此他们用各种方式在作品中为读者留下交流的空间。有时，作者会直接在作品中使用"you"，比如，T. S. Eliot在诗歌"The Love Song of J. Alfred Prufrock"的开头这样写道："Let us go then, you and I"。大部分诗歌都用间接的方式与读者交流，比如英国诗人Robert Browning在"My Last Duchess"中对公爵的话语不作任何评论，表明他对读者的阅读能力的信任，相信读者有足够的道德评判能力，能从公爵的一席话语中看透他丑恶的本性。我们可以通过提出下列问题来分析作者对读者的态度：

1. Is any person or group addressed by the speaker?

2. What attitude is expressed?

3. Does the work promote respect, admiration, dislike, or other feelings about character or situation?

赏　析：

我们不妨就"基调"问题对英国诗人 Robert Browning 的"My Last Duchess"作进一步分析。由于整首诗歌采用了戏剧独白的形式，因此诗人无法直接与读者对话，也无法直接表达他对公爵的评判——诗人是通过说话人和各种创作技巧的使用来表达说话人和诗人自己的态度的。从结构上看，我们可以根据话语主题的变化将整首诗歌分为三个部分：公爵介绍夫人的画像，公爵提出对本次婚嫁的要求，公爵介绍海神驯海马的塑像。在介绍夫人画像的时候，公爵对提亲人的语气比较客气，在介绍公爵夫人的画像时语气中充满了得意和炫耀。但是公爵在谈论公爵夫人本人时，言语中却充满了怨恨和怒气。这种怨恨的语气逐渐递增，直至最后说明他命人结束了公爵夫人的生命。从他的话语中，读者可以得知，导致怨恨的唯一原因只是因为公爵夫人对所有人都和颜悦色，而不是只敬重公爵、公爵的头衔和公爵的地位；在提出对本次婚嫁的要求时，公爵对提亲者的语气强硬而霸道，他不容置疑地提出了他的要求，大言不惭地声明，他的妻子不过是他的一份财物；在介绍海神驯海马的塑像时，公爵的语气变得得意而狂妄，似乎他就是那个海神。显而易见，这三部分在结构上是平行的，在语气上是递进的：第一部分用举例的方式间接表明了公爵对妻子的态度，第二部分直接说明了公爵对妻子的定位，第三部分着重强调了公爵驯服妻子的姿态。从这一角度切入，我们无疑听到了公爵内心的声音，公爵对提亲者发出的宣言和威胁。

那么，诗人的声音又在何处呢？诗人的语气又是如何的呢？诗人的声音就隐藏在公爵的话语中，它需要读者用自己的道德观和价值观作为参照作出自己的评判。诗人让读者从公爵的话语中认识了公爵夫人：她有灿烂的笑容、感恩的心情和温顺的个性。诗人使公爵的专断、自私、蛮横与公爵夫人的开朗、温柔、善良形成鲜明的对比，诗人辛辣的批评就隐藏在这种鲜明的对比之中，隐藏在公爵大言不惭的声明和不可理喻的暴行的背后，当然最最辛辣的批判隐藏在公爵夫人的"罪行"——微笑——与公爵炫耀的"业绩"——杀人——之间的对比。当杀人者可以津津乐道地谈论他杀戮的"正义"和"公正"却没有遭遇任何谴责和审判的时候，这时候的问题肯定不是一个公爵的问题，而是一个社会的问题。这个社会缺乏对生命的最基本的尊重。可以说，诗人的声音是响亮的，语气是很强烈的，但这种声音和语气只有在文明社会中才能够被听到和感觉到。

基调的重要性是不容置疑的。

小　结：

关注诗歌中的说话人，判断说话人是否是诗人的代言人。如果说话人不代表诗人，那么就要学会在倾听说话人的声音的同时，兼听诗歌中通过各种创作技巧发出的间接的声音或语气，并学会在众多的声音和语气中辨别出主要的声音和语气，用心体会这种语气所传递的情感，然后你就会发现，你距离诗歌的意义越来越近了。

Chapter 11　Poetic Rhetorical Devices

第十一章　诗歌的修辞方法

What oft was thought, but ne'er so well expressed.

Alexander Pope

简要介绍:

诗歌之所以能够超越语言的局限, 表达无以言说的情感和想象, 是因为它是一种用意象进行描绘、用修辞扩展内涵、用典故跨越时空的语言。

第一节: 意象 (Imagery)

Imagery, a critical term variable in meaning, basically refers to the use of perceptible or "concrete" objects, scenes, or actions in a literary work, which evokes sense-impressions, as opposed to abstract argument or exposition. The imagery of a literary work consists of a set of images that it uses, including both mental "pictures" and others that appeal to senses. The term also signifies vehicles of figurative language used in a work, especially those of metaphors and similes. Images suggesting further meanings and associations that go beyond the identifications of metaphor and simile are called symbols.

简　析:

"意象"是文学批评中最普通的一个术语, 也是最难以捉摸的一个术语。说它普通, 是因为它是形象地表达人的知觉和抽象思维的一种最基本的方法。比如, 说到"春天", 人们总是不由自主地"看见"破土的花蕾, "听见"小鸟的歌唱, "闻到"泥土的滋润, "感到"微风的轻拂; 说到"美丽", 人们会自然而然地联想到"鲜花"、"彩虹"等——这正是诗歌捕捉和描写客观世界和主体意识的基本方法。说它难以捉摸,是因为批评家们对它的界定显得模糊不清。批评家的界定大致可以分为三种：一种界定是由戴·路易斯在他的专著《诗歌的意象》（*Poetic Image*, 1948）中提出的，他认为意象就是"语词建构的图像"[1]，而"一首诗歌本身就是由多个意象构成的一个意象"[2]。这一界定侧重于从视觉的角度界定"意象"。一种界定认为文学作品中的"意象"包括能够激发所有知觉（即"视觉"、"嗅觉"、"触觉"、"听觉"、"味觉"）的语词。一种界定将"意象"等同于修辞，认为意象是修辞——特别是隐喻和明喻——的表现媒介。不过，不管批评家们在界定意象时的出发点有多么不同，他们对意象的本质的理解是一致的，那就是，意象使诗歌形象化。

上述界定吸收了前面所说的三种界定的内涵，将"意象"确定在激发人的"视觉"、"嗅觉"、"触觉"、"听觉"、"味觉"等全部知觉的语词的范围之内，说明"意象"不同于抽象语言的形象化本质，同时指出"意象"在语言修辞，特别是在隐喻、明喻、象征，中的媒介作用，也指出了隐喻和明喻与象征的区别。

作　品：

Meeting at Night

Robert Browning

The gray sea and the long black land;
And the yellow half-moon large and low;
And the startled little waves that leap
In fiery ringlets from their sleep,
As I gain the cove[3] with pushing prow,
And quench[4] its speed i' the slushy[5] sand.

Then a mile of warm sea-scented beach;
Three fields to cross till a farm appears;
A tap at the pane[6], the quick sharp scratch
And blue spurt[7] of a lighted match,

---

1 Abrams, M. H. *A Glossary of Literary Terms.* 7th ed. Harcourt Brace College Publishers, 1999: 121.
2 Ibid.
3 cove: a small bay.
4 quench: stop.
5 slushy: of snow that is lying on the ground and has started to melt.
6 pane: a flat piece of glass, used in a window or door.
7 spurt: flowing out suddenly and with force.

And a voice less loud, through its joys and fears,

Than the two hearts beating each to each!

赏　析：

　　阅读这首诗歌，读者感受到的是大量的"意象"。我们可以"看到"："The gray sea"、"the long black land"、"the yellow half-moon"、"the startled little waves"、"fiery ringlets"、"the cove"、"prow"、"the slushy sand"、"beach"、"a farm"、"pane"、"blue spurt"。如果将"看到"的景物相连接，我们可以得到一幅丰富的路线图：sea—land—moon—waves—ringlets—cove—prow—sand—beach—farm—pane，我们可以想象出诗歌中的"我"穿越大海和陆地，终于来到一户人家的门前的情景，而在这一过程中我们看到色彩的变化：gray（灰）—black（黑）—yellow（黄）—fiery（红）—slushy（白），不仅展示了自然界的缤纷绚丽，也暗示了时光的流逝以及"我"的情绪的变化。我们还可以"闻到"大海的气味（sea-scented），"听到"海浪的拍击声（leap），"我"轻轻的叩门声（tap），"她"急切的开门声（quick sharp scratch），"我们"惊喜的谈话声（voice，through its joys and fears）以及"我们"激动的心跳声（two hearts beating）。从这许多感觉中，我们多半已经猜出了这首诗歌的主题：爱情。诗歌中的"我"在经历了漫长的跋涉后，终于叩开了一扇"爱"的大门，点燃了"爱"的火焰，伴随着喜悦的话语，让两颗跳动的心紧紧靠在一起。

　　勃朗宁用丰富的意象阐释了爱的历程，爱的感受和爱的终点。而我们也用我们丰富的心灵，透过灰色的语言，体会到了爱的温暖和喜悦。我们与其说是在阅读诗歌，不如说是在体验诗歌，体验诗歌中所描写的生活。诗歌是用意象编织的情感。

第二节　修辞格（Figures of Speech）

> **Figure of Speech** is an ancient term for any form of expression, in which the normal use of language is manipulated or stretched in terms of the meaning of the words, or the syntactical pattern of the words.

简要介绍：

　　当我们看到我们的朋友被雨水淋透时，我们会调侃地称他为"落汤鸡"；当我们看到美丽女子从身边走过，我们会赞叹她"美若天仙"——这就是我们所说的语言修辞。语言修辞在日常口语和各类写作中运用极为广泛，在文学创作中尤为重要，是文学创作最基本的元素之一。

> 西方修辞学的历史源远流长，最早可追溯到亚里士多德。经过2000多年的思考和研究，有修辞学者认为从宽泛的意义上说，各类修辞方式大约有250种。但是从更为精确的角度考虑，我们所用的主要修辞手法大约只有10余种，其中诗歌中最常用的修辞手法是：simile（明喻）、metaphor（隐喻）、metonymy（换喻/转喻）、synecdoche（提喻）、personification（拟人手法）、apostrophe（呼语）、symbol（象征）。这些修辞手法的基本共性是：用一物指称另一物。

下面我们逐一介绍诗歌的主要修辞手法：

> **Simile** refers to a comparison between two distinctly different things, which is explicitly indicated by the word 'like' or 'as'.

简　析：

华兹华斯的诗歌"I Wondered Lonely as a Cloud"的第一句"I wondered lonely as a cloud"就是很典型的明喻。在这一诗行中的"我"被比喻成"一片云"，中间的关联词是"as"。明喻在文学作品中是最常见的修辞手法，其主要特征是直接用意象将抽象的事物形象化。

> **Metaphor** refers to a word or expression in the literary work, which denotes one kind of thing, is applied to a distinctly different kind of thing, without a comparison.

简　析：

隐喻发挥着与明喻一样的作用，它与明喻的区别主要体现在用法上：明喻是通过两物之间的比较，用一种事物说明另一种事物；而隐喻虽然也是用一物说明另一物，两物之间却没有明显的对比关系——大多数情况下，被指代的事物在语句中根本就不出现。

比如，如果我们将 Robert Burns 诗句"My luve's like a red, red rose"改写成"My luve's a red, red rose"，那么改写后的诗句就是典型的隐喻——也就是说，隐喻用"is"或"are"等系动词直接将两物对等起来。当然，这只是最简单的隐喻；更多的时候，隐喻以更为隐蔽的方式出现的。比如，William Blake 的诗歌"The Tyger"：

"Tyger! Tyger! Burning bright
In the forests of the night,"

这里的"Tyger"与动词"Burning"（火）是隐喻关系。正是通过"Burning"一词，诗句传达了老虎的力量、勇气、激情等等所有"火"可能带给我们的内涵。

> **Personification** is a figure of speech by which animals, abstract ideas, or inanimate things are referred to as if they were human.

简 析:

拟人化手法其实是隐喻的一种，只是隐在的比较对象始终是人类。比如：在诗歌"Tree"中，诗人通过使用"mouth"、"breast"等词，将"树"拟人化了：

"A tree whose hungry mouth is press
Against the earth's sweet flowing breast;"

> **Synecdoche** is a figure of speech in which a part of something is used to signify the whole, or (more rarely) the whole is used to signify a part.

简 析:

如果说上面三种修辞法突出了两种不同事物之间的对比，那么，提喻和换喻突出了同一事物或有关联事物之间的互相替换。提喻是一种用部分说明全部或用全部指代部分的修辞手法。比如：用"树"来代表"森林"，用"水果"来指称"苹果"等。

在William Shakespeare的诗歌"Spring"中，"a married ear"就是提喻，用来指代"a married man"。

"The cuckoo then, on every tree,
Mocks married men; for thus sings he,
    'Cuckoo!
Cuckoo, cuckoo!' O word of fear,
Unpleasing to a married ear!"

> **Metonymy** is a figure of speech that replaces the name of one thing with the name of some other thing which is closely associated with it.

简 析:

与提喻稍有些不同，换喻中两事物有密切关联，但并不是同一事物。比如，用"王冠"指代"国王"，用"眼睛"代表"心灵"。英国诗人华兹华斯的诗句"They flash upon that inward eye"就是最好的例子。在诗句中，诗人用"inward eye"代表人的内心、灵魂。

如果稍微留心一下，我们就会发现，提喻和换喻在日常用语和书写中频繁出现，几乎已经成为日常表达的一部分，其修辞成分已经不再引人注目。因此我们也称提喻和换喻为"死去的隐喻"。不过，在特别关注措辞的诗歌的语言中，提喻和换喻还是有其特殊的作用。比如，它们可以表达诗人特别的关注和情感，给人以生动的意象和想象的愉悦。

> **Apostrophe** refers to a direct and explicit address either to an absent person or to an abstract or nonhuman entity.

简　析：

例如，约翰·济慈的"Ode on a Grecian Urn"诗歌的开头就用"Thou"替代了"Grecian Urn"。

"Thou still unravished bride of quietness,
Thou foster child of silence and slow time,"

"呼语"的使用，一方面可以起到拟人化的作用，另一方面恰到好处地表达了诗人的情感。

> **Symbol** refers to an object or action or anything in a literary work that stands for or represents something beyond itself—usually an idea conventionally associated with it.

简　析：

当我们阅读诗句"my love is like a red, red rose"时，我们知道"rose"代表"爱"，诗句的修辞格是明喻；当我们阅读诗句"she was our queen, our rose, our star"时，我们知道"rose"是一个隐喻，暗示"她"的美丽；但是，当我们阅读诗句"O Rose, thou art sick"时，我们发现我们不能像阅读前两个诗句那样，从诗句中发现"rose"的比照物，比如"my love"或"she"，也就是说，我们无法从诗句中直接获得"rose"确切的含义。"rose"依然是"rose"，但是它的含义显然要超越它的本义，它就是一个象征。

更明确地说，象征的最大特点是它没有特定的比照物来限定它的意义，但它的确指向某种意义，这种意义大多源于社会传统或文化习俗。比如，"龙"在中国文化中象征王权，而在英语文化中却象征"凶恶"。

象征的媒介，与隐喻和明喻一样，都是意象，比如玫瑰花，知更鸟、村庄、山、河、海等等。象征与隐喻的不同主要体现在它的开放性、不确定性和与文化习俗的关联。

我们不妨阅读一首诗歌，来更好地认识象征。

作　品：

The Road Not Taken

Robert Frost

Two roads diverged in a yellow wood,
And sorry I could not travel both
And be one traveler, long I stood
And looked down one as far as I could
To where it bent in the undergrowth;

Then took the other, as just as fair,
And having perhaps the better claim,
Because it was grassy and wanted wear
Though as for that, the passing there
Had worn them really about the same.

And both that morning equally lay
In leaves no step had trodden black.
Oh, I kept the first for another day!
Yet knowing how way leads on to way,
I doubted if I should ever come back.

I shall be telling this with a sigh
Somewhere ages and ages hence:
Two roads diverged in a wood, and I—
I took the one less traveled by,
And that has made all the difference.

赏　析：

　　这首诗歌最主要的意象是"路"。"我"站在森林中，面对着两条通往不同方向的路，犹豫着不知该如何选择。"我"尽可能对两条路进行认真考察，却没有发现太大的区别。于是"我"幻想"我"可以先选择走一条路，然后再回头走另外一条路，但是理智告诉"我"这是不可能的。如果说，读到这里为止，诗歌中的"路"依然是指两条让我举棋不定的路的话，那么最后的诗节让我们感悟到，诗歌中的"路"是带有某种象征意义的。正因为"我"选择了其中的一条路，"我"的人生从此就完全不同了。显然，"路"象征着人生任何时刻都可能出现的两难的选择。正是选择决定了人的一生。

诗歌中的"我"终于作了选择。他选择了一条"人们不太走的路"（the one less traveled by），正是这一选择构成了他不同的人生。诗歌中的"我"叹息了一声，叹息中似乎带有一丝遗憾，但也有一分欣慰。看来，诗人还是就"面对两难境地该如何选择"这一问题作出了明确的回答。诗中的"我"的选择正是诗人弗罗斯特本人一生的写照。青年弗罗斯特从哈佛大学毕业后选择了一条与众不同的路：回老家的农庄写诗，希望能为美国文学做点什么。为了全身心投入写作，他甚至卖掉自己的农庄，举家迁往英国。最后他终于获得成功，也为推进美国诗歌的发展作出了贡献。

需要注意的是，象征并不是刻意造出来表达某种含义的，它应该是一种自然而然的表达和联想。关于这一点，英国诗人庞德的话很有启发作用。

"I believe that the proper and perfect symbol is the natural object, that if a man uses 'symbol' he must so use them that their symbolic function does not obtrude; so that a sense, and the poetic quality of the passage, is not lost to those who do not understand the symbol as such, to whom, for instance, a hawk is a hawk."[1]

小　结：

意象、明喻、隐喻和象征的区别

意象只指称意象本身，
明喻和隐喻只揭示它们的引申义，
象征同时保留本义和引申义，
只因缺少比照物，象征的意义丰富又开放。

---

1 Meyer, Michael. *The Compact Bedford Introduction to Literature.* 5th ed. Boston: Bedford/St. Martin's, 2000: 661.

第三节：典故（Allusion）

Allusion is an indirect or passing reference to a literary or historical event, person, place, or an artistic work or passage, without an explicit explanation of the nature and relevance. The function of allusion is to call upon the history or literary tradition economically, which is supposed to be shared by both author and reader.

简　析：

　　从定义中可以看出，典故其实是指那些直接嵌入在作品中而不加以任何说明的文学的或历史的事件、人物、地点，或者指直接嵌入在作品中的某些先前作品的诗行或段落等。采用典故是作者以最简练的方式将历史或文学传统与现时世界并置的一种有效方式，也是作者以最经济的方式将抽象的思想形象化的一种有效的途径。采用典故大都是为了形象地说明或鲜明地突出作品的主题，有时候也会通过典故与主题之间的反差来讽刺某事物。由于作者没有在作品中说明典故的内涵，因此要理解典故就需要读者拥有与作者一样丰富的历史、文化、文学知识，这正是我们中国读者阅读西方作品的难点。好在大多数典故都是比较常见，较难一点的典故，比如庞德、艾略特作品中的典故，也会有注释为我们作提示。但是，要很好地理解英语作品，需要我们尽可能多地熟悉英语文化和历史，因为文学文本之间、文学与文化之间、文学与历史之间，是互文的，或者说，是互相关联的。

作　品：

To Helen

Edgar Allan Poe (1809—1849)

Helen, thy beauty is to me
　　Like those Nicean barks of yore[1],
That gently, o'er a perfumed sea,
　　The weary, wayworn wanderer bore
　　To his own native shore.

---

1 yore: long ago.

On desperate seas long wont to roam,
　　Thy hyacinth hair, thy classic face,
Thy Naiad airs have brought me home
　　To the glory that was Greece
And the grandeur that was Rome.

Lo! in yon[2] brilliant window-niche
　　How statue-like I see thee stand,
　　The agate lamp within thy hand!
Ah! Psyche, from the regions which
　　Are Holy Land!

赏　析：

初次阅读这首诗歌，我们可能会有一种雾里看花的感觉，首先遭遇的是一头雾水。这主要是因为诗歌中有许多典故。要拨开浓雾，看清楚鲜花的形状，最简单的办法是破译每一个典故的内涵。

下面列出的就是诗歌中主要的典故及其内涵：

Helen: Helen of Troy, an embodiment of beauty.

Nicean: an adjective from the name of the town Nicaea, which was in ancient Bithynia, a little country colonized by Roman Empire when it expending, in present day Turkey.

Weary, wayworn wanderer: a line in Homer's epic, refers to warrior Odysseus.

Hyacinth: a kind of flower, according to Greek myth, hyacinth flower grew out of the blood of the dead Hyacinthus, the beloved of Apollo, whom God accidentally killed with his discus. Therefore, the word symbolizes rebirth.

Naiad: Naiad is a noun, referring to the nymphs in classical mythology that give life to lakes, rivers and streams.

Niche: recess in a wall for a statue or ornament

Agate lamp: symbolizes immortality

Psyche: "Psyche" was a mortal princess in Roman mythology who loved and was loved by Cupid, the immortal Roman God of love. Because Psyche was so spectacularly beautiful, and a mere mortal, she was jealously condemned by Venus, the Goddess of Love, to marry a hideous, ugly monster. Venus sent her son, Cupid, to ensure the deed

---

2 yon: yonder, over there.

was done but, instead, Cupid fell in love with Psyche and secretly kept her in a beautiful gardened palace. Visiting her only at night so that Psyche could not see his face, they lived and loved in darkness until Psyche, driven by curiosity and the jealous goading of her sisters, hid a lamp in her chamber so that when Cupid fell asleep, she could see his face. When Cupid fell asleep, she lit the lamp and as she gazed upon the handsome features of Cupid, hot oil dripped on his face and awoke him. Furious at her disobedience, Cupid left her alone. Poe's reference to the "agate lamp" is representative of the lamp used by Psyche. Desperate to regain his love and trust, Psyche ultimately went to Venus to beg forgiveness. Still angry and jealous, Venus was touched by Psyche's deference and despair and gave her three tasks to test Psyche's worthiness for her son. The last was for Psyche to enter Hades and retrieve some beauty potions from Persephone, Queen of the Underworld. The only way into Hades for a mortal was to die and as she prepared to throw herself from the highest tower of the Temple, Cupid intervened and showed her a secret passage to the underworld. There is much more to the tale but this should give you the drift of the story.

现在再次阅读这首诗歌，我们可以感觉到诗人借助家喻户晓的希腊美女海伦和耳熟能详的荷马英雄奥德赛的故事向我们传递了他对美的向往。

诗歌第一节，诗人用明喻的手法，将希腊神话中的美女海伦比喻为古罗马时期的一叶小舟，载着"我"轻轻地穿越散发着幽香的大海，像那位经历了千难万险终于抵达自己的出生地的荷马英雄奥德赛一样，终于回到了自己的故土。

诗歌第二节，诗人用提喻的手法，将海伦的美具化为风信子一般的头发，优雅古典的脸庞和宁馨儿一般的气质，正是这一切使"我"穿越汹涌的大海，来到了古希腊和古罗马的辉煌的故土。

诗歌第三节，诗人用隐喻的手法，将海伦喻为一尊端庄地耸立在远处的神龛中的女神，手持象征不朽的玛瑙灯，俨然是来自圣地的灵魂的化身。

Three Approaches to Edgar Allan Poe's "To Helen"

1. Traditional Approaches to Edgar Allan Poe's "To Helen"

1) Historical-Biographical Considerations

To get some knowledge about Poe's life experience and his historical background may help readers to apprehend this poem comprehensively.

Allan Poe lived in a period when English Romanticism was at full tide in America. Writers at that time paid much attention to imagination and emotion and tended to glorify the Nature and express personal feelings. They also showed admiration and love for ancient civilizations. Poe was one of them. But unlike his contemporaries who devoted to writing about the contemplation of nature and American realities, Poe tried to explore the world of dream and nightmare. He was also attracted to mythologies and long-departed ancient civilizations. These explain why there are so many allusions to legendary past in "To Helen".

His divorce from the society, and his isolation from other writers might attribute to his special life experience. Throughout his life, he was puzzled by the feeling of insecurity, isolation, and uncertainty of his identity. Born in Boston, Massachusetts, Edgar Poe was orphanized in his early childhood. His father was indulged in drinking and finally left the family, abandoning his wife and three children. Soon, Poe's mother died of tuberculosis. Deep sense of insecurity haunted the poor child. Actually, even when his parents were present and alive, Poe seldom enjoyed peaceful and settled life, since they both worked in a stage company and moved regularly from one place to another. After his mother's death, Edgar was taken in by his godfather, John Allan, a hot-tempered Scottish-born trader. Never being formally adopted, however, Poe failed to lead a normal and happy life in the new family. What's worse, his relationship with John was abominable. This guardian never showed any tender feelings toward the poor child, let alone placating him with security.

The direct consequence was Poe's frequent question about his own identity. No family accepted him sincerely or loved him wholeheartedly. He was just like a wanderer on the sea, lost and unable to find way home. Hence, Poe gradually formed a gloomy, negative and pessimistic character and attitude toward life. This stance became the basic tone of most of his works.

But, he still held the wish to be loved and guided, like other children. It was Mrs. Jane Staunard, the mother of one of Poe's classmate who partly fulfilled the poor child's wish and bestowed him with considerate love. To him, she suggested the beauty of the legendary past and temporarily drew him out of the misery reality. Unfortunately, however, this kindhearted woman died at a young age. In mourning for his boyhood idol, Poe wrote "To Helen" and imaged Mrs. Staunard as the renowned beauty Helen. His imagination corresponds to his real experiences. In the poem, Helen, with physical and spiritual beauty, guides the wanderer to a safe shore with splendid civilization, while in real life, Mrs. Staunard, with a virtuous soul, comforted Poe who was tortured by the sense of insecurity and isolation.

Generally speaking, the poem "To Helen", a tribute to Mrs. Staunard, can be deemed as a reflection of Poe's life and experiences.

2) Moral-Philosophical Considerations

Edgar Allan Poe was not given enough emphasis or due reputation in his lifetime. His values were only gradually recognized after his death. One reason is that though being a Romantic writer, he was not in whole conformity with his contemporaries, especially on the effect of moralization. He hated the "the heresy of the didactic" and his works were alienated from reality and national issues. He advocated "art for art's sake" and said highly of poem's aesthetic beauty on its own. Therefore, it is hard to find profound moral or philosophical implications in Poe's works.

But the function to teach morality can never be completely excluded from literary works. In "To Helen", Poe indirectly expresses his emphasis on the maintenance of humanity. In Poe's time, industry developed rapidly in America, but Poe, with some other Romanticists, detested the advancement of industrialization that turned men inhuman and mechanized. Hence, in this poem, Poe expressed his yearning for the greatest ancient civilizations—"the Glory that was Greece and the grandeur that was Rome"—where there was no pollution and the money-hunting desire caused by industrialization. To Poe, to retain humanity and dignity as men is the most important.

2. Diction, Symbol, Allusion: Motifs of Beauty, Guidance and Security in "To Helen"

As a literary man, Poe is at the same time poet, novelist and literary critic. His most renowned critical works like *Twice-Told Tales*, *Philosophy of Composition* and *The Poetic Principle* give detailed introductions of his theories for the short story and poetry.

In his opinion, the poem should be as short as possible, and as long as it can produce the designed effect. Before starting writing, a poet should form a preconcerted purpose for his poem and then each word and phrase should serve this purpose so as to realize the effect of unification. To Poe, the major aim of all poems is beauty or supernatural beauty. Hence, he advocates the use of polished language and specific poetic devices to reach this objective and enhance the musical effect of the poetry.

In "To Helen", all this theories are put into practice. Only with three stanzas and fifteen lines, it is readable at one sitting. Its sole theme is to pay a tribute to the unearthly beauty who can guide wanderer to security or even the divine. This theme decides all the motifs, namely beauty motif, guidance motif and security motif, which aim at communicating this effect. Mainly three devices are adopted to achieve the effect of these motifs: diction, symbol and allusion.

To emphasize the beauty motif, the most important one of the three, the means of diction and allusion are used frequently. Though a tribute to Mrs. Jane Staunard, this poem is entitled "To Helen" instead of "To Jane". Here is an allusion to the Helen of Troy, a legendary beauty in the Greek mythology, who was said to be the daughter of Zeus and Leda (or Nemesis, according to other legends). Her goodliness attracted many suitors and she finally married Menelaus. Later, she was abducted by Paris to Troy. Hence, Helen became the basic cause for the Trojan War and the fall of Troy. Her lilies and roses, however, were never denied. To strengthen the beauty motif, the poet chooses many exquisite words and phrase in the first and second stanzas. For example, "gently" and "perfumed" depict the characteristic female features. "Perfumed sea" delineates Helen's aroma and its immense extension on the sea. In the second stanza, words supporting the image of an ideal beautiful woman include "hyacinth", "classic" and "Naiad airs". Here are another two allusions. One is "Naiad" that presents the fair water nymphs and the other is "hyacinth" that is a kind of plant, said to be springing from blood of the slain Hyacinthus, a handsome youth Apollo loved. Both are traditional symbols of beauty. Also in the previous two stanzas, the delineation of seas as "desperate" and the wanderer as "weary, wayworn" is in contrast to Helen's beauty, which reemphasizes Helen's beauty from the opposite perspective. In the third stanza, the motif of beauty is elevated and apotheosized through the diction of "statuelike" and the allusion to Psyche, Cupid's lover, who personifies "the breath of life, the human spirit or soul". Therefore, beauty here means not only a fair appearance but also intelligence and knowledge about the truth of immorality and divinity. The word "brilliant", though used to describe the place where Helen stands, can also be considered as a modifier of beauty.

As to the guidance motif, two symbols deserve attention. The first one is "Nicean barks of yore". Though the poet likens it to Helen's beauty, it doesn't stop at being a mere metaphor. It is a symbol of guidance and transportation. "Nicean barks of yore" is a kind of vessel in antiquity. To the weary and wayworn wanderer on the sea who is tortured by the endless roaming, the appearance of a boat undoubtedly stands for hope and salvation. The boat can draw him out of the fruitless voyages and lead him to a safe harbor that is "his own native shore". To equate this symbol of guidance to the goodliness of Helen stresses that beauty in the poem represents not only good looks but also guidance. Besides, this power of beauty is also indicated in the phrases "perfumed the sea". It is the extension of Helen's fragrance that enables the wanderer to trace the right route home. The other symbol appears in the final stanza, that is, "the agate lamp". In most literary works, lamp symbolizes rosiness, hope and destination. "To Helen" is not an exception. On the lonely and distressing journey, the lamp is like a lighthouse. What's more important, this only guidance is in the hand of Helen, the incarnation of beauty. As a matter of fact, in some legends, Helen of Troy is considered to be the Protector of Voyagers. Hence, the guidance motif is closely connected to the motif of beauty and what's more, sublimes the effect of the latter one. Guidance is, in fact, a bridge linking beauty and the wanderer's destiny—a place with security.

Then comes the motif of security. The first stanza ends with the line "to his own native shore". Here the use of the word "native" beings the sense of belonging and returning home where there is safety and stabilization. In the following stanza, the sense of home or security is put forward with an allusion to two greatest civilizations in the history—Greece and Rome. According to some mythologies, the achievements made in both periods are more or less related to Helen of Troy. This again links the motifs of beauty and security. Besides, "the glory that was Greece" and "the grandeur that was Rome" also symbolize the humankind's perfection and maintenance of humanity. This symbol implicates that merely returning to "native shore" may be insufficient in providing the wanderer with the sense of security. What are more important are the feelings of perfection and humanity. This motif of security is further sublimed in the final stanza by referring to "Holy Land" and using the word "agate" which in antiquity is a symbol of immorality. Both images contain the sense of the divine. Thereby, beauty, incarnated in Helen and then in Psyche, fulfills its task to guide the perplexed wanderer toward immorality, divinity and supernatural beauty. Actually, the divine should always be found beyond beauty.

With the support of three coherent motifs and the assistance of three major devices, Poe succeeded in producing the intense effect of the single theme. At last, his adoption of other poetic devices to add the musical impact of the poem cannot be neglected. In each stanza, Poe strictly sticks to the rhyme-scheme. And the use of monosyllabic words at the end of each line makes the poem read compact and finger-popping. Another specific device is alliteration and the most obvious example is the "weary, wayworn wanderer" which produces the impact like strong chords.

3. Archetypes of Female and Return in "To Helen"

Though Allan Poe insists that poems should be exquisitely structured and poets should create "art for art's sake", this principle doesn't deny the application of archetypal and mythological approaches to "To Helen". The reason is that "[n]o literary work survives because it is merely clever, merely well written. It must partake somehow of the universal and, in doing so, may contain elements of the archetypal" (Guerin, 2004: 175). Besides, Poe is also enthusiastic in referring to the antique scenes and issues in his works. Hence, it is appropriate to exam "To Helen" with archetypal concern. This poem is about beauty, and centers on returning home where there is security and even immorality. Here, at least two archetypes are involved: one is the archetype of women and the other is that of return.

The image of an archetypal woman, as an incarnation of beauty, impenetrates the whole poem. In the first stanza, this image can be interpreted as Good Mother, who ensures the "wanderer" with life and bestows him with transportation (through those "Nicean barks of yore"), protection and safety ("bore to his own native shore"). Furthermore, in the second stanza, the image of Good Mother is enriched and becomes concrete. She has "hyacinth hair", "classic face" and "Naiad airs". Here the word "hyacinth" indicates another archetype—blue. In ancients, hyacinth was a blue gem, probably sapphire. Now it can be used to mean a deep purplish blue. The color of blue has a positive archetypal meaning, indicating truth and security. It is the color of Good Mother. Besides, the archetype of blue is also a symbol of spiritual purity. From the perspective of this implication, the archetypal female in the poem can also be understood as the Soul Mate, which in literary works is usually personified as fair ladies and is the "incarnation of inspiration and spiritual fulfillment" (Guerin, 2004: 163). This kind of the female archetype is proved especially in the third stanza and the later part of the second one. Helen, the beautiful lady, as a Soul Mate, aids the wanderer with inspiration to reach the shore with great civilizations—"the glory that was Greece and the grandeur that was Rome". What's more, she even guides him further to the "Holy Land" where he can get spiritual security and return to the divine. The archetype of women, in acting out its function and bringing this fulfillment, is in contrast to the archetype of sea presented in the first and second stanza. According to Jung's archetypal theory, water is the "commonest symbol for the unconscious"(ibid. 161), the "desperate seas" here be explained in this sense. The boundless dark sea tortures the wanderer in the similar way that unconsciousness bewilders the innocent man.

The second major archetype is the one of return. The archetypal return to one's "own native land" and "home" with glories is associated to the sense of "returning to paradise" that implies the achievement of perfection. This archetype recurs in all the three stanzas. Though the wanderer in the poem is mostly the passive receiver of the archetypal woman's help and guidance, he, in the process of returning, also represents some characteristics of the hero archetype. One feature is that he takes an exhausting journey on the sea, in search of the routes to get back home. Another one is that he experiences the phases of separation, quest and return. In the first stanza, he is isolated from his "native shore" and trapped in the confusing dark seas. Then, with Helen's guidance, he reaches home blessed with great civilizations and finally returns to "Holy Land" to realize transformation and even immorality. The archetypal immortality is indicated through the references to the "statuelike" Helen, "Psyche" and "Holy Land".

In the poem, the two major archetypes are not isolated but closely interrelated. Since humankind was "brought into existence by some supernatural Being or beings" according to the motif of archetypal creation, then the return of lost men is also to be achieved by the power of a similar being, which is, in "To Helen", the supernatural beauty incarnated in the archetypal female. Hence, the archetypes of female and return are connect and become a whole.

References:

[1] Guerin, W. et al. *A Handbook of Critical Approaches to Literature.* Beijing: Foreign Language Teaching and Research Press, 2004.

[2] Mednick, Fred. *An Introduction to American Literature: from Newcomers to Naturalists.* Henan: Henan Univeristy Press, 2002.

[3] 曹曼. 美国文学名著导读. 武汉：武汉大学出版社，1999.

[4] 左金梅. 美国文学. 青岛：青岛海洋大学出版社，2000.

(孙艳艳)

Chapter 12　Rhythm and Rhyme

第十二章　节奏和音韵

> Poetry withers and dries out when it leaves music…
> poets who are not interested in music are, or become, bad
> poets.
>
> Ezra Pound

> The sound (of poetry) must seem an echo to the
> sense.
>
> Alexander Pope

> Rhythm must have meaning.
>
> Ezra Pound

简要介绍：

诗歌是阅读的艺术，也是朗诵的艺术。阅读诗歌可以使我们感悟到它那深远的意境，而朗诵诗歌可以使我们享受它那悠然的韵律。几乎所有经典诗歌的措辞都不会只关注诗词的意而忽略诗词的音，因为音是意的回声壁，恰如其分的音可以使意的传达更为优雅，更为意味深长。诗歌的音与意之间的这种特殊关系其实并不难理解，从最初的诗歌，比如民谣、史诗，到现代的抒情歌曲，许多诗都是以说唱的形式流传的，诗歌中运用的节奏、音韵、重复等技巧不仅方便说唱者的记忆、观众的接受和乐器的配音，而且以一种独特的方式传达着诗歌特有的意蕴。诗歌始终是富有乐律的，始终是超越语言的。

对诗歌的节奏和音韵的系统研究称为韵律学（prosody or versification）：

Prosody refers to the systematic study of versification in poetry, in other words, it is a study of the principles and practice of meter, rhyme, stanza forms as well as speech-sound patterns and effects of alliteration, assonance, etc.

简 析：

韵律学的主要研究内容可分为两个方面：诗的节奏，比如音步、诗节等；诗的音韵，比如尾韵、头韵等。本章将分两节分别介绍诗的节奏、诗的音韵，以及诗的节奏和音韵与诗的意义的传达之间的微妙关系。

第一节　诗的节奏

> **Rhythm** refers to the recurrent pattern of sounds with equivalent 'beats' at more or less equal intervals. **Rhythm in poetry** indicates a sequence of measured beats and "offbeats" arranged in verse lines, which govern the alternation of stressed and unstressed syllables.

简 析：

所谓"节奏"，我们通常也称为"节拍"，其实不过是音的有规律的重复。我们的生活充满了各种节奏：比较简单的节奏包括我们的心跳声、我们的呼吸声、闹钟的滴答声、雨水的滴答声、海浪的拍击声；比较复杂的节奏包括激昂的鼓声、动听的乐曲、优雅的舞步等。诗歌的节奏属于后一种，是诗人用语言创造的美的旋律。

从我们对诗歌的节奏作的界定定义中，我们可以看出，英语诗歌的节奏是由重音（stressed syllable）和轻音（unstressed syllable）的组合在诗行中不断重复而构成的。英诗中的重音和轻音按一定规律组合构成诗歌节奏中的最小单位，我们称之为音步（foot）。音步的数量的不同构成不同的英诗的格律（meter）。

在西方诗歌的发展中，曾出现 4 种格律类型：有按音量记数的（quantitative），即根据诗行（line）中音节的长短组合成格律的最小记数单位，古希腊和拉丁诗歌多采用这种格律；有按音节记数的（syllabic），即单独根据诗行中的音节数来记数，不考虑音节的轻重，法语诗歌曾采用这种记数法；有单独按重音记数的（accentual），即根据诗行中的重音数记数，不考虑诗行中的轻音，古德语和古英语诗歌曾采用这种记数法；有按诗行中的轻、重音组合来记数的（accentual-syllabic），这种格律自 14 世纪以后成为英语诗歌的主导格律类型。本章节介绍的主要是最后一种格律类型。

既然 14 世纪之后英诗的格律以轻音和重音的组合为记数单位，在我们详细介绍轻、重音的组合类型之前，我们首先要学会如何判断音节的轻和重。我们通常依照 3 条准则来判断音节的轻重：

1）对于有两个以上音节的英语单词而言，音节的轻重根据英语单词原有的音节轻重来定，比如"tiger"，重音就落在前面一个音节。

　2）对于只有一个音节的英语单词而言，音节的轻重根据英语单词的语法功能来决定——在一般情况下，所有的实词都是重音，包括：名词、动词、形容词、副词、数量词、感叹词；所有的虚词都是轻音，包括：代词、冠词、介词、连接词。特别予以强调的单词往往是重音。

　　3）在同一首诗或同一诗行中，如果基本上已经形成一种主导的格律，那么上面两条中所确定的音节的轻重可以根据该诗歌主导格律的要求而进行调整。

　　下面是英诗中轻重音节——或者说"音步"——的几种常见的类型：

> 1. 抑扬格（iambic）：an unstressed syllable followed by a stressed syllable.

简　析：

　　抑扬格是一种由轻音转入重音的格律，在英语诗歌中最为常见，因为它其实就是我们日常语言最基本的节律。抑扬格可以用于主题严肃的诗歌，也可以用于主题轻松的诗歌。下面我们将以"v"表示"轻音"，以"/"表示"重音"，以"|"表示音步之间的分界线，用具体例子说明抑扬格在英诗中的运用。

```
  v   /  v   /  v   /
She lived | in storm | and strife,
  v/   v   /  v   /
Her soul | had such | desire
```

(William Butler Yeats, That The Night Come, 1912)

> 2. 扬抑格（trochaic）：a stressed syllable followed by an unstressed syllable.

简　析：

　　扬抑格由重音转入轻音，在诗歌中不太常见，可以用于表达激昂、悲壮的主题。许多扬抑格诗行的最后一个轻音都是没有的，就像下面的诗行。

```
 /v   /v   /  v  /
Tyger! | Tyger ! | Burning | bright
```

(William Blake, The Tyger, 1794)

> 3. 抑抑扬格（anapestic）：two unstressed syllables followed by a stressed syllable.

简　析：

　　抑抑扬格和下面的扬扬抑格要比上面的两种格律，即抑扬格和扬抑格，更轻快和流畅一些。它们也常常被穿插在以抑扬格或扬抑格为主要格律的诗歌中。

```
        v v  /    v v /
He is called | by thy name,
      v v    /   v /   v /
For he calls | himself | a Lamb.
```

(William Blake, The Lamb, 1789)

---

4. 扬扬抑格（dactylic）: a stressed syllable followed by two unstressed syllables.

简　析：

```
/   v v  /   v v  /   v v  /   v v
Green as our | hope in it, | white as our | faith in it
```

(Swinburne)

---

5. 扬扬格（spondaic）: it consists two stressed syllables; most often it is used as
   a substitute for an iamb or trochee; it neither rises nor falls.

简　析：

　　扬扬格和抑抑格在英语诗歌中不会以主导格律出现，它们通常是在上面 4 种格律的诗行中偶尔出现的一种音步，以替换原来的格律，对某些音节进行强调（比如下面诗界节中第一行的"Breeze sent"）或快速转入下一个重音（比如抑抑格例句中的"is to"和"with the"）。

```
      /    /v   /   v  /   v
Breeze sent | a wrink | ling dark |ness
      v/    v/   v/
Across | the bay. | I knelt
      v/    v/   v   /
Beneath | an up | turned boat,
      v    /   v   v/   v   /
And, mo | ment by mo | ment, felt
```

(Timothy Steele, Waiting for the Storm, 1986)

---

6. 抑抑格（pyrrhic）: it consists of two unstressed syllables, most often it is used
   as a substitute for an iamb or trochee; it neither rises nor falls.

简　析：

　　v /　　v v　　v /　　v v　　v / v
My way | is to | begin | with the | beginning

(Byron, Don Juan，1819—1824)

　　上面诗行中最后的音步"beginning"中最后"ning"称为"imperfect foot"，是由单个音节组成，一般在诗行的最后。

　　英国诗人 Samuel Taylor Coleridge 曾用一首诗巧妙概括了上面介绍的几种音步的主要特征：

　　　　Trochee trips from long to short;
　　　　From long to long in solemn sort
　　　　Slow Spondee stalks; strong foot yet ill able
　　　　Ever to come up with Dactylic trisyllable.
　　　　Iambics march from short to long—
　　　　With a leap and a bound the swift Anapests throng.

　　在结束对英诗中音步的介绍之前，需要说明的一点是：英语诗歌一般由一种音步为主导，但并不是说诗歌中的所有音步都完全一致，常常会有其他类型的音步穿插在其中。下面我们不妨挑选一首诗，对其音步进行分析。

作　品：

A Tiny Cry within the Night

Lynn Johnston

v /　 v /　 v /　 v 　 /
A ti | ny cry | within | the night,
v /　 v 　 /　 v /　 v 　/
A mo | ther's touch, | a gen | tle light,
v /　 v 　/　 v 　/　 v 　/
A ro | cking chair,| a cheek | caressed,
v /　 v v　 v /　 v 　/
A ba | by to | a bo | som pressed,

```
v /   v v v /   v   /
A bun | dle in | a cot | replaced,
v /   v   /   v   /   v /
A mo | ther's foot | steps, soft, | retraced—
v   /   v   v v   /   v   /
She whis | pers as | the sha | dows creep…
 /   /   v   /   /   /   v  /
"Now let | me sleep! | Please, let | me sleep!!!"
```

简　析：

　　整首诗主导的音步是"抑扬格"，稍稍穿插了几个"抑抑格"和"扬扬格"。每一诗行都是 4 个音步。4 个音步的格律英语称为"Tetrameter"，因此这首诗的格律是"iambic tetrameter"。

　　下面我们将英语诗歌格律（meter）的英文名称列表如下：

monometer:	one foot
dimeter:	two feet
trimeter :	three feet
tetrameter:	four feet
pentameter:	five feet
hexameter:	six feet
heptameter:	seven feet
octameter:	eight feet

　　每一首英诗的格律一般由两部分构成，即诗歌"音步的类型"和"音步的数量"，因此我们称上面的诗歌格律为"iambic tetrameter"。"iambic tetrameter"是英诗中比较常见的格律。

> **Stanza** refers to a group of verse lines forming a section of a poem, which shares the same lengths of lines, meter, and rhythm scheme with other sections of the same poem, or at least with some of the other sections. Stanzas are separated by spaces.

简　析：

　　我们知道，英语诗歌每隔几行就会有一行空格，这些由空格分割的诗行就称为诗节。在传统诗歌中，诗节一般具有以下特征：同一诗节中诗行的长度、格律大致相同，同一首诗歌中诗节的行数、音韵大致相同。

从英语诗歌发展的历史来看，诗节主要有下面几种类型：双行诗节（couplet）、三行诗节（triplet or tercet）、四行诗节（quatrain）。另外还有八行诗节（ottava rima）和斯宾诺塞诗节（Spenserian stanza）。

1）双行诗（Couplet）：a stanza of two lines, usually with end-rhymes

例：

> Poems are made by fools like me,
> But only God can make a tree.
>
> (Joyce Kilmer)

英雄双行诗（Heroic couplet）：a rhyming couplet of iambic pentameter

例：

> Some foreign writers, some our own despise;
> The ancients only, or the moderns, prize.
>
> (Pope)

2）三行诗节（Triplet or Tercet）：a three-line stanza, usually with one rhyme

例：

> You've seen a strawberry
> that's had a struggle; yet
> was, where the fragments met,
>
> (Marianne Moore)

三行连环韵诗（Terza rima）：a poem composed of tercets which are interlinked, in that each is jointed to the one following by a common rhyme: aba, bcb, cdc, and so on.

这类诗歌最典型的例子是雪莱的《西风颂》（*Ode to the West Wind*）。

3）四行诗节（Quatrain）：a four-line stanza, the most commonly used English versification, with various meters and rhyme schemes

例：

> Before man came to blow it right
> The wind once blew itself untaught,
> And did its loudest day and night
> In any rough place where it caught.
>
> (Robert Frost)

英雄四行诗节（Heroic Quatrain）：a four-line stanza, with iambic pentameter, rhyming abab

例：

> Now fades the glimmering landscape on the sight,
> And all the air a solemn stillness holds,
> Save where the beetle wheels his droning flight,
> And drowsy tinklings lull the distant folds;

（Thomas Gray）

4）八行诗节（ottava rima）：a stanza with 8 lines, rhyming ababdabcc

例：拜伦的 *Don Juan*。

5）斯宾诺塞诗节（Spenserian stanza）：a stanza devised by Edmund Spenser, with 9 lines, in which the first 8 lines are iambic pentameter and the last iambic hexameter, rhyming ababbcbcc.

例：斯宾诺塞的 *The Faerie Queene*。

第二节　诗的音韵

> **Rhyme** refers to the identity of sound between syllables or paired groups of syllables, usually at the ends of verse lines. Normally, it is the last stressed vowel in the line and all sounds following it that make up the rhyming element.
>
> For example:
>
> love/above (monosyllable，masculine rhyme)
>
> wh*ether* / tog*ether* (two syllables，feminine rhyme)
>
> gl*amourous* / *amorous* (three syllables，triple rhyme)

简　析：

诗的音韵是诗歌韵律学研究中另外一个重要部分。所谓"音韵"（rhyme），简单地说，就是指两个和两个以上的单词或词组中元音和元音之后的辅音的重复。

诗歌的音韵中最常见的是"尾韵"（end-rhyme），即诗行中最后的元音以及元音后的辅音与另一诗行中最后的元音以及元音后的辅音之间的重复。比如，下面这一诗节中的"sh*ake*"、"mist*ake*"和"fl*ake*"。这一诗节中的押韵我们可以用"aaba"来表示。

> He gives his harness bells a sh*ake*
> To ask if there is some mist*ake*.
> The only other sound's the sweep
> Of easy wind and downy fl*ake*.

（Robert Frost）

诗歌的音韵中另一种形式是"行间韵"（internal rhyme），即同一诗行中两个或两个以上单词之间最后的元音以及元音后的辅音的重复。比如，下面诗行中的"*napping*"和"*tapping*"。

> While I nodded nearly napping, suddenly there came a tapping

尾韵和行间韵由于所押韵的元音数量的不同，在英语中有三种不同名称，其中第一种最常见。

"masculine rhyme",	比如："sh*ake*"、"mist*ake*"、"fl*ake*"
"feminine rhyme" or "double rhyme",	比如："n*apping*"、"t*apping*"
"triple rhyme"	比如："gl*amourous*"、"*amorous*"

诗歌的音韵还有两种形式是"头韵"（alliteration）和"母韵"（assonance）。

"头韵"即诗行中相近的两个或两个以上单词的头一个辅音之间的重复。比如，下面诗行中的"black"、"blackberries"、"breakfast"。

> I love to go out in late September
> among the fat, overripe, icy, **b**lack **b**lackberries
> to eat **b**lackberries for **b**reakfast,

> (Galway Kinnell)

"母韵"即诗行中相近的两个或两个以上单词中的相同元音的重复。比如，下面诗行中的"bride"、"quietness"、"child""silence""time"。

> Thou still unravished bride of quietness,
>   Thou foster child of silence and slow time,

> (John Keats)

"头韵"和"母韵"可用于表达对某种意义的强调，或用于突出两个或多个相关词语之间的微妙关系，或用于突出某种色彩、语调、氛围等。

作 品：

Stopping by Woods on a Snowy Evening

Robert Frost

Whose woods these are I think I know.
His house is in the village though;
He will not see me stopping here

To watch his woods fill up with snow.

My little horse must think it queer
To stop without a farmhouse near
Between the woods and frozen lake
The darkest evening of the year.

He gives his harness bells a shake
To ask if there is some mistake.
The only other sound's the sweep
Of easy wind and downy flake.

The woods are lovely, dark, and deep,
But I have promises to keep,
And miles to go before I sleep,
And miles to go before I sleep.

赏　析：

　　这首诗歌共有 4 个诗节，每个诗节有 4 个诗行，这样的诗节在英诗中最为常见；诗歌的格律也是英诗中常见的 4 音步抑扬格（iambic tetrameter）。诗歌常见的格律形式与诗歌措辞的简洁和诗歌基调的恬淡形成一种和谐的氛围，让人在这个雪天的夜晚，目睹了一幅最为普通，却又是最美丽的乡村雪景画；聆听了一个最为普通，却又是最为典型的人面对自然所发出的感叹。第一诗节描绘了一种静态的美：诗歌中的我，在夜深人静的时刻，站在远离村庄，又不属于我的树林中，静静地观赏林中雪景。寥寥几笔，给人美的感受的同时，也给人留下了困惑：半夜？在别人的林中赏雪？第二诗节借用马的疑问，清楚地道出了这种常人的困惑，这一诗节特别点出了在这个隆冬的夜晚中，树林的黑暗和寒冷：这是一年中最黑的夜晚，而"我"正站在白雪覆盖的树林和结冰的湖水之间。于是，第三诗节让马儿轻轻摇动马具上的铃，发出了响亮的质疑，这铃声突出了树林的寂静：除了静静的风声和雪花悄然落地的声音，再没有其他的响动了。第四诗节用"The woods are lovely, dark, and deep"回答了上面三个诗节的疑问，让读者感受到了"我"对林中美景深深的留恋，这里的"lovely, dark, and deep"恰好是对前三个诗节的最精练的概括和提炼。然而，"我"终于用一个"But"终结了我对自然美景的依恋，带着我的"promises"继续前行。

　　对于诗歌的主题，我们通常都通过对一些关键词作象征意义的阐释，读出我们的理解，然而，你有没有注意到这首诗歌的尾韵正以一种独特的方式，向读者述说着诗歌的意韵。

诗歌的尾韵是：aaba, bbcb, ccdc, dddd。也就是说，诗歌的前 3 个诗节中，每个诗节中有 3 个诗行押韵，而该诗节中不押韵的诗行与下一个诗节中的 3 个诗行押韵，依此类推，直至第 4 个诗节中所有的诗行都押韵。这样循环押韵的模式使我们不断在新的音节和原有的音节之间来回往返，从音节的离去和回归之中感受诗歌的说话人在欲望与责任之间的艰难取舍。用音的循环来表达矛盾的心境，这的确是一种绝妙的方法，不过，这只是很多种方法中的一种，如果你细细品味每一首诗歌的音韵和节奏，你可以感受到诗歌独具匠心的美。

Chapter 13　Types of Poetry

第十三章　诗歌的基本类型

> **Narrative poetry** is the type of poems，including ballads, epics, and verse romances, that tell stories, as distinct from dramatic and lyric poetry.
>
> **Dramatic poetry,** originally referring to the class of verse composing for theatrical performance, is now extended to non-theatrical poems which involve a similar kind of impersonation, mainly used in the closet drama and the dramatic monologue.
>
> **Lyric poetry** refers to short poems expressing the personal mood, feeling, or meditation of a single speaker. It is now the most popular type of poetry since the decline of narrative and dramatic poetry in the 19th century in the west. The common traditional lyric forms include the sonnet, ode, elegy, and epigram, while the modern form may be composed in almost any meter and on almost any subject.

简　析：

　　诗歌的基本类型有三种，即叙事诗（Narrative poetry）、戏剧诗（Dramatic poetry）、抒情诗（Lyric poetry）。

　　根据定义，比较分析三种诗歌形式，可以看出三种诗不同的用途决定了它们的区别：叙事诗主要用于讲述故事，戏剧诗主要用于再现戏剧中的人物对话和独白，抒情诗则主要用于表达情感。19 世纪以后，叙事诗和戏剧诗相继衰微，唯有抒情诗依然广泛用于表达现代人的情感，诗的形式也早已经突破了传统的模式。

　　本节将简要介绍传统上最广泛使用的两种诗歌类型——叙事诗和抒情诗，并附上一些现代诗。

第一节　叙事诗

叙事诗的主要类型有两种，民谣（ballad）和史诗（the epic）。

民　谣

> **Ballad** is a folk song, orally transmitted, which tells a story directly or dramatically. The story, which is mostly derived from an incident in local history or legend, is always told simply, impersonally, and with dialogue. Ballads are normally composed in quatrains with alternating four-stress and three-stress lines, the second and fourth lines rhyming; but some ballads are in couplet form, or in six-line stanzas.

简　析：

　　形成于中世纪后期，民谣在当时的欧洲主要流行在没有文化的民众中间，以口头流传的方式的讲述着神秘的、历史的、传奇的悲剧故事。它的基本特征很明显：

　　1）它的创作者是无名氏，由于是口头流传，内容和曲调往往是经多人吟唱后定型。

　　2）它有比较固定的结构和形式，一般以 4 行为一个诗节，每一诗节中的第 2 行与第 4 行押韵，也有采用双行诗节的。

　　3）它的语言简洁，用词简单，常以非个人化的语调，以戏剧对白的方式展示故事情节的发展，短语和诗节的重复是最常用的修辞手段。

作　品：

Lord Randal

Anonymous

"O where hae ye been, Lord Randal, my son?
O where hae ye been, my handsome young man?"
"I hae been to the wild wood; mother, make my bed soon,
For I'm weary wi hunting, and fain wald lie down."

"Where gat ye your dinner, Lord Randal, my son?

Where gat ye your dinner, my handsome young man?"
"I dined wi my true-love; mother, make my bed soon,
For I'm weary wi hunting, and fain wald lie down."

"Where gat ye to your dinner, Lord Randal, my son?
Where gat ye to your dinner, my handsome young man?"
"I gat eels boiled in broo; mother, make my bed soon,
For I'm weary wi hunting, and fain wald lie down."

"What became of your bloodhounds, Lord Randal, my son?
What became of your bloodhounds, my handsome young man?"
"O they swelled and they died; mother, make my bed soon,
For I'm weary wi hunting, and fain wald lie down."

"O I fear ye are poisoned, Lord Randal, my son?
O I fear ye are poisoned, my handsome young man?"
"O yes! I am poisoned; mother, make my bed soon,
For I'm sick at the heart, and I fain wald lie down."

史　诗

> **Epic** is a long narrative poem celebrating the great and serious deeds of one or more legendary heroes or quasi-divine figures, in a formal, grand and elevated style. The hero or quasi-divine figure, who is usually protected by or even descended from gods, performs, with superhuman power, in battle or in marvelous voyages, to save or to found a tribe, a nation, or the human race itself.

简　析：

最著名的口头流传的"传统史诗"包括：
Homer's *Iliad* and *Odyssey* (8th century BC)
the Anglo-Saxon epic *Beowulf* (8th century AD)
the French epic *Chanson de Roland* (12th century AD)
the Spanish epic *Poema del Cid* (12th century AD)
the German epic *Nibelungenlied* (13th century AD)

最经典的书面流传的"文学史诗"包括：

Virgil's *Aeneid* (30—20 BC)

Milton's *Paradise Lost* (1667)

作为欧洲文学史上历史最悠久的文学类型，史诗曾被亚里士多德列为仅次于悲剧的体裁，被众多文艺复兴的诗人们誉为最伟大的体裁。作为英雄时代的时代精神和理想的最恢弘的记载方式，史诗不仅记录了古代神人和勇士的惊天动地的壮举和伟绩，也记录了人类历史最厚重的想象和理想。直至今天，我们还常常用"史诗式的"这样的形容词来赞誉那些描述人类英雄伟业的长篇小说和电影，比如托尔斯泰的小说《战争与和平》，比如电影《特洛伊》和《亚历山大大帝》。人类不能没有时代精神和理想。

史诗通常有下列创作特征：

1）史诗中的人物不是神人就是英雄，他们肩负着拯救国家、民族，甚至整个人类的重任。

2）史诗的故事背景宏大而开阔，故事的发生地可能是在国家范围内，也可能在世界范围内，甚至扩展到宇宙范围内。

3）史诗人物的行为常带有超自然的神力，因此他们的业绩通常是惊天动地的。

4）史诗故事发展的情节中常掺和着上帝、众神或其他超自然力量的干预。

5）史诗的叙述风格高雅，措辞正式，句法精妙，基调庄严。

作　品：

下面是英国著名诗人弥尔顿（John Milton）的《失乐园》（Paradise Lost）的开头部分：

Paradise Lost

John Milton

Of man's first disobedience, and the fruit

Of that forbidden tree whose mortal taste

Brought death into the world, and all our woe,

With loss of Eden, till one greater Man

Restore us, and regain the blissful seat,

Sing, Heavenly Muse, that, on the secret top

Of Oreb, or of Sinai, didst inspire

That shepherd who first taught the chosen seed

In the beginning how the Heavens and Earth

Rose out of Chaos: or, if Sion hill

Delight thee more, and Siloa's brook that flowed

Fast by the oracle of God. I thence

Invoke thy aid to my adventurous song,

That with no middle flight intends to soar

Above th' Aonian mount, while it pursues

Things unattempted yet in prose or rhyme.

And chiefly thou, O Spirit, that does prefer

Before all temples th' upright heart and pure,

Instruct me, for thou know'st; thou from the first

Wast present, and, with mighty wings outspread,

Dovelike sat'st brooding on the vast abyss,

And mad'st it pregnant: what in me is dark

Illumine; what is low, raise and support:

That, to the height of this great argument,

I may assert Eternal Providence,

And justify the ways of God to men.

第二节　抒情诗

抒情诗的主要类型有四种，警句诗（epigram）、哀歌（elegy）、颂歌（ode）、十四行诗（sonnet）。

警句诗

> **Epigram** refers to a statement in verse or prose, which is terse, pointed, and witty. The epigram may be on any subject, with mostly satirical style.

简　析：

在古希腊时期，"epigram"原指适合于刻在墓碑上的铭文，后来由罗马诗人马提雅尔发展为一种简短、精辟、诙谐、辛辣的诗歌的形式。17、18 世纪，警句诗在英国、法国、德国比较流行，一些著名的英国作家都曾写过警句诗，比如 John Donne、Ben Jonson、Alexander Pope、Samuel Taylor Coleridge、Oscar Wilde 等。

作　品：

What Is an Epigram?

Samuel Taylor Coleridge

What is an epigram? A dwarfish whole;
Its body brevity, and wit its soul.

Epigram Engraved on the Collar of a Dog
Which I Gave to His Royal Highness

Alexander Pope

I am his Highness' dog at Kew;
Pray tell me, sir, whose dog are you?

哀　歌

> **Elegy** is an elaborately formal lyric poem lamenting the death of a friend or public figure, or reflecting seriously on a solemn subject.

简　析：

在古希腊文学和拉丁文学中，"哀歌"是指一种用特定的哀歌格律写作的诗歌，题材不限。自 16 世纪以来，英国文学中的"哀歌"只用于指称表现哀伤内容的诗歌，或者哀悼亲朋好友或公众人物的去世，或者表达对死亡的残酷性的沉思，其格律不限。

较为著名的哀歌有：

Thomas Gray "Elegy Written in a Country Churchyard" (1751) (a lament for the passing of men and the things they value)

Alfred Tennyson "In Memoriam" (1850) (a lament for the death of his friend Arthur Hallam)

Walt Whitman "When Lilacs Last in the Dooryard Bloom'd" (1865) (a lament for the death of a public figure, Abraham Lincoln)

W. H. Auden "In Memory of W. B. Yeats" (1940)

作　品：

下面是 Thomas Gray "Elegy Written in a Country Churchyard" (1751) 的头两个诗节。

Elegy Written in a Country Churchyard

Thomas Gray

The curfew tolls the knell of parting day,

　　The lowing herd wind slowly o'er the lea,

The plowman homeward plods his weary way,

　　And leaves the world to darkness and to me.

Now fades the glimmering landscape on the sight,

　　And all the air a solemn stillness holds,

Save where the beetle wheels his droning flight,

　　And drowsy tinklings lull the distant folds.

颂　歌

> **Ode** is a long stately lyric poem which is serious in subject, elevated in style, and elaborate in structure.

简　析：

颂歌的源头有两个，一是由希腊诗人品达（Pindar）创建于公元前 5 世纪的希腊合唱颂歌，用于赞誉奥林匹克运动会中获胜的运动员，诗歌充满了激情，措辞正式。二是由贺拉斯用拉丁文创作的颂歌，创建于公元前 1 世纪，语调冷静，充满玄想，语言比较口语化。品达的颂歌由三部分组成：诗节、反诗节、结句，前面两个部分格律一致，最后一部分的格律与前两个部分不同；贺拉斯的颂歌是由格律相同的诗节多次重复构成。Thomas Gray、John Dryden、William Collins、William Wordsworth、P. B. Shelley 等诗人沿用或创新了品达的颂歌模式，而 John Keats 则采用了贺拉斯的颂歌模式。

著名的颂歌包括：

Wordsworth "Ode to Duty"

Coleridge "Dejection: An Ode"

Shelley "Ode to the West Wind"

John Keats "Ode on a Grecian Urn", "Ode to a Nightingale"

作　品：

Ode on a Grecian Urn

John Keats

1

Thou still unravish'd bride of quietness,

　Thou foster child of silence and slow time,

Sylvan historian, who canst thus express

　A flowery tale more sweetly than our rhyme:

What leaf-fring'd legend haunts about thy shape

　Of deities or mortals, or of both,

　　In Tempe or the dales of Arcady?

　What men or gods are these? What maidens loath?

What mad pursuit? What struggle to escape?

　What pipes and timbrels? What wild ecstasy?

2

Heard melodies are sweet, but those unheard

　Are sweeter; therefore, ye soft pipes, play on;

Not to the sensual ear, but more endear'd,

Pipe to the spirit ditties of no tone:

Fair youth, beneath the trees, thou canst not leave

Thy song, nor ever can those trees be bare;

Bold Lover, never, never canst thou kiss,

Though winning near the goal—yet, do not grieve;

She cannot fade, though thou hast not thy bliss,

Forever wilt thou love, and she be fair!

3

Ah, happy, happy boughs! That cannot shed

Your leaves, nor ever bid the Spring adieu;

And, happy melodist, unwearied,

Forever piping songs forever new;

More happy love! more happy, happy love!

Forever warm and still to be enjoy'd,

Forever panting, and forever young;

All breathing human passion far above,

That leaves a heart high-sorrowful and cloy'd,

A burning forehead, and a parching tongue.

4

Who are these coming to the sacrifice?

To what green altar, O mysterious priest,

Lead'st thou that heifer lowing at the skies,

And all her silken flanks with garlands dressed?

What little town by river or sea shore,

Or mountain-built with peaceful citadel,

Is emptied of this folk, this pious morn?

And, little town, thy streets forevermore

Will silent be; and not a soul to tell

Why thou art desolate, can e'er return.

5

O Attic shape! Fair attitude! With brede

Of marble men and maidens overwrought,

With forest branches and the trodden weed;

Thou, silent form, dost tease us out of thought

As doth eternity: Cold Pastoral!

When old age shall this generation waste,

Thou shalt remain, in midst of other woe

Than ours, a friend to man, to whom thou say'st,

"Beauty is truth, truth beauty,"—that is all

Ye know on earth, and all ye need to know.

十四行诗

> **Sonnet** is a lyric poem consisting of a single stanza of 14 iambic pentameter lines linked by an intricate rhyme scheme.

简　析：

　　十四行诗大约起源于 13 世纪西西里诗派宫廷诗人，14 世纪在意大利诗人彼特拉克笔下基本成型，其主要结构特征是：前 8 行说一件事或提出一个问题，后 6 行解决或回答问题；前 8 行称为 "octave"，其尾韵为 "abbaabba"，后 6 行称为 "sestet"，其尾韵为 "cdecde" 或 "cdcdcd"。这一类型的诗歌被统称为意大利十四行诗或彼特拉克体十四行诗（Petrarchan sonnet），其主题主要是爱情。到 16 世纪，意大利十四行诗被引入欧洲其他国家，在英、法、德等国出现了各种变体，其中英国十四行诗流传十分广泛。英国十四行诗或称莎士比亚体十四行诗（Shakespearean sonnet）由 3 个 4 行诗句和最后 1 个押韵的对句组成，其基本韵式为"abab cdcd efef gg"，主要的变体为"abab bcbc cdcd ee"。最后的对句通常要求简洁有力地概括前 3 个 4 行诗句。到 17 世纪英国诗人多恩（Donne）突破十四行诗原有的爱情主题，创作了宗教主题的十四行诗，弥尔顿创作了以政治、宗教或个人经历为主题的十四行诗，此后，十四行诗开始用于表达各种主题。18 世纪时，十四行诗曾遭冷落，到 19 世纪又开始盛行，英国诗人 Wordsworth，Keats 等都曾用这一诗体写出著名诗句。

作　品：

Italian sonnet:

On First Looking into Chapman's Homer[1]

John Keats

Much have I travell'd in the realms[2] of gold,	a
And many goodly states and kingdoms seen;	b
Round many western islands have I been	b
Which bards[3] in fealty[4] to Apollo[5] hold.	a
Oft of one wide expanse had I been told	a
That deep-brow'd Homer ruled as his demesne[6];	b
Yet did I never breathe its pure serene[7]	b
Till I heard Chapman speak out loud and bold:	a
Then felt I like some watcher of the skies	c
When a new planet swims into his ken[8];	d
Or like stout Cortez[9] when with eagle eyes	c
He star'd at the Pacific—and all his men	d
Look'd at each other with a wild surmise[10]—	c
Silent, upon a peak in Darien.	d

简　析：

Rhyme scheme: abba abba cdc dcd

The first eight lines of the sonnet compares the speaker's wide reading with traveling. Lines 9-14 vividly illustrate the speaker's feelings upon his first reading of Chapman's translation of Homer's great epic poems, *The Iliad* and *The Odyssey*. The octave and the

---

1 Chapman's Homer: The translation of Homer's *Odyssey* by George Chapman.
2 realm: a general area of knowledge, interest and thought.
3 bard: a poet.
4 fealty: loyalty to a king, queen, etc.
5 Apollo: god of sun and poetic inspiration.
6 demesne: domain.
7 serene: atmosphere.
8 ken: knowledge.
9 Cortez: Spanish conqueror of Mexico who was the first European to see the Pacific from Darien in Panama.
10 surmise: to guess that something is true.

sestet differ in diction and syntax. The diction in octave is formal and elevated, with some archaic words like "bards" and "goodly". Such diction creates an impression of the remoteness, and the grandeur. The syntax is smooth and complete. In the sestet, the diction is simple and direct; the syntax is somewhat broken through the use of dashes. (Dashes are used to indicate the speaker's emotion.) Moreover, comparisons are used to convey the excitement of the discovery. In line 12 and line 13, the description of actions "stared" and "looked", and the depiction of reaction "wild surmise" and "silent" vividly express the speaker's excitement.

作　品：

English sonnet or Shakespearean sonnet:

Sonnet 18

William Shakespeare

Shall I compare thee to a summer's day?
Thou art more lovely and more temperate:
Rough winds do shake the darling buds of May,
And summer's lease hath all too short a date;
Sometime too hot the eye of heaven shines,
And often is his gold complexion dimmed;
And every fair from fair sometime declines,
By chance or nature's changing course untrimmed;
But thy eternal summer shall not fade,
Nor lose possession of that fair thou ow'st;
Nor shall death brag thou wander'st in his shade,
When in eternal lines to time thou grow'st:
　So long as men can breathe, or eyes can see,
　So long lives this, and this gives life to thee.

Rhyme scheme: abab cdcd efef gg

第三节 现代诗

> **Open form** refers to the form of a poem which is not written in a fixed or predominant meter or rhyme. Many poets, especially those in and after the 20th century, have resisted the limitations of the poem with a consistent and specific metrical pattern or rhyming scheme. They either use the traditional fixed forms in more flexible ways, or create their own unique form. Open form does not indicate formlessness, it organizes its rhythmic qualities through the repetition of words, phrases, grammatical structures, or other specific ways.

简要介绍：

许多诗歌，特别是创作于20世纪的诗歌大都只能被称为自由诗（free verse）或开放诗（open form），因为它们不再像传统诗歌那样遵循一种固定的模式，束缚于特定的韵律和节奏。不过，这并不是说现代诗就毫无韵律和节奏，只是它们的韵律和节奏通过其他更为自由奔放、无拘无束的方式来表现，比如词句的重复、特殊的语法结构、特殊的形式等更为内在的方式。我们不妨来欣赏几首。

作 品：

The Soul, Reaching, Throwing Out for Love

Walt Whitman

The Soul, reaching, throwing out for love,
As the spider, from some little promontory, throwing out filament after filament,
tirelessly out of itself, that one at least may catch and form a link, a bridge,
a connection
O I saw one passing along, saying hardly a word—yet full of love I detected
him, by certain signs
O eyes wishfully turning! O silent eyes!
For then I thought of you o'er the world,
O latent oceans, fathomless oceans of love!
O waiting oceans of love! yearning and fervid! and of you sweet souls perhaps
in the future, delicious and long:
But Death, unknown on the earth—ungiven, dark here, unspoken, never born:

You fathomless latent souls of love—you pent and unknown oceans of love!

(1862)

The Red Wheelbarrow

William Carlos Williams

so much depends
upon

a red wheel
barrow

glazed with rain
water

beside the white
chickens.

(1923)

l(a

E. E. Cummings

l(a

le
af
fa

ll

s)
one
l

iness

简　析：

It is a visual poem, which strikes the eye as a series of letters flowing from the page, for the most part two to a line. If we rearrange the poem, we find these words: "l (a leaf falls) oneliness". When we rearrange the poem, we find that the poem consists of two parts: "loneliness" and "a leaf falls". The falling of a leaf is usually a symbol of loneliness, it is not special, what is unique is that e. e. cumming separates the words into fragments, indicating that separation is the primary cause of loneliness. And through separation, e. e. cumming singles out the word "one", suggesting his understanding: loneliness is oneliness. And the similarity between the initial letter "l" and the number "1" further stresses the theme of the poem.

Chapter 14　Poems for Further Reading

第十四章　延伸阅读诗歌选

Trees

Joyce Kilmer

I think that I shall never see
A poem lovely as a tree.

A tree whose hungry mouth is press
Against the earth's sweet flowing breast;

A tree that looks at God all day;
And lifts her leafy arms to pray;

A tree that may in summer wear
A nest of robins in her hair;

Upon whose bosom snow has lain;
Who intimately lives with rain.

Poem are made by fools like me,
But only God can make a tree.

Questions:

1. What does the poet compare the poem with?
2. What kind of writing technique is adopted in the poem?
3. How lovely is a tree?
4. What is the theme of the poem?

Loveliest of Trees

A. E. Housman

Loveliest of Trees, the cherry now
Is hung with bloom along the bough,
And stands about the woodland ride[1]
Wearing white for Eastertide[2].

Now, of my threescore[3] years and ten,
Twenty will not come again,
And take from seventy springs a score[4],
It only leaves me fifty more.

And since to look at things in bloom
Fifty springs are little room,
About the woodlands I will go
To see the cherry hung with snow.

Questions:

1. How old is the speaker?
2. How do you understand the following words: cherry, white, spring, bloom, snow?
3. What is the theme of the poem?

---

1 ride: path.
2 Eastertide: the Easter holidays, a Christian holy day in March and April when Christians remember the death of Christ and his return to life.
3 threescore: old use for 60.
4 score: 20.

Tree at My Window

Robert Frost

Tree at my window, window tree,

My sash[1] is lowered when night comes on;
But let there never be curtain drawn
Between you and me.

Vague dream-head lifted out of the ground,
And thing next most diffuse[2] to cloud,
Not all your light tongues talking aloud
Could be profound.

But, tree, I have seen you taken and tossed,
And if you have seen me when I slept,
You have seen me when I was taken and swept
And all but lost.

That day she put our heads together,
Fate had her imagination about her,
Your head so much concerned with outer,
Mine with inner, weather[3].

Questions:

1. What is the dominant tone of the words?
2. What does "she" refer to?
3. What is the relationship between "you" and "me"?
4. What is the theme of the poem?

---

1 sash: a wooden frame that has a sheet of glass fixed into it to form part of a window.
2 diffuse: scatter.
3 weather: the temperature and other conditions such as sun, rain, cloud, and wind.

A Christmas Tree

William Burford

Star,
If you are
A love compassionate[1],
You will walk with us this year.
We face a glacial[2] distance, who are here
Huddld[3]
At your feet.

Questions:

1. What does "star" refer to?
2. What is the relationship between "you" and "we"?
3. What is the theme of the poem?

Woman Work

Maya Angelou

I've got the children to tend
The clothes to mend
The floor to mop
The food to shop
Then the chicken to fry
The baby to dry
I got company to feed
The garden to weed
I've got the shirts to press
The tots to dress
The cane to cut

---

1 compassionate: (adj.) feeling sympathy for people who are suffering.
2 glacial: extremely cold.
3 Huddld: misspelling for huddled, gathered together, especially because of cold or fright.

I gotta clean up this hut
Then see about the sick
And the cotton to pick.

Shine on me, sunshine
Rain on me, rain
Fall softly, dewdrops
And cool my brow again.

Storm, blow me from here
With your fiercest wind
Let me float across the sky
'Til I can rest again.

Fall gently, snowflakes
Cover me with white
Cold icy kisses and
Let me rest tonight.

Sun, rain, curving sky
Mountain, oceans, leaf and stone
Star shine, moon glow
You're all that I can call my own.

Questions:

1. What is the feature of the punctuation in the poem? How do you interpret it?
2. Who is the speaker? What is she/he seeking?

If Thou Must Love Me

Elizabeth Barrett Browning

If thou must love me, let it be for naught
Except for love's sake only. Do not say
"I love her for her smile—her look—her way

Of speaking gently—for a trick of thought

That falls in well with mine, and certes brought

A sense of pleasant ease on such a day"—

For these things in themselves, Beloved, may

Be changed, or change for thee-and love, so wrought,

May be unwrought so. Neither love me for

Thine own dear pity's wiping my cheeks dry—

A creature might forget to weep, who bore

Thy comfort long, and lose thy love thereby!

But love me for love's sake, that evermore

Thou mayst love on, through love's eternity.

Questions:

1. Who is the speaker, a man or a woman? Why?

2. How does she/he understand love?

3. How does she/he express her philosophy of love?

Blackberry Sweet

Dudley Randall

Black girl black girl

lips as curved as cherries

full as grape bunches

sweet as blackberries

Black girl black girl

when you walk you are

magic as a rising bird

or a falling star

Black girl black girl

what's your spell to make

the heart in my breast

jump   stop   shake

Questions:

1. What make the poem unique?
2. How does the speaker exactly want to say?

To Spring

Henry Wadsworth Longfellow

Oh you, sweet spring, alight from cherub's wing,
And put the ugly winter full to flight;
And rouse the earth to smile, and larks to sing,
With skies so bright and hearts of youth so light.
Your gentle and genial breaths each blossom blow,
While bees in gardens hum the lullabies.
The hills and dales are stripped of mantles of snow,
And streams and rivers freed from irons of ice.
May seasons all be spring—the pride of years,
That all the things would e're in glories gleam!
May man be ever in the prime of the year!
But dream, however sweet, is but a dream.
If happy when you come and sad when gone,
Would that you'd never gone or never gone!

Questions:

1. Who is the speaker?
2. What is the tone? How do you know?

Crossing the Bar[1]

Alfred Tennyson

Sunset and evening star,
And one clear call for me!

---

1 Although not the last poem written by Tennyson, it appears, at his quest, as the final poem in all collections of his work.

And may there be no moaning of the bar,
    When I put out to sea.

But such a tide as moving seems asleep,
    Too full for sound and foam,
When that which drew from out the boundless deep
    Turns again home.

Twilight and evening bell,
    And after that the dark!
And may there be no sadness of farewell,
    When I embark;

For though from out our bourne[1] of Time and Place
    The flood may bear me far,
I hope to see my Pilot face to face
    When I have crossed the bar.

Questions:

1. What is the poem talking about? What does the "bar" symbol?
2. What is the tone of the poem? How do you know?

A Red, Red Rose

Robert Burns

O my luve's like a red, red rose,
    That's newly sprung in June;
O my luve's like the melodie
    That's sweetly played in tune.
As fair art thou, my bonnie lass,
    So deep in luve am I;
And I will luve thee still, my dear,
    Till a' the seas gang dry.

---

1 bourne: boundary.

Till a' the seas gang dry, my dear,
　And the rocks melt wi' the sun:
O I will love thee still, my dear,
　While the sands o' life shall run.

And fare thee weel, my only luve,
　And fare thee weel awhile!
And I will come again, my luve,
　Though it were ten thousand mile.

Questions:

1. What is the subject-matter of the poem?
2. What is the tone? How does the poet create the tone?

Spring

William Shakespeare

When daisies pied and violets blue,
　And lady-smocks all silver-white,
And cuckoo-buds of yellow hue
　Do paint the meadows with delight,
The cuckoo then, on every tree,
Mocks married men; for thus sings he,
　　　　"Cuckoo!
Cuckoo, cuckoo!" O word of fear,
Unpleasing to a married ear!

When shepherds pipe on oaten straws,
　And merry larks are plowmen's clocks,
When turtles tread, and rooks, and daws,
　And maidens bleach their summer smocks,
The cuckoo then, on every tree,
Mocks married men; for thus sings he,

"Cuckoo!

Cuckoo, cuckoo!" O word of fear,

Unpleasing to a married ear!

Questions:

1. What are the images used to describe spring?

2. Why is the sound "cuckoo" unpleasing to a married man? (pay attention to the similarity between the words "cuckoo" and "cuckold")

3. What is the tone of the poem? Why?

The Sick Rose

William Blake

O rose, thou art sick!

The invisible worm

That flies in the night,

In the howling storm,

Has found out thy bed

Of crimson joy,

And his dark secret love

Does thy life destroy.

Questions:

1. What is the symbolic meaning of the word "rose"?

2. What are the implications of colours?

Player Piano

John Updike

My stick finger click with a snicker

And, chuckling, they knuckle the keys;

Light-footed, my steel feelers flicker

And pluck from these keys melodies.

My paper can caper; abandon
Is broadcast by dint of my din,
And no man or band has a hand in
The tones I turn on from within.

At times I'm a jumble of rumbles,
At others I'm light like a moon,
But never my numb plunker fumbles,
Misstrums me, or tries a new tune.

Questions:

1. Can you point out alliteration and assonance in the poem?
2. Analyze the effects of alliteration and assonance.

Song

John Donne

Go and catch a falling star
　Get with child a mandrake root,[1]
Tell me where all past years are,
　Or who cleft the Devil's foot,
Teach me to hear mermaids singing,
　Or to keep off envy's stinging,
　　　And find
　　　What wind
Serves to advance an honest mind.

If thou be'st borne to strange sights,
　Things invisible to see,
Ride ten thousand days and nights,
　Till age snow white hairs on thee,

---

1 mandrake root: this V-shaped root resembles the lower half of the human body.

Thou, when thou return'st, wilt tell me

All strange wonders that befell thee,

And swear

Nowhere

Lives a woman true, and fair.

If thou findst one, let me know,

Such a pilgrimage were sweet—

Yet do not, I would not go,

Though at next door we might meet;

Though she were true, when you met her,

And last, till you write your letter,

Yet she

Will be

False, ere I come, to two or three.

Questions:

1. What is the speaker's view of a woman's love?
2. Does the speaker take his argument seriously or humorously? Why?
3. What is the rhyme scheme of the poem? Does it helpful to the understanding of the poem?

A Light Exists in Spring

Emily Dickenson

A light exists in spring

Not present on the year

At any other period—

When March is scarcely here

A Color stands abroad

On Solitary Fields

That science cannot overtake

But Human Nature feels.

It waits upon the Lawn,
It shows the furthest Tree
Upon the furthest Slope you know.
It almost speaks to you.

Then as Horizons step
Or Noons report away,
Without the Formula of sound
It passes, and we stay—

A quality of loss
Affecting our Content
As Trade had suddenly encroached
Upon a Sacrament.

Questions:

1. What is the tone of the poem?
2. How do you understand the "light" described?

Section 3　Reading Drama
第三部分　阅读戏剧

The tragic poet is an imitator, and therefore, like all other imitators, he is thrice removed from the king and from the truth.

Plato

Chapter 15　About Drama

第十五章　关于戏剧

简要介绍：

　　"**Drama**, the general term for performances in which actors impersonate the actions and speech of fictional or historical characters (or non-human entities) for the entertainment of an audience, either on a stage or by means of a broadcast: or a particular example of this art, i.e. a play. Drama is usually expected to represent stories showing situations of conflict between characters, although the monodrama is a special case in which only one performer speaks. Drama is a major genre of literature, but includes non-literary forms (in mime[1]), and has several dimensions that lie beyond the domain of the literary dramatist or playwright. The major dramatic genres in the west are comedy and tragedy, but several other kinds of dramatic work fall outside these categories (drame[2], history play, masque, melodrama, morality play, mystery play, tragicomedy)." [3]

　　Like fiction, drama has its plot and characters to develop a theme and arouse audience's emotion; and many traditional plays are written in the form of poetry, but drama has its own feature, that is, it is written to be performed by actors and actresses on a stage before the audience.

　　Since drama is performed through actors and actresses, playwrights must keep in mind not only the audience but also actors, directors, costumers, designers, and technicians, etc. And it is through dialogue, facial expression, gesture, speech rhythm and intonation of the performers, the meaning of a play is expressed to the audience, who need imagination before they develop a good understanding of the play.

　　Since a play is showed on the stage, it must be written objectively or

---

1 哑剧。
2 法语 "戏剧" 的表述方式，专用于指称介于悲剧与喜剧之间的戏剧。
3 Baldick, Chris. *Oxford Concise Dictionary of Literary Terms*, 上海：上海外语教育出版社，2000: 61-62.

dramatically. The playwright cannot directly comment on the action or characters, nor can he tell directly what is going on, in other words, almost everything is unfolded by performers.

The essential elements of drama include plot, character, dialogue, staging, and theme.

Plot is the structure of a play's actions, the arrangement of all the incidents in a play. Plot is traditionally made up of four parts: exposition, rising action, climax, and ending. Plot involves more than simply what happens, it also involves how and why things happen.

Characters are the vital center of a play, which bring play to life. Their human dimension is specifically displayed with the help of the performers. Characters are fully developing through their dialogue.

Dialogue refers to the verbal exchanges between characters. Dialogue in a play has four major functions at least: to advance the plot, to establish setting (the time and place of the action), to reveal characters and to develop the theme.

Staging refers to the visual spectacle a play presents in performance. This includes such things as the positions of actors on stage, their nonverbal gestures and movements, the scenic background, the props and costumes, lighting, and sound effects. It is usually described through narrative as well as descriptive way.

Theme is the play's meaning or significance we derive from plot, characters, dialogue and staging.

简　析：

戏剧不同于小说和诗歌，我们可以从戏剧的性质、内容、体裁等几个方面探讨戏剧的特性：

1）不同于诗歌和小说，戏剧是表演性的，通过舞台或广播，由演员以表演的方式将故事演绎给观众，因此它在创作上有许多限制。

2）戏剧主要通过人物之间的对话来演绎故事。

3）戏剧是文学的主要形式之一，其基本表现形式有喜剧和悲剧两种，但在戏剧发展史上曾出现过多个剧种，比较有影响的包括：历史剧、假面剧、情节剧、道德剧、神秘剧、悲喜剧等。

4）戏剧的要素包括主题、人物、情节、对话和舞台背景。

我们可以更深入地了解一下欧美戏剧史上主要的戏剧类型：

奇迹剧（miracle play），欧洲中世纪 3 种主要戏剧之一（另两种为神秘剧和道德剧），11 到 13 世纪盛行于欧洲，主要描述一个圣徒一生的种种奇迹或以身殉教的故事，比如贞女马利亚或主教圣·尼古拉的故事。

　　神秘剧（mystery play），13 到 16 世纪盛行于欧洲，由拉丁语表演的戏剧发展而来，题材通常是选自《圣经》的故事，比如亚当和夏娃，末日审判等。

　　道德剧（morality play），15 到 16 世纪初盛行于欧洲，是一种戏剧化的寓言，其人物代表某种抽象概念，比如善、恶、正义、怜悯等人性美德或弱点。剧情围绕一个正面人物，如"人类"，展开，描述他如何将自己的灵魂从罪的恶魔中拯救出来，最终获得上帝的女儿（正义、真理、节欲等）的帮助的过程。

　　假面剧（masque），16 到 17 世纪时期盛行于欧洲的一种集唱歌、音乐、舞蹈、道具和舞台效果为一体的室内剧，演员们开始演出时脸上戴着面具，装扮成神话人物，表演寓言情节，最后以演员取下面具，与观众一起跳舞结束。

　　历史剧（history play），其情节全部或部分取自历史记载，通常特指那些按时间顺序叙述的戏剧，如莎士比亚的历史剧。

　　悲喜剧（tragicomedy），一种同时具有悲剧和喜剧成分的戏剧作品，或者为悲剧续上大团圆的结局，或者将严肃和轻松的氛围同时糅合在同一部作品中。此术语由罗马剧作家首创，后在欧洲文艺复兴时期发展成为主要戏剧体裁之一，莎士比亚的许多戏剧都被后人归于此类体裁，比如《冬天的故事》、《辛白林》等。19 世纪后期，受批判现实主义的影响，悲喜剧增添了讽刺的成分，使其显得更为扣人心弦，比如易卜生的《野鸭》、《群鬼》等；20 世纪的现代悲喜剧成了荒诞剧的同义词，贝克特的《等待戈多》和品特的《送菜升降机》通常被认为是此类剧作的典型。

　　情节剧（melodrama），19 世纪流行于欧洲剧场，以夸张的情节冲突表达人的强烈情感，以善恶之间的冲突为主题，最终以惩恶扬善结局。20 世纪的情节剧主要表现在惊险电影和电视连续剧中。

Chapter 16   Tragedy and Comedy

第十六章   悲剧和喜剧

> Tragedy is an imitation of an action that is serious, complete, and of a certain magnitude.
>
> Aristotle

简要介绍：

Drama is essentially of two types: one is comedy, the other is tragedy. Comic plays elicit laughter, tragic plays evoke tears. They stand for two different ways to look at the world. In comedy, the major characters look at the world affirmatively and joyfully, and regard themselves common and ordinary, as a result, their human weakness and errors do not lead to calamity but happiness; in tragedy, the protagonist views the world seriously and solemnly, who is a hero with noble thought and awesome social responsibility, as a result, their human weakness and errors result in fatal calamity. Both comedy and tragedy involve changes of fate, with the former turning from bad to good and the latter from good to bad.

TRGEDY

Tragedy refers to a serious play, presenting a courageous protagonist who confronts powerful forces within or outside himself with dignity, and finally undergoes a disastrous downfall. It is written to reveal the breadth and depth of the human spirit in face of failure, defeat or even death.

In his *Poetics,* Aristotle defined tragedy, based on the works of the Greek dramatists such as Aeschylus, Euripides and Sophocles, as "the imitation of an action that is serious, complete, and of a certain magnitude", which involves "incidents arousing pity and fear, wherewith to accomplish the catharsis of such emotions."

Before the beginning of the 18th century, tragedies were mostly written in accordance with Aristotle's theory, which, written in verse, usually dealt with the downfall of the protagonist, who is either a member of the royal family (like Shakespeare's *King Lear*, *Hamlet*) or of high social rank (*Othello*), as a result, his fate affect the fortune of a state. The protagonist's determination to complete some task or goal make him admirable and heroic, but it does not mean he is infallible. According to Aristotle, tragic hero will most effectively evoke both our pity and fear if he is a person neither thoroughly good nor thoroughly bad, or if he is a hero better than the ordinary. The latter may achieve stronger tragic effect. Pity is elicited, for the protagonist's fatal calamity, which is led by his error of judgment or only a mistaken choice, is greater than he deserves; fear is evoked, for the audience recognize similar possibilities of error in their own fallible selves.

Aristotle remarks that the protagonist is led into a fatal calamity by a "hamartia" (error). The major internal tragic flaw of the protagonist, which leads to his tragic downfall, is an excess of pride, ambition and passion, or a misjudgment of other characters, events and reality.

As to the effect of tragedy, Aristotle uses "catharsis" (purgation or purification) to refer to the remarkable fact that many tragic representations leave the audience not depression but relief. In other words, Aristotle arouses our attention to the peculiar effect of a tragedy on the audience, namely "the pleasure of pity and fear'. Aristotle observes that it is the basic way to distinguish the tragic from comic or other forms, and it is the ultimate effect a playwright is seeking. The accomplishment of the tragic effect usually depends on the protagonist's recognition of what has happened to him, that is, the hero discovers something previously unknown or something he knew but misconstrued; and the audience's awareness of admirable qualities in the protagonist, which are wasted terribly in the fated disaster.

Shakespeare's *Othello* is one of the few plays, which accords closely with Aristotle's basic concepts of the tragic hero and plot, that is, a good man who commits a tragic error experiences a fatal catastrophe. The fatal flaw of Othello is his misjudgment, which mistakes the villain Iago for an honest, loving friend; and mistakes his faithful wife, Desdemona, for a person committing adultery. It is through Othello's recognition of his mistakes at the end, the tragic play reaches it climax.

Modern tragic drama, however, normally presents, in prose, a protagonist of middle or lower social rank undergoing a commonplace or domestic misfortune, which arouses compassionate understanding from the audience rather than pity and fear, as in the plays of Henrik Ibsen and Arthur Miller. Arthur Miller's *The Death of a Salesman* (1949), for example, delineates a salesman who is bewildered and defeated by life.

COMEDY

Comedy refers to a play written chiefly to interest and amuse the audience, based on the audience's sense of confidence that no great disaster will occur in the end. Like tragedy, the characters in comedy are also persons with internal flaws, for instance, misunderstanding and misjudgment, and there are obstacles and conflicts too that the characters must confront, but in comedy, these errors and forces lead not to calamity as in tragedy, but to laughter and happiness, for the characters delight the audience by overcoming all difficulties.

The first general principle a comedy tends to follow is that, it begins with problems and ends with their resolution. The second general principle to follow is that, comic heroes are ordinary people, who are less grand and noble than tragic protagonists. The third general principle to follow is that, a comedy is closer to the representation of everyday life than a tragedy, for it describes ordinary people's failings rather than tragic heroes' disastrous downfall. The fourth general principle to follow is that, its ending is usually happy for the major characters.

There are several kinds of comedy, the major ones including romantic comedy, satiric comedy, comedy of manners.

Romantic comedy represents mainly the love affairs of the young lovers and the complicated obstacles they are confronting, for instance, parents' disapproval, deceptions, jealousies, disguises, and misunderstandings, which always ends with a lighted-hearted and happy union. The lightness is the basic tone of the play, and life is a celebration in the play, for the sense of humor gives the audience a good taste of the various possibilities of life. Discord and misunderstanding finally give way to concord and love. The well-known examples are Shakespeare's *A Midsummer Night's Dream, As You Like it, Twelfth Night*, etc.

Satiric comedy ridicules the weakness of human nature, follies of politics, vices of philosophical doctrines, hypocrisy of religion or flaws of morals, and aims to correct them and celebrate virtue. Moliere's *Tartuffe* is a good example.

Comedy of manners is a kind of comedy representing the complex and sophisticated relations and intrigues of men and women living in an upper-class society. Its plot usually develops around intrigues of lust and greed, and its humor relies on its verbal wit. The English comedy of manners was early exemplified by Shakespeare's *Love's Labour's Lost* and *Much Ado about Nothing*, and flourished in Restoration comedy. Although it lapsed in the early 19th century, it was revived by Oscar Wilder and George Bernard Shaw at the end of the 19th century.

简 析:

悲剧和喜剧是戏剧两种最基本的形式。它们在共享戏剧的基本要素的基础上,在多个方面表现出差异:

1)悲剧和喜剧有着各不相同的主题设定:悲剧重在表现英雄人物面对困境、失败、死亡时所表现的精神上的悲壮和崇高;喜剧旨在描写普通人物面对生活中的问题、困难、挫折时所表现的乐观、幽默,以及生活所给予的多种机会和惊喜。

2)悲剧和喜剧有着各自的人物定位:悲剧人物或者出身高贵,或者有着很高的社会地位,他们品德高尚,但是都有自身的弱点,其中最为普遍的弱点是"过于骄傲"或"自视过高"。喜剧的人物大都出生中产阶级,甚至来自社会下层,他们有着普通人的善良和淳朴,也有着普通人的愚蠢和自私,因此面对生活的挫折,做过蠢事,也闹过笑话,但是最终总能获得幸福。

3)悲剧和喜剧有着各自的情节模式:悲剧的情节以顺境开头,以逆境结束,以悲壮和震撼达到净化观众的心灵的效果;喜剧的情节以逆境开头,以顺境结束,以喜庆和轻松给观众一种大团圆的幸福感觉。

4)悲剧和喜剧各有自己的背景设置:悲剧的背景大都设置在权力的中心地带,比如在皇宫,在豪门世家;喜剧的背景大都设定在普通人生活的闹市区,社区,或自然景区。

5)悲剧和喜剧各有自己的语言风格:悲剧的措辞高雅、凝重,句式规范、冗长,以突出思想的深刻和精神的悲壮;喜剧的措辞诙谐、幽默,句式灵活、精练,以描写生活的轻松和现实的多种可能性。

作 品：

WILLIAM SHAKESPEARE

[1564—1616]

Othello

THE MOOR OF VENICE

(1604)

Scene. *Venice and Cyprus*

ACT I

Scene I [Venice. A street]

RODERIGO: Tush! Never tell me? I take it much unkindly
            That thou, Iago, who hast had my purse
            As if the strings were thine, shouldst know of this[1].

IAGO: 'Sblood[2], but you'll not hear me! If ever I did dream
            Of such a matter, abhor me.

RODERIGO: Thou told'st me
            Thou didst hold him in thy hate.

IAGO: Despise me
            If I do not. Three great ones of the city,
            In personal suit to make me his lieutenant,
            Off-capped[3] to him; and, by the faith of man,
            I know my price; I am worth no worse a place.
            But he, as loving his own pride and purposes,
            Evades them with a bombast circumstance[4],
            Horribly stuffed with epithets of war;

Nonsuits[5] my mediators. For, "Certes," says he,
"I have already chose my officer." And what was he?
Forsooth, a great arithmetician[6],
One Michael Cassio, a Florentine,
(A fellow almost damned in a fair wife)
That never set a squadron in the field,
Nor the division of a battle knows
More than a spinster; unless the bookish theoric,
Wherein the tongued[7] consuls can propose
As masterly as he. Mere prattle without practice
Is all his soldiership. But he, sir, had th' election;
And I, of whom his eyes had seen the proof
At Rhodes, at Cyprus, and on other grounds
Christian and heathen, must be belee'd and calmed[8]
By debitor and creditor. This counter-caster[9],
He, in good time, must his lieutenant be,
And I—God bless the mark!—his Moorship's ancient[10].

RODERIGO: By heaven, I rather would have been his hangman.

IAGO: Why, there's no remedy. 'Tis the curse of service:
Preferment goes by letter and affection[11].
And not by old gradation[12], where each second
Stood heir to th' first. Now, sir, be judge yourself,
Whether I in any just term am affined[13]
To love the Moor.

RODERIGO: I would not follow him then.

IAGO: O, sir, content you.
I follow him to serve my turn upon him.
We cannot all be masters, nor all masters
Cannot be truly followed. You shall mark
Many a duteous and knee-crooking knave
That, doting on his own obsequious bondage,
Wears out his time, much like his master's ass,
For naught but provender; and when he's old, cashiered[14].
Whip me such honest knaves! Others there are
Who, trimmed in forms and visages of duty,

Keep yet their hearts attending on themselves,

And, throwing but shows of service on their lords,

Do well thrive by them, and when they have lined their coats,

Do themselves homage. These fellows have some soul;

And such a one do I profess myself. For, sir,

It is as sure as you are Roderigo,

Were I the Moor, I would not be Iago.

In following him, I follow but myself.

Heaven is my judge, not I for love and duty,

But seeming so, for my peculiar end;

For when my outward action doth demonstrate

The native[15] act and figure of my heart

In complement extern[16], 'tis not long after

But I will wear my heart upon my sleeve

For daws to peck at; I am not what I am.

RODERIGO: What a full fortune does the thick-lips owe[17]

If he can carry't thus!

IAGO: Call up her father,

Rouse him. Make after him, poison his delight,

Proclaim him in the streets, incense her kinsmen,

And though he in a fertile climate dwell,

Plague him with flies; though that his joy be joy,

Yet throw such chances of vexation on't

As it may lose some color.

RODERIGO: Here is her father's house. I'll call aloud.

IAGO: Do, with like timorous[18] accent and dire yell

As when, by night and negligence, the fire

Is spied in populous cities.

RODERIGO: What, ho, Brabantio! Signior Brabantio, ho!

IAGO: Awake! What, ho, Brabantio! Thieves! Thieves!

Look to your house, your daughter, and your bags!

Thieves! Thieves!

BRABANTIO *above [at a window].*

BRABANTIO: What is the reason of this terrible summons?

What is the matter there?

RODERIGO: Signior, is all your family within?

IAGO: Are your doors locked?

BRABANTIO: Why, wherefore ask you this?

IAGO: Zounds, sir, y'are robbed! For shame. Put on your gown!

Your heart is burst, you have lost half your soul.

Even now, now, very now, an old black ram

Is tupping your white ewe. Arise, arise!

Awake the snorting[19] citizens with the bell,

Or else the devil will make a grandsire of you.

Arise, I say!

BRABANTIO: What, have you lost your wits?

RODERIGO: Most reverend signior, do you know my voice?

BRABANTIO: Not I. What are you?

RODERIGO: My name is Roderigo.

BRABANTIO: The worser welcome!

I have charged thee not to haunt about my doors.

In honest plainness thou hast heard me say

My daughter is not for thee; and now, in madness,

Being full of supper and distemp'ring draughts[20],

Upon malicious knavery dost thou come

To start[21] my quiet.

RODERIGO: Sir, sir, sir—

BRABANTIO: But thou must needs be sure

My spirits and my place[22] have in their power

To make this bitter to thee.

RODERIGO: Patience, good sir.

BRABANTIO: What tell'st thou me of robbing? This is Venice,

My house is not a grange[23].

RODERIGO: Most grave Brabantio,

In simple and pure soul I come to you.

IAGO: Zounds, sir, you are one of those that will not serve God if the devil bid you. Because we come to do you service and you think we are ruffians, you'll have your daughter covered with a Barbary[24] horse, you'll have your nephews[25] neigh to you, you'll have coursers for cousins[26], and gennets for germans[27].

BRABANTIO: What profane wretch art thou?

IAGO: I am one, sir, that comes to tell you your daughter and the Moor are making the beast with two backs.

BRABANTIO: Thou art a villain.

IAGO: You are——a senator.

BRABANTIO: This thou shalt answer. I know thee, Roderigo.

RODERIGO: Sir, I will answer anything. But I beseech you,
If't be your pleasure and most wise consent,
As partly I find it is, that your fair daughter,
At this odd-even[28] and dull watch o' th' night,
Transported, with no worse nor better guard
But with a knave of common hire, a gondolier,
To the gross clasps of a lascivious Moor——
If this be known to you, and your allowance,
We then have done you bold and saucy wrongs;
But if you know not this, my manners tell me
We have your wrong rebuke. Do not believe
That from the sense of all civility[29]
I thus would play and trifle with your reverence.
Your daughter, if you have not given her leave,
I say again, hath made a gross revolt,
Tying her duty, beauty, wit, and fortunes
In an extravagant and wheeling[30] stranger
Of here and everywhere. Straight satisfy yourself.
If she be in her chamber, or your house,
Let loose on me the justice of the state
For thus deluding you.

BRABANTIO: Strike on the tinder, ho!
Give me a taper! Call up all my people!
This accident[31] is not unlike my dream.
Belief of it oppresses me already.
Light, I say! Light!   *Exit [above].*

IAGO: Farewell, for I must leave you.

It seems not meet, nor wholesome to my place,

To be produced—as, if I stay, I shall—

Against the Moor. For I do know the State,

However this may gall him with some check^{32},

Cannot with safety cast^{33} him; for he's emarked

With such loud reason to the Cyprus wars,

Which even now stands in act^{34}, that for their souls

Another of his fathom^{35} they have none

To lead their business; in which regard,

Though I do hate him as I do hell-pains,

Yet, for necessity of present life,

I must show out a flag and sign of love,

Which is indeed but sign. That you shall surely find him,

Lead to the Sagittary^{36} that raised search:

And there will I be with him. So farewell.   [*Exit.*]

Enter BRABANTIO [*in his nightgown*], *with* SERVANTS *and torches.*

BRABANTIO: It is too true an evil. Gone she is;

And what's to come of my despised time

Is naught but bitterness. Now, Roderigo,

Where didst thou see her?—O unhappy girl!—

With the Moor, say'st thou?—Who would be a father?—

How didst thou know 'twas she?—O, she deceives me

Past thought!—What said she to you? Get moe^{37} tapers!

Raise all my kindred!—Are they married, think you?

RODERIGO: Truly I think they are.

BRABANTIO: O heaven! How got she out? O treason of the blood!

Fathers, from hence trust not your daughters' minds

By what you see them act. Is there not charms

By which the property^{38} of youth and maidhood

May be abused? Have you not read, Roderigo,

Of some such thing?

RODERIGO: Yes, sir I have indeed.

BRABANTIO: Call up my brother.—O, would you had had her!—

Some one way, some another.—Do you know

Where we may apprehend her and the Moor?

RODERIGO: I think I can discover him, if you please

To get good guard and go along with me.

BRABANTIO: Pray you lead on. At every house I'll call;

I may command at most.—Get weapons, ho!

And raise some special officers of night.—

On, good Roderigo; I will deserve your pains[39].   [*Exeunt.*]

Scene II [A steeet.]

Enter OTHELLO, IAGO, ATTENDANTS *with torches.*

IAGO: Though in the trade of war I have slain men,

Yet do I hold it very stuff[40] o' th' conscience

To do no contrived murder. I lack iniquity

Sometime to do me service. Nine or ten times

I had thought t' have yerked[41] him here, under the ribs.

OTHELLO: 'Tis better as it is.

IAGO: Nay, but he prated,

And spoke such scurvy and provoking terms

Against your honor, that with the little godliness I have

I did full hard forbear him. But I pray you, sir,

Are you fast[42] married? Be assured of this,

That the magnifico[43] is much beloved,

And hath in his effect a voice potential

As double as the Duke's. He will divorce you,

Or put upon you what restraint or grievance

The law, with all his might to enforce it on,

Will give him cable[44].

OTHELLO: Let him do his spite.

My services which I have done the Signiory[45]

Shall out-tongue his complaints. 'Tis yet to know[46]—

Which when I know that boasting is an honor

I shall promulgate—I fetch my life and being

From men of royal siege[47], and my demerits[48]
May speak unbonneted to as proud a fortune
As this that I have reached[49]. For know, Iago,
But that I love the gentle Desdemona,
I would not my unhoused[50] free condition
Put into circumscription and confine
For the seas' worth. But look, what lights come yond?

Enter CASSIO, *with* [OFFICERS *and*] *torches.*

IAGO:	Those are the raised father and his friends.
	You were best go in.
OTHELLO:	Not I. I must be found.
	My parts, my title, and my perfect soul[51]
	Shall manifest me rightly. Is it they?
IAGO:	By Janus, I think no.
OTHELLO:	The servants of the Duke? And my lieutenant?
	The goodness of the night upon you, friends.
	What is the news?
CASSIO:	The Duke does greet you, general;
	And he requires your haste-posthaste appearance
	Even on the instant.
OTHELLO:	What is the matter, think you?
CASSIO:	Something from Cyprus, as I may divine.
	It is a business of some heat. The galleys
	Have sent a dozen sequent[52] messengers
	This very night at one another's heels,
	And many of the consuls, raised and met,
	Are at the Duke's already. You have been hotly called for.
	When, being not at your lodging to be found,
	The Senate hath sent about three several[53] quests
	To search you out.
OTHELLO:	'Tis well I am found by you.
	I will but spend a word here in the house,
	And go with you. [*Exit.*]

CASSIO: Ancient, what makes he here?

IAGO: Faith, he tonight hath boarded a land carack[54].

    If it prove lawful prize, he's made forever.

CASSIO: I do not understand.

IAGO: He's married.

CASSIO: To who?

[*Enter* OTHELLO.]

IAGO: Marry, to—Come captain, will you go?

OTHELLO: Have with you.

CASSIO: Here comes another troop to seek for you.

Enter BRABANTIO, RODERIGO, *with* OFFICERS *and torches.*

IAGO: It is Brabantio. General, be advised.

    He comes to bad intent.

OTHELLO: Holla! Stand there!

RODERIGO: Signior, it is the Moor.

BRABANTIO: Down with him, thief! [*They draw swords.*]

IAGO: You, Roderigo? Come, sir, I am for you.

OTHELLO: Keep up your bright swords, for the dew will rust them.

    Good signior, you shall more command with years

    Than with your weapons.

BRABANTIO: O thou foul thief, where hast thou stowed my daughter?

    Damned as thou art, thou hast enchanted her!

    For I'll refer me to all things of sense,

    If she in chains of magic were not bound,

    Whether a maid so tender, fair, and happy,

    So opposite to marriage that she shunned

    The wealthy, curled darlings of our nation,

    Would ever have, t'incur a general mock[55],

    Run from her guardage to the sooty bosom

    Of such a thing as thou—to fear, not to delight.

    Judge me the world if 'tis not gross in sense[56]

That thou hast practiced[57] on her with foul charms,
Abused her delicate youth with drugs or minerals
That weaken motion[58]. I'll have't disputed on;
'Tis probable, and palpable to thinking.
I therefore apprehend and do attach[59] thee
For an abuser of the world, a practicer
Of arts inhibited and out of warrant[60].
Lay hold upon him. If he do resist,
Subdue him at his peril.

OTHELLO:　Hold your hands,
Both you of my inclining and the rest.
Were it my cue to fight, I should have known it
Without a prompter. Whither will you that I go
To answer this your charge?

BRABANTIO:　To prison, till fit time
Of law and course of direct session[61]
Call thee to answer.

OTHELLO:　What if I do obey?
How may the Duke be therewith satisfied,
Whose messengers are here about my side
Upon some present[62] business of the state
To bring me to him?

OFFICER:　'Tis true, most worthy signior.
The Duke's in council, and your noble self
I am sure is sent for.

BRABANTIO:　How? The Duke in council?
In this time of the night? Bring him away.
Mine's not an idle[63] cause. The Duke himself,
Or any of my brothers[64] of the state,
Cannot but feel this wrong as 'twere their own;
For if such actions may have passage free,
Bondslaves and pagans shall our statesmen be.　　　　[*Exeunt.*]

Scene *III* [*A council chamber.*]

Enter DUKE, SENATORS, *and* OFFICERS
[*set at a table, with lights and* ATTENDANTS].

DUKE: There's no composition[65] in this news
That gives them credit[66].
FIRST SENATOR: Indeed, they are disproportioned.
My letters say a hundred and seven galleys.
DUKE: And mine a hundred forty.
SECOND SENATOR: And mine two hundred.
But though they jump[67] not on a just accompt[68]—
As in these cases where the aim[69] reports
'Tis oft with difference—yet do they all confirm
A Turkish fleet, and bearing up to Cyprus.
DUKE: Nay, it is possible enough to judgment.
I do not so secure me in the error,
But the main article[70] I do approve
In fearful sense.
SAILOR (Within): What, ho! What, ho! What, ho!

Enter SAILOR.

OFFICER: A messenger from the galleys.
DUKE: Now? What's the business?
SAILOR: The Turkish preparation makes for Rhodes.
So was I bid report here to the State
By Signior Angelo.
DUKE: How say you by this change?
FIRST SENATOR: This cannot be
By no assay of reason. 'Tis a pageant[71]
To keep us in false gaze[72]. When we consider
Th' importancy of Cyprus to the Turk,
And let ourselves again but understand

	That, as it more concerns the Turk than Rhodes,
	So may he with more facile question bear[73] it,
	For that it stands not in such warlike brace,
	But altogethet lacks th' abilities
	That Rhodes is dressed in. If we make thought of this,
	We must not think the Turk is so unskillful
	To leave that latest which concerns him first,
	Neglecting an attempt of ease and gain
	To wake and wage[74] a danger profitless.
DUKE:	Nay, in all confidence he's not for Rhodes.
OFFICER:	Here is more news.

Enter a MESSENGER.

MESSENGER: The Ottomites, reverend and gracious,
　　　　　　Steering with due course toward the isle of Rhodes,
　　　　　　Have there injointed them with an after[75] fleet.
FIRST SENATOR: Ay, so I thought. How many, as you guess?
MESSENGER: Of thirty sail; and now they do restem[76]
　　　　　　Their backward course, bearing with frank appearance
　　　　　　Their purposes toward Cyprus. Signior Montano,
　　　　　　Your trusty and most valiant servitor,
　　　　　　With his free duty[77] recommends[78] you thus,
　　　　　　And prays you to believe him.

DUKE:	'Tis certain then for Cyprus.
	Marcus Luccicos, is not he in town?

FIRST SENATOR: He's now in Florence.

DUKE:	Write from us to him; post-posthaste dispatch.

FIRST SENATOR: Here comes Brabantio and the valiant Moor.

Enter BRABANTIO, OTHELLO, CASSIO, IAGO, RODERIGO, *and* OFFICERS.

DUKE:	Valiant Othello, we must straight[79] employ you
	Against the general enemy Ottoman.
	[*To* BRABANTIO] I did not see you. Welcome, gentle signior.

We lacked your counsel and your help tonight.

BRABANTIO: So did I yours. Good your grace, pardon me.

Neither my place, nor aught I heard of business,

Hath raised me from my bed; nor doth the general care

Take hold on me; for my particular grief

Is of so floodgate[80] and o'erbearing nature

That it engluts[81] and swallows other sorrows,

And it is still itself.

DUKE: Why, what's the matter?

BRABANTIO: My daughter! O, my daughter!

SENATORS: Dead?

BRABANTIO: Ay, to me.

She is abused, stol'n from me, and corrupted

By spells and medicines bought of mountebanks;

For nature so prepost'rously to err,

Being not deficient, blind, or lame of sense,

Sans[82] witchcraft could not.

DUKE: Who'er he be that in this foul proceeding

Hath thus beguiled your daughter of herself,

And you of her, the bloody book of law

You shall yourself read in the bitter letter

After your own sense; yea, though our proper[83] son

Stood in your action[84].

BRABANTIO: Humbly I thank your Grace.

Here is the man—this Moor, whom mow, it seems,

Your special mandate for the state affairs

Hath hither brought.

ALL: We are very sorry for't.

DUKE [To OTHELLO]: What in your own part can you say to this?

BRABANTIO: Nothing, but this is so.

OTHELLO: Most potent, grave, and reverend signiors,

My very noble and approved[85] good masters,

That I have ta'en away this old man's daughter,

It is most true; true I have married her.

The very head and front[86] of my offending

Hath this extent, no more. Rude[87] am I in my speech,

And little blessed with the soft phrase of peace.

For since these arms of mine had seven years' pith[88]

Till now some nine moons wasted[89], they have used

Their dearest[90] action in the tented field;

And little of this great world can I speak

More than pertains to feats of broils and battle;

And therefore little shall I grace my cause

In speaking for myself. Yet, by your gracious patience,

I will a round[91] unvarnished tale deliver

Of my whole course of love—what drugs, what charms,

What conjuration, and what mighty magic,

For such proceeding I am charged withal,

I won his daughter—

BRABANTIO: A maiden never bold,

Of spirit so still and quiet that her motion

Blushed at herself[92], and she, in spite of nature,

Of years, of country, credit, everything,

To fall in love with what she feared to look on!

It is a judgment maimed and most imperfect

That will confess perfection so could err

Against all rules of nature, and must be driven

To find out practices[93] of cunning hell

Why this should be. I therefore vouch[94] again

That with some mixtures pow'rful o'er the blood

Or with some dram, conjured to this effect,

He wrought upon her.

DUKE: To vouch this is no proof,

Without more wider and more overt test

Than these thin habits[95] and poor likelihoods

Of modern[96] seeming do prefer against him.

FIRST SENATOR: But, Othello, speak.

Did you by indirect and forced courses

Subdue and poison this young maid's affections?

Or came it by request, and such fair question

As soul to soul affordeth?

OTHELLO: I do beseech you,

Send for the lady to the Sagittary

And let her speak of me before her father.

If you do find me foul in her report,

The trust, the office, I do hold of you

Not only take away, but let your sentence

Even fall upon my life.

DUKE: Fetch Desdemona hither.

OTHELLO: Ancient, conduct them; you best know the place.

[*Exit* IAGO, *with two or three* ATTENDANTS.]

And till she come, as truly as to heaven

I do confess the vices of my blood,

So justly to your grave ears I'll present

How I did thrive in this fair lady's love,

And she in mine.

DUKE: Say it, Othello.

OTHELLO: Her father loved me; oft invited me;

Still[97] questioned me the story of my life

From year to year, the battle, sieges, fortune

That I have passed.

I ran it through, even from my boyish days

To th' very moment that he bade me tell it.

Wherein I spoke of most disastrous chances,

Of moving accidents by flood and field,

Of hairbreadth scapes i' th' imminent[98] deadly breach.

Of being taken by the insolent foe

And sold to slavery, of my redemption thence

And portance[99] in my travel's history,

Wherein of anters[100] vast and deserts idle[101],

Rough quarries, rocks, and hills whose heads touch heaven,

It was my hint to speak. Such was my process.

And of the Cannibals that each other eat,

The Anthropophagi[102], and men whose heads
Grew beneath their shoulders. These things to hear
Would Desdemona seriously incline;
But still the house affairs would draw her thence;
Which ever as she could with haste dispatch,
She'd come again, and with a greedy ear
Devour up my discourse. Which I observing,
Took once a pliant hour, and found good means
To draw from her a prayer of earnest heart
That I would all my pilgrimage dilate[103],
Whereof by parcels she had something heard,
But not intentively[104]. I did consent,
And often did beguile her of her tears
When I did speak of some distressful stroke
That my youth suffered. My story being done,
She gave me for my pains a world of kisses.
She swore in faith 'twas strange, 'twas passing[105] strange;
'Twas pitiful, 'twas wondrous pitiful.
She wished she had not heard it; yet she wished
That heaven had made her such a man. She thanked me,
And bade me, if I had a friend that loved her,
I should but teach him how to tell my story,
And that would woo her. Upon this hint I spake.
She loved me for the dangers I had passed,
And I loved her that she did pity them.
This only is the witchcraft I have used.
Here comes the lady. Let her witness it.

Enter DESDEMONA, IAGO, ATTENDANTS.

DUKE: I think this tale would win my daughter too.
Good Brabantio, take up this mangled matter at the best.
Men do their broken weapons rather use
Than their bare hands.
BRABANTIO: I pray you hear her speak.

If she confess that she was half the wooer,

Destruction on my head if my bad blame

Light on the man. Come hither, gentle mistress.

Do you perceive in all this noble company

Where most you owe obedience?

DESDEMONA: My noble father,

I do perceive here a divided duty.

To you I am bound for life and education;

My life and education both do learn me

How to respect you. You are the lord of duty,

I am hitherto your daughter. But here's my husband,

And so much duty as my mother showed

To you, preferring you before her father,

So much I challenge[106] that I may profess

Due to the Moor my lord.

BRABANTIO: God be with you. I have done.

Please it your Grace, on to the state affairs.

I had rather to adopt a child than get[107] it.

Come hither, Moor.

I here do give thee that with all my heart

Which, but thou hast already, with all my heart

I would keep from thee. For your sake[108], jewel,

I am glad at soul I have no other child,

For thy escape would teach me tyranny,

To hang clogs on them. I have done, my lord.

DUKE: Let me speak like yourself and lay a sentence[109]

Which, as a grise[110] or step, may help these lovers.

When remedies are past, the griefs are ended

By seeing the worst, which late on hopes depended[111].

To mourn a mischief that is past and gone

Is the next way to draw new mischief on.

What cannot be preserved when fortune takes,

Patience her injury a mock'ry makes.

The robbed that smiles, steals something from the thief;

He robs himself that spends a bootless[112] grief.

BRABANTIO: So let the Turk of Cyprus us beguile:

We lose it not so long as we can smile.

He bears the sentence well that nothing bears

But the free comfort which from thence he hears;

But he bears both the sentence and the sorrow

That to pay grief must of poor patience borrow.

These sentences, to sugar, or to gall,

Being strong on both sides, are equivocal.

But words are words. I never yet did hear

That the bruised heart was pierced through the ear.

I humbly beseech you, proceed to th' affairs of state.

DUKE: The Turk with a most mighty preparation makes for Cyprus. Othello, the fortitude[113] of the place is best known to you; and though we have there a substitute[114] of most allowed[115] sufficiency, yet opinion[116], a more sovereign mistress of effects, throw a more safer voice on you. You must therefore be content to slubber[117] the gloss of your new fortunes with this more stubborn and boisterous[118] expedition.

OTHELLO: The tyrant Custom, most grave senators,

Hath made the flinty and steel couch of war

My thrice-driven[119] bed of down. I do agnize[120]

A natural and prompt alacrity

I find in hardness and do undertake

These present wars against the Ottomites.

Most humbly, therefore, bending to your state,

I crave fit disposition for my wife,

Due reference of place, and exhibition[121],

With such accommodation and besort

As levels with[122] her breeding.

DUKE: Why, at her father's

BRABANTIO: I will not have it so.

OTHELLO: Nor I.

DESDEMONA: Nor would I there reside,

To put my father in impatient thoughts

By being in his eye. Most gracious Duke,

To my unfolding[123] lend your prosperous[124] ear,

And let me find a charter[125] in your voice,

T' assist my simpleness.

DUKE: What would you, Desdemona?

DESDEMONA: That I love the Moor to live with him,

My downright violence, and storm of fortunes,

May trumpet to the world. My heart's subdued

Even to the very quality of my lord.

I saw Othello's visage in his mind,

And to his honors and his valiant parts

Did I my soul and fortunes consecrate.

So that, dear lords, if I be left behind.

A moth of peace, and he go to the war,

The rites for why I love him are bereft me,

And I a heavy interim shall support

By his dear absence. Let me go with him.

OTHELLO: Let her have your voice[126].

Vouch with me, heaven, I therefore beg it not

To please the palate of my appetite,

Nor to comply with heat[127] the young affects[128]

In me defunct—and proper satisfaction;

But to be free and bounteous to her mind;

And heaven defend[129] your good souls that you think

I will your serious and great business scant

When she is with me. No, when light-winged toys

Of feathered Cupid seel[130] with wanton dullness

My speculative and officed instrument[131],

That my disports corrupt and taint my business,

Let housewives make a skillet of my helm,

And all indign[132] and base adversities

Make head[133] against my estimation[134]!

DUKE: Be it as you shall privately determine,

Either for her stay or going. Th' affair cries haste,

And speed must answer it.

FIRST SENATOR: You must away tonight.

OTHELLO: With all my heart.

DUKE:	At nine i' th' morning here we'll meet again.
	Othello, leave some officer behind,
	And he shall our commission bring to you,
	And such things else of quality and respect
	As doth import[135] you.
OTHELLO:	So please your grace, my ancient;
	A man he is of honesty and trust.
	To his conveyance I assign my wife,
	With what else needful your good grace shall think
	To be sent after me.
DUKE:	Let it be so.
	Good night to every one. [To BRABANTIO] And, noble signior,
	If virtue no delighted[136] beauty lack,
	Your son-in-law is far more fair than black.
FIRST SENATOR:	Adieu, brave Moor. Use Desdemona well.
BRABANTIO:	Look to her, Moor, if thou hast eyes to see:
	She has deceived her father, and may thee.

[*Exeunt* DUKE, SENATORS, OFFICERS, & c.]

OTHELLO:	My life upon her faith! Hoenst Iago,
	My Desdemona must I leave to thee.
	I prithee let thy wife attend on her,
	And bring them after in the best advantage[137].
	Come, Desdemona. I have but an hour
	Of love, of worldly matter, and direction
	To spend with thee. We must obey the time.

Exit [MOOR *with* DESDEMONA].

RODERIGO:	Iago?
IAGO:	What say'st thou, noble heart?
RODERIGO:	What will I do, think'st thou?
IAGO:	Why, go to bed and sleep.
RODERIGO:	I will incontinently[138] drown myself.

IAGO: If thou dost, I shall never love thee after. Why, thou silly gentleman?

RODERIGO: It is silliness to live when to live is torment; and then have we a prescription to die when death is our physician.

IAGO: O villainous! I have looked upon the world for four times seven years, and since I could distinguish betwixt a benefit and an injury, I never found man that knew how to love himself. Ere I would say I would drown myself for the love of a guinea hen, I would change my humanity with a baboon.

RODERIGO: What should I do? I confess it is my shame to be so fond, but it is not in my virtue to amend it.

IAGO: Virtue? A fig! 'Tis in ourselves that we are thus, or thus. Our bodies are our gardens, to the which our wills are gardeners; so that if we will plant nettles or sow lettuce, set hyssop and weed up thyme, supply it with one gender of herbs or distract[139] it with many—either to have it sterile with idleness or manured with industry—why, the power and corrigible[140] authority of this lies in our wills. If the balance of our lives had not one scale of reason to poise another of sensuality, the blood and baseness of our natures would conduct us to most prepost'rous conclusions. But we have reason to cool our raging motions, our carnal sting or unbitted[141] lusts, whereof I take this that you call love to be a sect or scion[142].

RODERIGO: It cannot be.

IAGO: It is merely a lust of the blood and a permission of the will. Come, be a man! Drown thyself? Drown cats and blind puppies! I have professed me thy friend, and I confess me knit to thy deserving with cables of perdurable toughness. I could never better stead[143] thee than now. Put money in thy purse. Follow thou the wars; defeat thy favor[144] with an usurped[145] beard. I say, put money in thy purse. It cannot be long that Desdemona should continue her love to the Moor. Put money in thy purse. Nor he his to her. It was a violent commencement in her and thou shalt see an answerable sequestration[146]—put but money in thy purse. These Moors are changeable in their wills—fill thy purse with money. The food that to him now is as luscious as locusts shall be to him shortly as bitter as coloquintida[147]. She must change for youth; when she is sated with his body, she will find the errors of her choice. Therefore, put money in thy purse. If thou wilt needs damn thyself, do it a more delicate way than drowning. Make all the money thou canst. If sanctimony[148] and a frail vow betwixt an erring[149] barbarian and supersubtle Venetian be not too hard for my wits, and all the tribe of hell, thou shalt enjoy her. Therefore, make money. A pox of drowning thyself, it is clean out of the way. Seek thou rather to be hanged in compassing thy joy than to be drowned and go without her.

RODERIGO: Wilt thou be fast to my hopes, if I depend on the issue?

IAGO: Thou art sure of me. Go, make money. I have told thee often, and I retell thee again and again, I hate the Moor. My cause is hearted[150]; thine hath no less reason. Let us be conjunctive[151] in our revenge against him. If thou canst cuckold him, thou dost thyself a pleasure, me a sport. There are many events in the womb of time, which will be delivered. Traverse[152], go, provide thy money! We will have more of this tomorrow. Adieu.

RODERIGO: Where shall we meet i' th' morning?

IAGO: At my lodging.

RODERIGO: I'll be with thee betimes.

IAGO: Go to, farewell. Do you hear, Roderigo?

RODERIGO: I'll sell all my land.   *Exit.*

IAGO: Thus do I ever make my fool my purse;
For I mine own gained knowledge should profane
If I would time expend with such snipe[153]
But for my sport and profit. I hate the Moor,
And it is thought abroad that 'twixt my sheets
H'as done my office. I know not if't be true,
But I, for mere suspicion in that kind,
Will do, as if for surety[154]. He holds me well;
The better shall my purpose work on him.
Cassio's a proper man. Let me see now:
To get his place, and to plume up[155] my will.
In double knavery. How? How? Let's see.
After some time, to abuse Othello's ears

That he is too familiar with his wife.

He hath a person and a smooth dispose[156]

To be suspected—framed to make women false.

The Moor is of a free and open nature

That thinks men honest that but seem to be so;

And will as tenderly be led by th' nose

As asses are.

I have't! It is engendered! Hell and night

Must bring this monstrous birth to the world's light. *[Exit.]*

注 释:

1. **this**: Desdemona's elopement.

2. **'Sblood**: by God's blood.

3. **Off-capped**: took off their caps—as a mark of respect.

4. **bombast circumstance**: roundabout speech.

5. **Nonsuits**: rejects.

6. **arithmetician**: theorist.

7. **tongued**: eloquent.

8. **Blee'd and calmed**: left in the lurch.

9. **counter-caster**: bookkeeper.

10. **ancient**: an under-officer.

11. **letter and affection**: recommendations and personal preference.

12. **old gradation**: seniority.

13. **affined**: obliged.

14. **cashiered**: turned off.

15. **native**: natural.

16. **complement extern**: outward appearance.

17. **owe**: own.

18. **timorous**: frightening.

19. **snorting**: snoring.

20. **distemp'ring draughts**: unsettling drinks.

21. **start**: disrupt.

22. **place**: rank as a senator.

23. **grange**: isolated house.

24. **Barbary**: Arabian, referring to the Moor.

25. **nephews**: grandsons.

26. **cousins**: relatives.

27. **gennets for germans**: Spanish horses for near kinsmen.

28. **odd-even**: between night and morning.

29. **sense of all civility**: feeling lf what is proper.

30. **extravagant and wheeling**: vagrant and roving.

31. **accident**: happening.

32. **check**: restraint.

33. **cast**: discharge.

34. **stands in act**: takes place.

35. **fathom**: capacity.

36. **Sagittary**: probably the name of an inn.

37. **moe**: more.

38. **property**: nature.

39. **pains**: efforts.

40. **stuff**: essence.

41. **yerked**: stabbed.

42. **fast**: securely.

43. **magnifico**: nobleman.

44. **cable**: scope.

45. **Signiory**: the rulers of Venice.

46. **yet to know**: still unknown.

47. **siege**: rank.

48. **demerits**: deserts.

49. **May...reached**: I modestly assert, are the equal of the family I have married into.

50. **unhoused**: unconfined.

51. **perfect soul**: stainless conscience.

52. **sequent**: successive.

53. **several**: separate.

54. **carack**: treasure ship.

55. **general mock**: public shame.

56. **gross in sense**: obvious.

57. **practiced**: used tricks.

58. **motion**: thought.

59. **attach**: arrest.

60. **inhibited and out of warrant**: prohibited and unlawful.

61. **direct session**: regular trial.

62. **present**: immediate.

63. **idle**: trifling.

64. **brothers**: refers to the other senators.

65. **composition**: consistency.

66. **gives them credit**: makes them believable.

67. **jump**: agree.

68. **just accompt**: exact counting.

69. **aim**: conjecture.

70. **article**: substance.

71. **pageant**: show.

72. **in false gaze**: looking a false way.

73. **with facile question bear**: easily capture.

74. **wake and wage**: rouse and risk.

75. **after**: following.

76. **restem**: steer again.

77. **free duty**: unlimited respect.

78. **recommends**: informs.

79. **straight**: at once.

80. **floodgate**: torrential.

81. **engluts**: devours

82. **Sans**: without.

83. **proper**: own.

84. **stood in your action**: were accused by you.

85. **approved**: tested by past experience.

86. **head and front**: extreme form.

87. **Rude**: unpolished.

88. **pith**: strength.

89. **wasted**: past.

90. **dearest**: most important.

91. **round**: plain.

92. **her motion/Blushed at herself**: she blushed at every thought.

93. **practices**: plots.

94. **vouch**: assert.

95. **habits**: appearances.

96. **modern**: trivial.

97. **still**: continually.

98. **imminent**: threatening.

99. **portance**: action.

100. **anters**: caves.

101. **idle**: sterile.

102. **Anthropophagi**: man-eaters.

103. **dilate**: recount in full.

104. **intentively**: with full attention.

105. **passing**: surpassing.

106. **challenge**: claim the right.

107. **get**: beget.

108. **For your sake**: because of you.

109. **lay a sentence**: provide a maxim.

110. **grise**: step.

111. **late on hopes depended**: was supported by hopes until lately.

112. **bootless**: valueless.

113. **fortitude**: fortification.

114. **substitute**: referring to the viceroy.

115. **allowed**: acknowledged.

116. **opinion**: general opinion.

117. **slubber**: sully.

118. **stubborn and boisterous**: rough and violent.

119. **thrice-driven**: softest.

120. **agnize**: know in myself.

121. **exhibition**: allowance of money.

122. **levels with**: corresponds to.

123. **unfolding**: explanation.

124. **prosperous**: favorable.

125. **charter**: permission.

126. **voice**: agreement.

127. **heat**: passion.

128. **affects**: passions.

129. **defend**: forbid.

130. **seel**: blind.

131. **speculative and officed instrument**: perceptive and responsible sight.

132. **indign**: unworthy.

133. **make head**: attack.

134. **estimation**: reputation.

135. **import**: concern.

136. **delighted**: delightful.

137. **advantage**: opportunity.

138. **incontinently**: at once.

139. **distract**: vary.

140. **corrigible**: corrective.

141. **unbitted**: uncontrolled.

142. **sect or scion**: offshoot.

143. **stead**: serve.

144. **defeat thy favor**: disguise your face.

145. **usurped**: assumed.

146. **sequestration**: estrangement.

147. **coloquintida**: a medicine derived from a bitter apple.

148. **sanctimony**: sacred bond (of marriage).

149. **erring**: wandering.

150. **hearted**: deep seated in the heart.

151. **conjunctive**: joined.

152. **Traverse**: forward march.

153. **snipe**: fool.

154. **surety**: certainty.

155. **plume up**: gratify.

156. **dispose**: manner.

Questions:

1. Please compare Othello's character between the one in Iago's description and the one delivers speech. Can you sketch his disposition through the comparison? What might be the tragic flaw of Othello? Is he a person with a jealous disposition or a noble hero? Why is he so vulnerable to Iago's intrigue at the end of the play?

2. What makes Iago so eager to manipulate people, and to intrigue against Othello? Why does he hate Othello so passionately? What is his character like?

3. How do Othello and Desdemona understand love? Has it anything to do with their ultimate tragedy?

4. What are the differences between the presentations of male characters and female characters in the play? Do you think Shakespeare depicts man and woman equally?

5. How shall we perform the play?

Bibliography

Abrams, M. H. *A Glossary of Literary Terms*. 7th ed. Fort Worth: Harcourt Brace College Publishers, 1999.

Abrams, M. H. *The Norton Anthology of English Literature* (Vol.1, 2). 5th ed. New York: W. W. Norton & Company, 1995.

Arp, Thomas R. *Perrine's Literature: Structure, Sound and Sense*. 7th ed. Fort Worth: Harcourt Brace College Publishers, 1998.

Baldick, Chris. *Oxford Concise Dictionary of Literary Terms*. 上海：上海外语教育出版社，2000.

Brooks, C., Robert P. Warren. *Understanding Fiction*. 3rd ed. Beijing: Foreign Language Teaching and Research Press, 2004.

Brooks, C., Robert P. Warren. *Understanding Poetry*. 4th ed. Beijing: Foreign Language Teaching and Research Press, 2004.

Cassill, R. V. *The Norton Anthology of Short Fiction*. 5th ed. New York: W. W. Norton & Company, 1995.

Di Yanni, Robert. *Literature: Reading Fiction, Poetry, Drama, and Essay*. New York: Random House, 1986.

Dolley, Christopher, ed. *The Penguin Book of English Short Stories*. Beijing: Foreign Languages Press, 1989.

Ellmann, Richard. *Norton Anthology of Modern Poetry*. New York: W. W. Norton & Company, 1973.

Fyre, Joanne S. *Tillie Olsen: A Study of the Short Fiction*. New York: Twayne Publishers, 1995.

Garraty, John. *A Short History of the American Nation*. 4th ed. New York: Harper & Row, Publishers, 1985.

Guerin, Wilfred L., et al. *A Handbook of Critical Approaches to Literature*. Beijing: Foreign Language Teaching and Research Press, 2004.

Hall, Donald. *To Read Literature: Fiction, Poetry, Drama*. New York: Holt, Rinehart and Winston, 1983.

Jaworski, Adam. *The Power of Silence*. London: Sage Publications, 1993.

Lacan, Jacques. *Ecrits: A Selection*. Trans. Alan Sheridan. Tavistock, Publications, 1977.

Mednick, Fred. *An Introduction to American Literature: From Newcomers to Naturalists*. Henan: Henan Univeristy Press, 2002.

Mellow, James. *Hemingway: A Life Without Consequence*. Boston: Houghton Mifflin Company, 1992.

Meyer, Michael. *The Compact Bedford Introduction to Literature*. 5th ed. Boston: Bedford/St. Martin's,

2000.

Olsen, Tillie. *Silences.* New York: Dell Publishing Co., Inc., 1979.

Roberts, Edgar V. *Writing Theme About Literature.* 7th ed. New Jersey: PrenticeHall, 1991.

Sapiro, Virginia. *Women in American Society: An Introduction to Women's Studies.* [S.l.]: Mayfield Publishing Company, 1986.

Scott, Ian and Kilvert, ed. *British Writers* (Volume VII). New York: Charles Seribner's Sons, 1984.

Shrodes, Caroline et al. *The Concious Reader.* 8th ed. Boston: Allyn and Bacon, 2001.

Stubbs, Patricia. *Woman & Fiction : Feminism & the Novel 1880—1920.* [S.l.]: The Harvester Press Ltd, 1979.

Ward, A. C. *Longman Companion to Twentieth Century Literature.* Essex: Longman House, 1981.

Wordsworth Classics. *Introduction to Mrs. Dalloway.* London: Wordsworth Editions Limited, 1996.

阿尔伯斯 A. 一次轻率的旅行：凯瑟琳•曼斯菲尔德的一生. 冯洁音译. 上海：知识出版社，1993.

曹曼. 美国文学名著导读. 武汉：武汉大学出版社，1999.

陈晓兰. 女性主义批评与文学诠释. 兰州：敦煌文艺出版社，1999.

丁丽军. 《白象似的群山》与"冰山原则"——海明威小说艺术特色探析. 南昌航空工业学院学报，2003，3.

方文开，李祖明. 《白象似的群山》解读. 荆州师范学院学报，2002，1.

付灿邦. 论曼斯菲尔德的《苍蝇》.四川师范学院学报（哲社版），1994，4.

傅子柏. 论曼斯菲尔德的《苍蝇》. 重庆师范学院学报（哲社版），1995，3.

甘文平."梦"的建构、消解与幻灭——《白象似的群山》与《雨里的猫》的主题比较. 四川外语学院学报，2002，2.

霍冬克. 从《白象似的群山》看海明威小说创作的艺术风格. 丹东师专学报，2002，3.

刘建成. 海明威《白象似的山峦》叙事技巧和主题. 乌鲁木齐职业大学学报，2003，3.

上官燕. 海明威笔下之另类反英雄——评《白象似的群山》和《雨里的猫》中男性形象. 三峡大学学报，2003，4.

申丹. 叙述学与小说文体学研究. 北京：北京大学出版社，1998.

徐凯. 巧妙的象征•深刻的内涵. 名作欣赏，2000，5.

叶华年等. 英语短篇小说导读：结构与理解. 上海：华东师范大学出版社，1999.

费伦 J. 作为修辞的叙事. 陈永国译. 北京：北京大学出版社，2002.

张首映. 西方二十世纪文论史. 北京：北京大学出版社，1999.

赵敏霞. 论曼斯菲尔德短篇小说的主题特征. 学术交流，1999，4.

朱刚. 二十世纪西方文艺批评理论. 上海：上海外语教育出版社，2001.

左金梅. 美国文学. 青岛：青岛海洋大学出版社，2000.